PUBLIC WORKS IN INDIA

PUBLIC WORKS IN INDIA:

THEIR IMPORTANCE

WITH SUGGESTIONS

FOR

THEIR EXTENSION AND IMPROVEMENT

SIR ARTHUR COTTON

GYAN

Published by

Gyan Publishing House
5, Ansari Road
Daryaganj, New Delhi-110002
Phone: 011-47034999, 9811692060
E-mail: books@gyanbooks.com

Distribution Network
gyanbooks.com
India, USA, Canada, UK, Australia

ISBN: 978-93-7014-067-7 (PB)

First Published, 1854

2nd Impression 2025

Printed at: Gyan Press, Delhi.

PUBLIC WORKS IN INDIA
Author: SIR ARTHUR COTTON

PUBLIC WORKS IN INDIA,

THEIR IMPORTANCE;

With Suggestions

FOR

THEIR EXTENSION AND IMPROVEMENT.

BY

LIEUT.-COLONEL A. COTTON.

Second Edition, with considerable additions.

LONDON:

RICHARDSON BROTHERS, 23, CORNHILL.

1854.

ADVERTISEMENT

TO THE

LONDON EDITION.

THIS treatise on "Public Works in India," was written for private circulation. It contains such a mass of information, and of powerful reasoning, upon a subject of vital importance to India, that the friends of the writer to whom it was addressed think it their duty to give it publicity. How we shall best spend our money upon public works in India, is a subject in which England, also, has a deep interest; for it involves, amongst other things, the great cotton question. By a judicious expenditure, we may render ourselves independent of the slave-grown cotton of America. On the other hand, we may spend millions without approximating to such a result; and as the interest of these millions is to be paid by the people of India, it is our obvious duty to spend it in a manner that will be most conducive to their advantage. How this may be done is a question that is thoroughly discussed in the following pages.

PREFACE

TO THE

INDIAN EDITION.

THE following Work has been undertaken under an urgent sense of the importance, at this crisis, of a right understanding of the principles upon which the material improvement of India should be conducted. Our responsibility for the just and judicious development of the resources of the country is now generally acknowledged: but it is not so clear that we have yet perceived and entered upon the right path to accomplish that object. A great system of railways has been projected, not after investigation of the specific condition, resources and wants of the different provinces and districts, but, it would appear, rather as a sort of infallible means of improvement, adapted *à priori* to this country as to every other. This may be ascribed in a considerable measure to the total absence of popular action in the country. In England and America, and other countries possessing effective Municipalities, improvements are projected chiefly by those who, being immediately interested in them, can fully comprehend their relative value and importance, and cannot be deceived by theories contradicted by their own knowledge and experience. It is therefore of great importance that in India, the voice of whose millions of inhabitants on subjects most nearly concerning their welfare is never uttered, or is at least inaudible, those friends of India who have reason to believe from the peculiar circumstances in which they have been placed, that they understand the country and its peculiar wants, should do their part to direct into the right channel the thoughts and plans of the Authorities whose decision is absolute: for the best intentions will never supply the place of just ideas.

What pretensions the writer has to offer advice and instruction on these subjects, will appear from the following pages; but whatever may be the value of his investigations, he has been actuated by a sincere desire to build them upon undoubted truth, and to conduct them to true results. It is only right to add that a work composed amidst the numerous distractions of very onerous public duty will necessarily be found to contain many faults, which more leisure might have enabled the author partly to correct; but though the composition has been hurried, the matter is the fruit of anxious thought and study, extending over many years of experimental acquaintance with the subjects treated of. The Work is therefore given to the public with a confidence in the soundness of its principles and conclusions, which mature consideration may entitle the Author to entertain.

Since the first part of these papers was written, what a change has taken place in the prospects of India! Who would have thought a year ago that England would take such an interest in her affairs, and that such fundamental changes should be made in the constitution of her Government, fairly opening the door to every improvement, and loudly demanding of every real friend of India, that he should put forth all his energies, encouraged by the hope, the certainty, that with God's blessing we shall no longer labour in vain? The battle has been fought and won, especially in respect of Public Works. The Madras Public Works Report is like the last general advance at Waterloo. Henceforth the chief difficulty will be to discern friends from foes, for the latter will have no choice, but to hurry on in the same direction as the former; their only safety will be in moving at the same speed, and if any hesitate, they will only be trampled under foot. Already we see unmistakeable evidences of this; and very shortly both parties will be seen intermixed and swept along in one mass. If any from fool hardiness or from not yet perceiving how the matter has really gone, attempt to make a stand, their efforts will scarcely have even a momentary effect, and will certainly bring upon themselves destruction. The tide of Indian improvement has now fairly set in, and woe be to him who attempts to stem it.

The writer would not have it supposed that he means these papers to be put forward as any attempt at an actual construction; he only offers them as containing *materials*, which in common with many other persons, he has been collecting during 30 years of conflict, often apparently hopeless. It is to be hoped that some Solomon, some man of peace, will now appear to construct this temple of peace for India. The time has now arrived for the application of these and other materials to the actual building, and all who have materials in their possession, should place them at the public disposal.* The Author on his part feels like an old soldier after a long battle, sitting down quietly in the enemies' position and in the midst of the slain, to eat his rice and talk over the incidents of the day, in the full assurance that the enemy are irrecoverably overthrown; leaving it to his younger companions who are in pursuit, to scatter the debris of the broken columns, and waiting for the accounts they bring in from time to time as they return, of the dispersion and destruction of those fugitives, who from exhaustion or infatuation, were found in the way of the pursuers.

* Already we have several most important contributions from the hearty friends of India. The Madras P. W. Report,* Mr. Norton's "Madras," and Mr. Mackay's Western India especially, should be thoroughly digested by those who are really anxious that England should do her duty and improve the privilege offered to her, of giving India a share of her own advantages.

* Parliamentary Paper No. 407—1 of 1853.

CONTENTS.

CHAPTER III.

CHAPTER IV.

CHAPTER V.

CHAPTER VI.

CHAPTER VII.

CHAPTER VIII.

Page.

CHAPTER IX.

CHAPTER X.

Irrigation.

8 Pice to a Penny.

1 P.	=	$\frac{1}{8}$*d.*
2	=	$\frac{1}{4}$*d.*
3	=	$\frac{3}{8}$*d.*
4	=	$\frac{1}{2}$*d.*
5	=	$\frac{5}{8}$*d.*
6	=	$\frac{3}{4}$*d.*
7	=	$\frac{7}{8}$*d.*
8	=	1*d.*

1 Anna	=	$1\frac{1}{2}$*d.*
$1\frac{1}{4}$	=	2*d.*
$1\frac{1}{2}$	=	$2\frac{1}{4}$*d.*
$1\frac{3}{4}$	=	$2\frac{1}{2}$*d.*
2	=	3*d.*
$2\frac{1}{2}$	=	$3\frac{3}{4}$*d.*
3	=	$4\frac{1}{2}$*d.*
1 Rupee	=	2*s.*
12 Pice	=	1 Anna.
16 Annas	=	1 Rupee.

100,000 Rupees = 1 Lack = £10,000
100 Lacks = 1 Crore = £1,000,000

1 Cawnie = 57600 sq. ft. = 6840 sq. yards = 1·32,2316 Acres.
1 Acre = 43560 sq. ft. = 4840 sq. yards = 0·75625 Cawnies.
640 Acres or 484 Cawnies = 1 sq. mile.

CHAPTER I.

GENERAL CONSIDERATIONS ON THE IMPORTANCE OF COMMUNICATIONS TO THE IMPROVEMENT OF INDIA, AND THE STRANGE NEGLECT OF THEM BY THE BRITISH GOVERNMENT.

The utter want of appreciation of the Subject hitherto.

THE object of the present Book is to try and lead those who are capable of such an undertaking, to investigate the subject of communications in India as a whole. I cannot find that this has ever been attempted. So far as I have been able to ascertain, whatever has been done in the case hitherto has been done as a patch. One man has thought it would be very nice to travel at the rate of 40 miles an hour from such a place to such a place, and he begins to examine whether this can be accomplished; and if he thinks that a Railroad on that line would pay the interest of the Capital expended on it, or if it will pay part of it and he can get the Government to make up the deficiency, the whole subject is exhausted. Whether it is the best way of accomplishing his object, whether *his* object is *the* object even on that particular line, whether this work will form part of a whole system of works adapted to India, whether it will hinder or help forward the welfare of India generally, so far as that will be affected by suitable communications, and many other points of a general nature, have not been at all considered. So far as the shareholders are concerned, it may be thought sufficient for them if there be a fair presumption that good interest will be returned for their money; but that cannot be the whole of the question to the Government and those who are interested in the welfare of India: nor is it in fact even the whole of the subject to the shareholders. They have not only to ascertain that such a work will pay, but that it is so nearly the best and most suitable means, considering the peculiar circumstances of the case, that it will not be in danger from a better planned rival.

Of the superficial way in which the question has been considered hitherto, even taking it in its narrowest view, and thinking only of the point whether a Railroad on a certain line will pay, we have a curious instance in the Calcutta Railway. The traffic is there, and it is proposed to construct the Railway, and calculations are given to show that such a traffic on such a Railway will pay such interest, but whether the Railway when it is ready can carry the traffic, has not been considered. The traffic is 1½ million tons a year or 5,000 tons a day, on an average of the whole line and of the year; which of course implies that at the busy time of the year and near Calcutta, there will be at least 10,000 tons a day besides 1,600 passengers. Can a double Railway carry 10,000 tons a day besides 1,600 passengers? The busiest Passenger Railroad in England only carries 700 tons a day on an average according to Lardner, or one-seventh of the quantity upon which these calculations are based. We have no data as to what amount of goods a Railway worked at high speed for passengers can carry, but we know certainly that it could not carry 10,000 tons of goods a day; so that when the road is finished, either only a small part of the goods can be carried, or additional Rails must be laid, or it must be worked at one speed for all, both goods and passengers, and that a very low one; any of which expedients, however, entirely overthrow the calculations of profit.

If a great national question is thus taken up, without a careful investigation of the whole subject, there can be no hope of its being wisely managed. We must form some distinct idea of the actual importance of the subject, the extent of the loss in the present state of things, the precise nature of the evil, the amount of labour and expenditure required to counteract it, the difficulties that we may expect to encounter, the value of time in applying a remedy, &c., before we can set about the matter in an effective way; in short we must count the cost, if we hope to finish the work. If we have not some tolerable measure of the amount of evil before us, we shall either be continually liable to give up the attempt to obtain a remedy upon every difficulty that we encounter; or on the other hand, we shall be wasting our money and our energies, on a remedy for an evil which is not worth so great efforts and sacrifices.

There cannot be any greater proof of the evil consequences of doing things without any general investigation, than the history of communications in India up to this time; the desultory way in which the matter has been attended to, and the consequent failures and waste of money that we have seen. While the loss from want of communications was so great, that there were a thousand ways and a thousand plans in which money might have been expended with the greatest advantage, perhaps crores of Rupees (millions sterling) have been thrown away from a total want of judgment in managing the expenditure.

The history of communications in the Madras Presidency, is one of the most curious of all the odd things that have occurred in the management of India. A sketch of this may be of great use as a warning to us in our future proceedings. The first roads made probably were those in Tanjore. When it was proposed to open one or two lines in that impassable sheet of irrigation, it was immediately objected, "Well this is a fine proposition; to make fine roads where there is not a horse or a cart to be found." There was not a mile in the whole Delta along which a horse or a cart could have moved. After some struggling however a first attempt was made, and it was discovered, that when there were cart roads, carts were used. But what was done in Tanjore, was done without the least reference to any other part of the country. The questions were never asked; "But if roads are to be made, " where are they most wanted? where will capital so expend- " ed produce the greatest results? which ought to be made " first, &c. &c.?" Tanjore, possessing the most active Government Officers, got roads; and the rest of the country generally remained without them, as it is to this day. The next roads were probably those made by the Pioneers. The arrangements for these works placed the whole management in the hands of the Officer commanding the Battalion, who had probably obtained the post by private favor, and certainly without any special qualification. He had never considered a made road; for he had left England before he was old enough to entertain a thought about the roads he travelled over there. He had not an idea on the whole subject, nor a book to refer to. Of the principles on which the lines should be selected, as well as those on which the roads should be constructed, he was utterly ignorant. He soon found that 1,000 men were lost upon a hundred miles of road, and obtained permission to employ a few thousand coolies; and thus besides the cost of the Pioneers, a few lacks of Rupees were spent by a man who had not the slightest knowledge of, or even natural turn for the work he was employed upon.

The road from Masulipatam on the Coast (300 miles north of Madras) to Hyderabad, a distance of 220 miles, was one of those executed in this manner. When about eight lacks of Rupees (£80,000) had been spent upon it, besides the pay of the Pioneers, the Court of Directors put a stop to it; and as no metal of any kind was put on most of it, the road has never yet been practicable in the wet season, and even in the dry season the communication is very little better, if at all, than it was

There is not the slightest exaggeration in this; it is a literal statement of the *usual* course of proceedings, in times past. No check of the remotest kind was exercised over these works; not a single professional Officer had any thing whatever to do with them. The Quarter Master General under whom they were carried on, was as perfectly ignorant of the matter, and probably at least as inexperienced, as the Executive Officers. Of the state of things a very distinct idea may be formed by the following anecdote. One of the Officers commanding the Pioneers employed as above described, drew up a Memorandum on the best construction for a road on cotton soil, (black alluvial mud without sand or gravel mixed with it;) and highly pleased with the knowledge he had attained, he sent it to the Quarter Master General. Struck by the remarkable talent displayed in the paper, the Quarter Master General sent a copy of it to all Officers employed in that Department; and that the utmost possible use might be made of it, he also sent a copy to the Chief Engineer, that he might circulate it through that corps. The plan was this; first a complete layer of large stones, about a foot or a foot and a half thick was to be laid over the whole surface to be occupied by the road, and over them was then to be laid three feet thick of the black cotton soil, to raise the road to a sufficient height and prevent its being flooded. By this admirable arrangement almost any amount of money might be spent, as in such a situation the stones would have to be brought several miles, and at the same time the surface of the road being formed of the natural soil, but thoroughly loosened by being dug and thrown up, would be ten times worse than the original surface of the country. Such was the state of knowledge of road making, among those who conducted the undertakings, and who were entrusted without check or supervision, with the expenditure of many lacks of Rupees. Only about 120 miles of the whole distance to Hyderabad was meddled with: the money spent for a very imperfect work, was therefore nearly £700 (7,000 Rupees) a mile, or twice as much as would make an excellent metalled road, and quite as much as would have made a good horse Railroad, (for there is not a single difficulty on the line,) which would have reduced the cost of transit to one-twelfth of what it was and still is. The road from Madras to Poonamallee, eleven miles, was a similar case; and as in this case the Pioneer Officer was able to communicate constantly with the authorities in person, he was not so restricted about expenditure as in the other case, and accordingly £45,000 (4,50,000 Rs.) was spent on this line, or £5,000 (50,000 Rs.) a mile. The Court of Directors now saw that it was necessary to apply a remedy; and that was, to order that no more roads should be made.

However, after some years another line of road was nevertheless commenced by the Government; and this time the really most important direction in the Presidency was selected, viz., that leading from Madras directly into the interior 120 miles. But exactly the same mistakes were made about its execution. It was put under a non-professional Officer, not a single Engineer was employed upon it, there was no open discussion about it, the line was badly selected, enormous labour was wasted on it, and it was not in any sense completed. The whole evil lies in the snug way in which things are done in India. In England no work is undertaken without endless discussions. The wits and experience of hundreds of professional Engineers are brought to bear upon it, and of tens of thousands of others, men of common sense and local knowledge, and yet after all great mistakes are often made: what must be the case then, when not a single man of professional knowledge and experience is employed upon a public work, and not the least attempt is made to get the opinions and help of the public generally? This road cost £1,000 (10,000 Rs.) a mile; much more than a horse Railroad need have cost; and the Court repeated their former orders with much more determination, when they heard of this work. It was however a work of immense value; imperfect as it was, there has been an enormous traffic on it, and it has saved in the cost of traffic, much more than 100 per cent. on its cost; the rate of transit having been reduced to about one-third of what it was previously.

These desultory proceedings however of course upon the whole, only retarded the general improvement of the communications. At length something like a systematic attempt was made to introduce roads into Madras. A Road Department was formed with the approval of the Court; but the same error was committed of having no thorough investigation or open discussion. A professional Officer was indeed appointed; but as he had charge of all the main roads of the Presidency, and only two assistants, he was completely lost in his duties; and every thing was still done in the same way without open discussion. Some work however was really done. The great road from Madras abovementioned was much improved, and some other lines commenced. But now a new difficulty arose. The local Government were reluctant to sanction the expenditure which the Court had authorized; and the Superintendent of Roads was so cramped in every way, that though he wore himself out in his work, but little was effected.

This outline is of great importance to show what the real state of things has been, and why no real progress has been made here and generally in India in opening the country.

The great line from Calcutta to the North West is almost the only important work that has yet been executed, and after all it is but a common road. Some real progress has however also been made of late years in the North West in improving the roads, and one step of real progress has been commenced upon, in the cutting of the Ganges Canal. When this work is opened, there will be 400 miles of cheap and expeditious communication on one of the most important lines in India. The cost of transit in this will probably not exceed ¼ farthing (½ Pie) per ton per mile. This is certainly the first, and at present the only step towards opening India. Till such *cheap* communications are opened, nothing at all is done.

Had the Court of Directors taken up this subject systematically, and had they had before them in figures the tremendous incubus that the cost of transit is upon the country, it is impossible that matters could have gone on in this way. A real apprehension of the importance of communications would have certainly led to such an attention to the subject, that the Department of Public Works would have been considered one of the very first in the State.

Certainly, without any exaggeration, the most astonishing thing in the history of our rule in India, is that such innumerable volumes should have been written by the ablest men in the Service on *the mode of collecting the land Revenue*, while the question of a thousand times more importance, how to enable people to pay it, was literally never touched upon. And yet even the question of the *amount* of taxation was utterly insignificant in comparison with that. While the Court of Directors, the Councils, the Boards, and the local authorities, have been labouring for a hundred years to discover how to get twenty lacks (£20,000) out of a district which is not able to pay it, not the least thought has been bestowed on the hundreds of lacks (millions) it was losing from the enormous cost of transit, which swallowed up all the value of the Ryots' produce, if they raised it. The roads are not the only Public Works that are wanted, irrigation also is in this country of the very first importance; but no irrigation will bring the country to a state of great prosperity without the means of conveying produce to a market, and cheap communications will have an immense effect even in enabling one part of the country to help another in the matter of food if local rains fail.

The question is, not whether a Railroad will pay on a certain line of 100 or 1,000 miles, but rather, "What is the importance of providing all India with communications, and the best mode of doing so, considering the various circumstances which affect the case?" Till the subject is taken up on this ground, nothing effectual will be done; and any particular lines improved will be just as likely to hinder, as to help the great work. It is certain that up to the commencement of the Railroads, the individual works undertaken in this Presidency were the main hindrances to a general system of communications. The Court instead of learning from the mistakes that were made, how to set about this important work in future, only concluded to do nothing. For the last four years, since the agitation about Railroads commenced, the consideration of this question has completely blinded Government and others; effectually preventing any real attempt to open out India. While millions of words, and lacks of Rupees, have been expended on a few miles of road, in two corners of the country,* the whole of India has been lying untouched in the same miserable and disgraceful state as before; whereas, if this ill-considered expenditure had not been going on, perhaps the Government or the English Public might have employed their time in commencing upon a real and general project, for giving all India *cheap* communications.

Some symptoms of a change of views in the matter have now indeed begun to appear; but nothing whatever that gives the least indication of a really right understanding of the state of the case. The sanction of 4 lacks (£40,000) to be spent where 400 lacks (4 millions sterling) would be insufficient,

* Since this was written, a third line has been commenced in the Madras Presidency.

the attempt to accomplish these vast works by means of the present Revenue, the appointment of one Officer to do more than twenty could do, and the fact of the local Government not laying out on communications even the comparatively small sum ordered by the Court of Directors for that purpose, —all these circumstances distinctly show that the whole thing is misapprehended by the Court of Directors, and that they still cling to the old idea, that if only the subject of *collecting the Revenue* be attended to, every thing else will follow as a matter of course; whereas, the converse is very nearly true. If a Collector were only allowed and required to spend liberally on Public Works, the Revenue would undoubtedly follow in general, though certainly some intelligence would be required in managing the collection. A Collector would then require no sanction for money from the treasury as his district would provide the interest for whatever money he required, and abundance of increase of Revenue besides. The saving in the cost of transit on the Western road from Madras is fully cent. per cent. on the Capital expended, and the average return on most of the new Irrigation Works in the Madras Presidency for the last fourteen years, is 70 per cent. taking the whole of the years since their execution; and the *present* annual profit is at least cent. per cent. and that without counting the improvement of private property.

All the imaginary importance of Revenue systems has been imbibed from the Natives; the proposition was, "How is a certain amount of Revenue to be collected when the people have not the means of paying it?" No wonder a satisfactory result has not yet been arrived at. But if only the communications, Irrigation Works, and Ports were properly attended to, then the questions about Revenue systems would almost solve themselves; at least they would certainly be as little thought of as they are in England, where we do not hear of nine-tenths of the time of Parliament being taken up in investigating a mere question such as whether the land tax shall be collected Ryotwar or Mowzawar. If the people were abundantly able to pay the taxes, the mode of arranging for the payment of the land tax, would become soon a very secondary question. For instance, a Tassildar of a Talook which was in good order, said to me "All the Revenue comes into my treasury of itself by the day it is due, without my sending out a Peon to call for it." The system of imbibing erroneous ideas from the Natives instead of teaching them, pervades every branch of the Indian service, and is at the bottom of all our blunders. The fact is, up to this day, the *country is governed by Natives.* Wherever you go, it is the Native ideas that are in operation. Nominally, Europeans are in authority; but they have insensibly imbibed the ideas of the Natives. Every European in the country has learnt in England the essential importance of communications and other public works; but yet he acts exactly as if he knew nothing about it. If intelligent Natives went to England, they would be astonished beyond measure when seeing the inconceivable effect of cheap transit, that the English in this country should have been content to throw away all their own ideas on the subject, and adopt the ignorant narrow ideas of their subjects and that instead of bringing their western knowledge, energy, activity, and common sense to bear, they should have adopted the views of a people without books or science. When the English begin to think for themselves, and bring their own Anglo-Saxon notions fairly to bear upon India, there will then be a wonderful change. A Native is by nature a very intelligent being, but he is utterly without our advantages. Imagine what a nation of Anglo-Saxons would be, who had not one single book worth reading in their language; and who had learnt nothing from books but drivellings such as are found in the Hindoo religious writings, which they themselves could see to be utter nonsense. And yet, such are the people we are content to learn from, instead of teaching them.

Where did the notion come from, that the grand point upon which the whole body of men entrusted with the government of the country were to employ their wits day and night, was "*how to collect a Revenue which the people could not pay under the present system,*" instead of the question being "*how to enable them to pay it?*" The former is purely a Native idea, and that of the lowest kind. The old Public Works of Irrigation now existing, show plainly that at some previous time and in some places, Natives have had some idea that there were things of more importance than *collecting Revenue;* but so low have the Europeans sunk, that they have not even been roused by the sight of these valuable works, so far as to make it a point to keep them in repair. The very name of the local controllers of the Revenue shows unmistakeably how low an idea was formed of the duties of Government; they were called simply *Collectors,* clearly implying that *Collection* was the leading idea, and the supposition that all other things could take care of themselves. With a right view of the case, they would have been called *Directors of Public Works,* or some such title, and the *collection of the Revenue* would have been understood to be quite a secondary matter, and a thing that would follow of course, *when the people were enabled easily to pay it.* What wonderful infatuation is shown to this day in this matter! In the district of Tanjore which is taken care of, irrigated, protected from floods, drained, and provided with common roads, (though not with better communications,) the Revenue steadily rises, till from 30 (£300,000) it becomes 50 lacks (£500,000) a year; the population increases from 7 or 8 lacks to 15 lacks (1½ millions), and the land reaches a saleable value of at least 4 millions sterling, equal, considering the difference in the value of money in India, to 24 millions in England. In the district of Guntoor on the other hand, all such works are utterly neglected, and in one year a famine occurs which sweeps away 2,50,000 people out of 5,00,000, and causes a loss of Revenue in the next 10 or 12 years of 80 lacks (£800,000); while not an acre of land is saleable. The sole cause of this difference between these two districts, is the different degree of attention given to Public Works. I challenge the most brilliant Collector, (let him belong to any class of Revenue men you please, Ryotwar, Village Settlement, Zemindaree or any thing else), to show how he could have saved the unhappy district of Guntoor from these inconceivable horrors, and the treasury from this enormous loss; and on the other hand send the most stupid or indifferent Civilian that ever fattened upon India, to Tanjore, and see if he could have prevented its progress, if only the Public Works had been attended to. A difference he might have made certainly, but he would have found it hard to reduce the population to 3,00,000, and the Revenue to 15 lacks (£150,000), or to have kept the land unsaleable.

And what would have been the progress of Tanjore, if, instead of the miserable petty expenditure that has been allowed it, (about 80,000 Rs. a year or one-fiftieth of the Revenue) a really liberal expenditure, equal only to one-tenth of the Revenue, had been reserved for this purpose. Probably the district is at this moment paying at least 30 lacks (£300,000) a year for the actual cost of transit, and losing much more in the value of things that cannot be moved from where they are produced to where they would be saleable; so that at the very lowest estimate, it is expending a sum equal to the whole Revenue, or 50 lacks (£500,000) a year for want of proper communications. And ought not Englishmen to know, that communications are an essential, if not the fundamental element, of national prosperity and wealth? Is this a thing that is now to be brought forward as a discovery? Could any man born and bred in England suppose that the subject of communications was a matter of utter insignificance, not worth a thought in comparison with that of *collecting the Revenue?* How could the whole body of our Rulers and *Collectors* have found room in their heads for such a notion, if they had not first surrendered all their English wits? Now suppose such a system of communications to have been introduced into Tanjore, as would have taken away nine-tenths of the cost of transit, and enabled the people to convey at a trifling expense every article worth a Rupee (2 shillings) a ton more in one part of the district than in another, so as to give an additional income equal to the whole present Revenue; what would have been the state of the district by this time, and how small a degree of skill and effort would have been required in a *Collector* to *collect* the present amount of Revenue, when it formed so small a portion of the annual income! One would think it would be intelligible to every one, that the shortest way to remove the difficulties in *collecting the Revenue* of 50 lacks (£500,000), would be, to increase the income of the district by 150 (1½ millions) or 200 lacks (2 millions). On the other hand, suppose we were to destroy the Roads, Canals, Railroads, Harbours, Steam Engines, &c., in England, and then try to obtain a Revenue of 50 millions by means of a splendid Revenue system and crack *Collectors*, could all the wisdom of Parliament extort 50 or even 5 millions a year out of the country? and yet this is the only expedient that has been tried, to facilitate the *collection* of the Revenue in India.

And this too after the indisputable proofs of the effects of attention to Public Works on the spot.* A statement (already alluded to) has lately been printed of the returns from 40 Works of Irrigation, including all of any consequence executed in fourteen years in the Madras Presidency, and the result is, a net average annual return of 70 per cent. on all

* See First Report of the Madras Public Works Commissioners printed by order of the House of Commons.—Appendix (Z), page 371.

the works (including the few failures); and the average being taken from the year of the execution of the works, the returns at the present time must be at least 100 per cent., on the outlay. But this is exclusive of the increase in the indirect taxes, for of course the improved condition of the people and land causes an increase of Revenue from all articles paying duty; so that the whole actual returns in *Revenue* to Government from all sources at this moment, must be much more than 100 per cent.; and to this is to be added the increase of private property, which much exceeds that of the Revenue, so that at the very least we are certain that these works now return on an average 200 per cent. on their cost. The increase in private property is shown by the increase of the saleable value of land in Tanjore for instance, since the great works were executed in 1836, the 7,00,000 acres of irrigated land are now sold, on an average, at least 20 Rupees (£2) an acre more than before; showing an increase of Capital of 1½ millions sterling.

CHAPTER II.

THE VIEWS OF THE HOME INDIAN GOVERNMENT ON THE SUBJECT OF PUBLIC WORKS, AS EXHIBITED IN THE FINANCIAL DESPATCHES FROM THE COURT OF DIRECTORS.

Government views on Finance and Public Works.

WHAT has been the effect of this astonishing gain from Public Works of Irrigation? Has this at last roused the Court of Directors to a sense of the grievous mistake that has been made, in doing so little in this way, and brought them at last to see the necessity in future of making Public Works the very first object of their attention, and led them to look out in future for crack *producers* of Revenue, rather than for crack *Collectors?* Have the Despatches of late run thus: "We cannot too often or too earnestly impress upon "you the absolute necessity of our now setting ourselves in "earnest, to repair with the least possible loss of time the "grievous error we have hitherto committed in our manage-"ment of India, in leaving its millions without those Public "Works, in the absence of which not only no increase of "Revenue can possibly be expected, but we cannot even "preserve the lives of this vast population. Neither can "the loss of population and Revenue in Guntoor, nor the

" Revenue returns of the few improvements that have been " made, leave any room for doubt now on this head. The " imaginary difficulty about the money for these works is now " also seen to have no existence, for where works return " 100 per cent. and Capital can be obtained to any amount " at 5 per cent., to say nothing of the 13½ millions sterling " that we have at this moment in the Treasury, no one can " doubt about what should be done, &c." Whether common sense should not dictate such a Despatch as the foregoing, let the reader judge.

The following however, are the words of the actual Finance Despatch of 25th October 1848:—" The Land Revenue, the " great source of Permanent Income to Government, appears " from the statement in the margin to be on the whole in a sa- " tisfactory state." The statement in question shows an increase from about 12¼ crores in 1839, to 14 crores (14 millions) in 1848; but it omits to show how much of this was owing to increase of Territory; without which it shows nothing at all. And in a further para., " The Madras Land Revenue ex- " hibits a considerable improvement since 1844-45. In the " ten years from 1829-30 to 1838-39, the depression in this " most important branch of Revenue was such as to occasion " us great anxiety, the average receipts during that period " having been upwards of 24 lacks (£240,000) per annum *less* " than the average of the 15 years preceding 1829-30. Since " 1838-39 the aspect has materially brightened. In 1845 " the receipts more than equalled the average amount rea- " lized from 25 to 30 years ago, or before the deterioration " already alluded to commenced; and in 1846 there was " further improvement of eight lacks (£80,000), while the " actual receipts of 1847, and the estimate for 1848, were " still more favourable. We therefore hope, that we may " safely pronounce the condition of the great bulk of the " people employed under the Presidency of Madras in agri- " culture, to have been much improved of late, and our anxiety

" for the permanent prosperity of the Land Revenue is con-
" sequently relieved."

But in this Extract not one word is said to show, whether this increase is owing to increased severity of taxation, or to increased ability to pay. We may make a tenant pay us 10£ a year instead of 8£, and say, " see how much richer he is!" Neither does the Statement show, whether this increase be really the result of the Capital expended by Government in improvements, or whether any increase has also been derived from land for which Government have done nothing.

Who could suppose from this, that in one case at least in this interval, (from 1839 to 1848) the local Government had brought expressly to the notice of the Court, that on an expenditure for an extensive improvement in a Public Work, an enormous return had been received! It appears from this Despatch, that such unanswerable proofs of what is wanted to put the finances to rights, do not produce one remark from the Court, when the subject of finance is expressly under investigation! How often do their servants erroneously imagine, that when they have proved by actual results the wisdom and necessity of a large system of improvement of the country, the grand point is gained; and that now at length a beginning will be made towards wiping off this abominable disgrace of our rule, that our only thought is, how to grind out of the poor ignorant people a little more Revenue, without an attempt even to enable them to pay it or to show them the incalculable advantages we have obtained in England by facilitating production and transit.

In the same Despatch, in examining the Charges, the whole Civil Expenditure is lumped together; and not one single word is said, to distinguish what has been expended on permanent improvements, however great the returns, from the ordinary current expenditure. What would be thought of a merchant who should add up together, the salaries of his clerks, his office expenses, and the price of a new ship which yielded him 100 per cent. per annum, and then call the total his annual expenditure? The practical result is, that the Court again and again simply urge *economy;* by which they mean reducing expenditure, whether productive or non-productive; whether the money be spent on a salary of 5,000£ a year, on the repair of works upon which the very lives of the population depend, or on the construction of new works which would yield 100 or 200 per cent.

Though the Court have had so many proofs of the immense losses resulting from neglect of Public Works, and the enormous profit derived from the execution of them, it is evident that the object mentioned in the 66th para. of the Despatch, viz., "*the equalization of your Revenue and expenditure,*" has never yet been taken a right view of; the Court considering that it is to be attained by *reduction of expenditure,* instead of by increasing the *sources of income* to the people and thus *enabling the country to pay a better Revenue.* There can be no mistake on this point; if the latter idea had been in existence, indications of it must have appeared in this deliberate review of the finances of India by the Court of Directors. Who could believe that although one solitary district, Tanjore, exhibits the example of a system of moderate but actual improvement steadily pursued for fifty years with unvarying success, raising the Revenue from 30 to 50 lacks (£500,000) a year, while the saleable value of the land has equally advanced, till it is now (allowing for the difference in the value of money) equal to the value of land in England;—all this being accomplished not by a sudden extensive outlay of Capital producing even temporary difficulty to Government, but by an average annual expenditure of only about 40,000 Rupees (£4,000) a year, besides current expenses for the repair of existing works—who would believe that the same system had not been applied to all the other districts of the country? The total sum expended in

Tanjore is about 20 lacks (£200,000) and the increase of Revenue per annum is the same; the increase of private property in the value of land, is also about 3 or 3½ crores, (3 to 3½ millions) indicating an addition of private income of 18 or 20 lacks (£200,000) a year. The money was expended in embanking rivers, cutting channels for the distribution of water and for drainage, constructing weirs, sluices, aqueducts and other masonry works connected with irrigation and drainage; building many hundred bridges, and making 1,000 miles of common road for facilitating transit. This one district standing alone amidst all the districts of India, shows the cause why there is yet no "*equalization of income and expenditure;*" and yet it fails to call forth a single remark from the Court of Directors. All the districts around have remained almost stationary, although some have, in a minor degree, had similar advantages granted to them. And the expenditure in Tanjore has been so inadequate to its requirements, that the whole of its immense traffic is still carried by common roads: whereas, had a system of canals been added to the other works, the district would probably have benefited to the extent of another 20 lacks (£200,000) a year.

And if this improvement takes place in a single isolated district, what would it be, if improvement were so far general, that the people of each district could send to distant markets the produce best cultivated by themselves, obtaining in return from distant places such things as their district could only produce at increased cost? It must be allowed that Tanjore has benefited very greatly by one improvement beyond its own limits, viz. the opening of the Paumbam Channel, between Ceylon and the Peninsula, which enables it to send its produce to Colombo one-third cheaper than before; thus producing a saving in freight on its 70,000 tons of exported rice, of more than 4 lacks (£40,000) a year. This shows how necessary it is to carry on these improvements generally, and how every district is interested in those executed in others. The sole reason why England has been paying to America instead of to India, millions a year for cotton, wheat, and rice, thus giving the former a monopoly, is, that Public Works have been energetically carried on in America, whereas they have NOT in India. And so long as the population of India are liable to scarcity and famine, and are obliged to carry their produce over hundreds of miles at a cost of *3d.* or *4d.* a ton per mile, (equal, from the greater value of money, to 1*s.* 6*d.* or 2*s.* in England,) and so long as the ports remain without shelter for shipping or depth of water for boats to land cargo, so long will the question of "*equalization of income and expenditure*" remain unsolved, even though all the wisdom of England were consumed in devising *modes of collecting Revenue*, and *reducing expenditure.* Whereas, by the general application throughout India of the Tanjore system, the country will be enabled to pay two-thirds more Revenue than it now does, with an equal increase of private property besides; and the question will then be, *how to apply a surplus*, instead of, *how to make up a deficit.*

How strange it seems that it should be necessary to argue over all this, again and again! At present two persons out of every four are employed in growing food, and a third in carrying goods; and one would suppose it would be obvious to all, that if by irrigation or any other means, one person instead of two could grow food for the whole four, and if by means of cheap transit one person could carry for 40 instead of for 4, thus leaving two and nine-tenths instead of only one out of every four persons, at liberty to labour either in providing luxuries for the four, or in producing things for sale to foreign states—then the worth of the country and its ability to pay an increased Revenue, would be enormously increased. Nobody can deny that by means of irrigation, &c., one person can grow as much food as two do now, or that by means of improved transit the same labourer would convey many times as much goods as he can with the present means; nor can it be denied that these advantages can be obtained at an outlay which would provide many times its interest: for all these points have already been proved again and again by actual results. And yet, all our Financiers are writing Despatches which imply, that there is but one way of "*equalizing your income and expenditure,*" and that nearly an impossible one, viz., *reducing the expenditure.*

The Financial Despatch of the 18th June 1852 is similar to the one already noticed, excepting in one remarkable point, viz., that it does mention as separate items, the expenditure on canals in the N. W. and on repairs of tanks in Madras; and although not a single remark is made on the results of this expenditure, yet the very notice of these works seems as if the first ray of light had dawned. Many are sure to think it really indicates the approach of daylight and one can hardly help flattering himself that it does; though after so many bitter disappointments, it is with fear and trembling that one admits the approach of such a hope. There is still however no distinction made between necessary current expenditure on repairs, and additional Capital sunk in new works; and consequently not one word about the increase of actual annual Revenue, as the return for such outlay. This is still therefore like a merchant adding together in his accounts, the current expenses of his establishment, and the cost of a new ship, or of 100 tons of goods. What merchant could tell whether he was likely to appear in the Gazette or not, if he did not keep his books in a better manner?

The only remark made by the Court on this outlay is as follows in para. 113 of the Despatch:—"We have not "overlooked the compensating circumstances, that within "the period under review, considerable outlays have been "made in the prosecution of Public Works, such as must

" eventually contribute largely to the improvement of Her " Majesty's Indian Territories." " But as the larger por- " tion of the cost of these Public Works is applicable to " such as are in progress only, and which will call for simi- " lar outlays in future years, we cannot but regard with " much anxiety the existing deficiency; and we feel the im- " portance of impressing in the strongest manner upon your " consideration, the necessity of using your most strenu- " ous endeavours to effect by every practicable economy and " retrenchment consistent with the due administration of the " public service, *such reductions of charge and debt* as may " conduce to the restoration of a favourable balance between " the receipts and expenditure of the Indian Finances." This in such a connection, is understood to mean, that Public Works must be stopped. On a late occasion when an estimate was submitted to the Madras Government for an outlay of 5,000 Rupees (£500) to run some of the Steamers employed at the Godavery works up the rivers, in order to ascertain more exactly what is required for making that magnificent river fully available, the local Government declined to sanction the expenditure upon their own responsibility, and under the impression that the object in view would cost at least Rs. 10,000 (£1,000), referred the matter to the Supreme Government, who rejected the application for this insignificant outlay, (upon which hang possible and indeed almost certain incalculable benefits to England and India) adding a few lines to the effect, that it was inexpedient in the then state of finances, to sanction money for an object of doubtful utility. With reference to these sentiments the following passage from the Court's Despatch above quoted, affords a noticeable comment:—" We have likewise found " it necessary on several occasions to remark that a considerable part of the money recently borrowed, remains in " your treasuries, and has augmented your cash balances " which have been gradually increasing for some time past,

" and are of higher amount by some crores of Rupees, " (millions sterling) than we consider the exigencies of the " public service require. While adverting to this point, " we may remark, that the latest estimate of their amount " on the 30th April 1852, exhibits the large and we believe " the unprecedented sum of 13½ crores as expected to be ly- " ing in the Indian treasuries at that date, &c. We invite " *your most earnest attention to these circumstances,* and to " the urgent expediency of applying the excess of your cash " balances to the liquidation of a portion of your debt, " or to an extensive reduction of the rate of interest now " payable upon it." But if the amount of interest were reduced without the payment of a portion of the debt, it is clear that the cash must still remain in the treasuries, and the question of the disposal of this enormous superfluity will still be where it was. It is very curious that under urgent circumstances, so small a sum as 10,000 Rupees (£1,000) could not be granted out of the 60 millions of Rupees (6 millions sterling) lying idle in the treasuries, over and above the 75 millions of Rupees (7½ millions sterling) required to veer and haul upon, with the present system of financial arrangements. It would be interesting to ascertain what portion of this latter sum would actually be necessary for the current expenditure, if only a better system of financial administration were followed.

Thus it is with this unfortunate country. It is labouring at once under two opposite evils; treasuries overflowing with millions of Rupees, and as many more ready as it chooses to accept at 4 per cent. interest, and at the same time, a want of 10,000 Rs. (£1,000) for the important object of examining an opening, by which it is well known, some of the greatest requirements both of England and India could be obtained.

It thus appears after all, that not only is it in the power of Government to obtain money for the purpose of throwing open India and relieving it from an annual expense of several millions sterling, now actually incurred in the conveyance of goods across the unimproved face of the country, but that even supposing no better system of management could be arranged than one requiring the enormous sum of 7½ millions sterling to be always in hand to meet current expenses, there are still six millions sterling now actually lying totally useless in the treasuries: quite sufficient to give 20,000 miles of lines of transit, at a cost not exceeding one-tenth of the present rate.

The examination of these financial letters is of the greatest importance, as showing exactly where the evil lies, viz., that there is an utter misapprehension of this fundamental point. No notice is taken by the Court of the only thing which can by any possibility put the finances of India to rights. How wonderful an oversight this is, when probably there is not one of the authorities who, if asked, "Do "you think England could pay a Revenue of 50 millions, if "she had no Public Works or Machinery, no Roads, Canals, "Railways, Ports, Steam and Water Power, and nothing "that enables the human power of the community to accomplish a hundred times as much as it could without "those aids?" but would answer, "She certainly could not "pay a tenth of it, without those things;" and yet, when the Court of Directors all consult together what can be done to enable India to meet her expenses, they are totally at a loss, to devise the only true remedy for existing deficiencies. If this be not one of the most extraordinary things connected with our management of India, it is at least wholly inexplicable to the Public. It cannot be that the Court believe a due attention to Public Works would set the finances to rights but think that attention unattainable, otherwise they would certainly have at least mentioned the subject; and five minutes' examination of the subject would have satisfied them that there could not be the smallest difficulty about it. Instances are before them of common roads, canals, irrigation works, &c., producing an annual return to the country of more than cent. per cent. upon the outlay; and as any amount of money, for making every sort of improvement in India, can be obtained at 5 per cent., the practicability of executing these essential works is undeniable.

The Western road from Madras, constructed by Lord Elphinstone, cost about 10,000 Rs. (£1,000) a mile (with a great waste of money), and the rate of transit has been reduced from 4¼ to 1¼ annas, (6¾ to 1¾ Pence) per ton per mile; and as there are now about 300 tons a day carried along it (besides travellers), there is an annual saving to the country from this work, of 18,500 Rupees (£1,850) a mile or nearly 200 per cent.; and had a canal been cut on the same line for 20,000 Rupees (£2,000) a mile, the traffic would probably have been increased five-fold, and the cost reduced to one-thirtieth of what it is now. Again, Cochrane's Canal, (about 10 miles of communication) costing originally perhaps 150,000 Rs. (£15,000) yields 30,000 Rupees (£3,000) a year, or 20 per cent. to Government, besides the saving to the community. Again, the opening of the Paumbam Channel, which has cost about 2½ lacks (£25,000) has reduced the cost of freight between Tanjore and Ceylon to one-third, producing in the carriage of grain alone a saving of more than 4 lacks (£40,000) a year, or 160 per cent., besides the reduction of Interest and Insurance from a shorter and safer voyage. Again, *all* the important and some minor Hydraulic Works executed in Madras during the last 14 years (exclusive of the Godavery works), have cost in all 5½ lacks (£55,000) and yielded on an average a net return to Government of 3¾ lacks (£37,000), or nearly 70 per cent. per annum from the time of their construction; and they are now yielding at least 100 per cent., besides all the profit to private individuals.* These are specimens of the effects of Public Works in India. How can it be otherwise? Does not common sense tell us, that a country in almost its natural state, occupied by millions of orderly and industrious people, must necessarily present openings for the employment of Capital in the improvement of natural advantages, far beyond what can be expected, either in a country like England where all the most obvious openings have already been taken advantage of, or in one like America where there is a deficient population?

And yet, the Court's Despatches imply first, that if the works are executed at all the cost must be defrayed out of the current Revenue; and secondly, that there is no other way of relieving the country than by paying off the debt already existing. With respect to the first, nothing can be more unreasonable and unjust; it is nothing more nor less, than the man's determination not to go into the water till he can swim. Until these works are executed the Revenue cannot seriously improve; and therefore if we wait for a surplus, we must wait for ever. And what can be more unjust even if it were possible to accomplish it, than to grind out of the present generation, the whole cost of works in which they only have a life interest? If the Capital required for the works be worth only 5 per cent., this is all that can justly be demanded of the present generation; and not one Rupee more should be taken from them. Let future generations who succeed to the possession of the works, pay their share of the cost, by meeting the current demand for Interest. Even if there were a surplus Revenue, both common sense and justice show us, that the taxes should rather be reduced, instead of such surplus being spent on Public Works of this very remunerative character.

With respect to the second point, viz., there being no way of relieving the country but by paying off the debt, let us suppose that we met a poor famished cooly fainting under

* See Statement Z. in Appendix to Madras Public Works Report.

a load of 20 lbs. from want of food, and had it in our power either to carry his load for him, or by feeding him restore him to his full strength, and enable him to carry 80 lbs. with ease; which would be the best thing to do for him? Even if all the taxes of India were taken off it would still be in a miserable state without Irrigation, Communications, Ports, &c. And to increase the income of the country, 25 millions sterling by means of these improvements, would be an incomparably greater benefit than to take off the present 25 millions of taxes; and a complete system of communications throughout India, would undoubtedly increase the income of the country by far more than 25 millions a year. Let us once more take the case of Tanjore, and suppose that instead of 40,000 Rupees (£4,000) a year being spent on improvements in Public Works, the same amount of taxes had been remitted; the district would, it is true, have had 40,000 Rupees (£4,000) a year less to pay, but it would on the other hand, have remained without those works which have raised the value of its land to 3 or 3½ crores (3½ millions sterling), indicating an increase of income of 18 or 20 lacks (£200,000) a year. Ask a sick man which he would rather a doctor should do for him; relieve him from a small part of his work? or restore him to his full health, so that his labour would be a pleasure to him? can there be any question which he would prefer? The present debt of India would be utterly insignificant to a fertile country containing 100 millions of people in a state of perfect peace; if only they had the means of cheap transit. It only amounts to half a Rupee per head per annum. The improvement in the Revenue of Tanjore alone, pays one-tenth of the interest of the debt trifling as the works are that have been executed there, and the increase in the value of private property there is equal to more than a tenth of the debt; so that if five districts out of thc 90 or 100 were thus positively improved, it would be equal to wiping off the whole debt.

When this point was expressly brought before the Court by the Madras Government, viz., the executing Public Works by means of a loan, it was not objected to, but still, nothing was done about it; the usual fate of all suggestions for the benefit of India. Debt, whether incurred for wars entailing a permanent charge upon the country without any good to counterbalance it, or for the execution of Public Works yielding 100 per cent., or 20 times the interest, is equally called a *burthen;* both are treated alike, and the same reasoning is applied to both, though one is the load on a bullock's back, and the other the wings of a bird, which instead of being a burthen, carry the body. We may safely say that there is in India an almost unlimited field for the employment of Capital that would yield at the lowest calculation 50 per cent. to the community; so that every million borrowed and spent, will in the present rate of interest (4 per cent.) be equivalent to paying off 11½ millions of debt; and this is all the *burthen* it will be to the country. A *burthen* is not an absolute, but a relative thing; and the present debt of India is a greater burthen to it with its 100 millions of inhabitants, than ten times the amount is to England with a quarter of that number of people, because India is starved to death and has no strength to bear even so trifling a burthen. A million of people in Berar are paying annually 200 or 300 lacks (2 or 3 millions sterling) a year, for rice which they grow themselves, while they could obtain it from Rajahmundry for 50 or 70 lacks (£70,000), if the Godavery navigation were opened. No wonder they cannot bear the burthen of these taxes when they have to bear this load of 150 or 200 lacks (1½ or 2 millions sterling) unnecessarily; whereas, if they could get their food so much more cheaply from Rajahmundry, they might employ their labourers in growing cotton for Manchester. And so also with respect to the sums actually paid for transit. The city of Madras for instance, pays for the carriage of firewood,

&c., at least 12 lacks (£120,000) a year, perhaps as much as 20 lacks (£200,000); nineteen-twentieths of which might be saved by improved communications. With this load, equivalent to 2 or 3 Rupees (4 or 6 shillings) a head, (more than ten times as much as their share of the interest of the Indian debt), no wonder the people are not able to bear the load of the taxes, light as they really are.

If we estimate the whole loss to India from want of communications at only 25 millions sterling, it is still twelve times as great a burthen as the interest of the debt. How is it that there are such endless discussions about relieving India from the debt, and not one word about getting rid of a load, in comparison with which, the debt is very trifling? How much easier would it be, to increase the strength of the country so that the debt shall be scarcely any burthen to it, than to get rid of the debt; and how much better to have a country in health and strength with a light load to carry, than to have a population miserable, sickly and starved, though without a load; even supposing it were *possible* to get rid of the burthen of debt, which it certainly is *not*, excepting by this one means of Public Works. India has been dealt with like a patient by an ignorant doctor, who in order to cure him of some complaint connected with the unwholesome state of his room, persists in physicing him, and thus reduces his strength more and more; whereas, if he would only give the sick man a change of air, his system would gather strength to throw off the disease of itself. What India requires is, *not* more financial doctors; but a change of circumstances. It requires no such physic as the financial Despatches prescribe, but something to invigorate the system; it wants to have the light and air let into it by means of communications. If this were only tried, it could soon throw off its present debt.

Alas for India! whatever happens, war or peace, famine or plenty, success or failure, increase of receipts or falling off, all lead to only one result, all tend to generate the lamentably false conclusion that *nothing can be done* to remedy existing evils. At the very time that a Despatch is written to India, treating with such indifference the subject of Public Works, the boast in England is, that such large sums are expended on them. The Statement above referred to, shows, for a period of 14 years throughout the whole Madras Presidency, an expenditure of only 5½ lacks of Rupees (£55,000) or 4,000£ a year (one-thousandth part of the Revenue) on new Works of Irrigation or improvements in old ones; and upon this a return of at least 200 per cent., including the benefits derived by the country, is obtained on the whole: and yet, a financial letter professing to submit a view of the whole subject, does not say one word about such an astonishing opening for relieving the finances. How often have we thought, "Well, now at any rate, the real state "of the case is proved so that it is impossible but that it "should be rightly understood, and we shall now at length "see a real energetic attention to Public Works." But hitherto we have suffered repeated disappointments; and when we have arrived at the end of 1852, this Despatch shows the results of all the efforts that have been made to awaken the Government, to a sense of the importance of these things.

It is indeed heart-breaking work; and the first impression is, what is the use of labouring for the good of India and the enrichment of the Treasury? Is it not much better to leave our rulers to go on in the old way, and India to its famines, poverty, and ignorance? But the longest night is followed by daylight at last; and surely there are symptoms of day-breaking already, at least in the North West. Surely there are manifest proofs of some increase of interest being taken in India by the people of England, and at all events the present enquiry offers an opportunity, which it would be the height of folly and wickedness to let pass without an effort to bring these matters more prominently to notice. Many at home now take a real interest in India, and there is a rapidly increasing body of men who begin to see and feel that England also is deeply concerned in the progress of this vast empire, as the prosperity of 100 millions of British subjects must powerfully affect that of the whole empire; in short that Englishmen are personally interested in India, and that whatever vitally affects that country is their personal concern. This at least gives an opening for hope, that the weight of England may be brought to bear upon this matter.

Manchester especially has made its voice heard, and its power felt in Indian matters; and there is even some evidence that it is sensible of its remarkable power as the proper substitute for a free and powerful Public voice in India itself. To its commercial population at least, the progress of things in India is a vital question; whether the country is to be dependent on America alone for cotton and cheap bread, or whether it is to have two strings to its bow, and two competitors for its custom and goods. If Manchester suffers such a state of things as above described without the most determined efforts to bring about a great change, certainly it will deserve to find itself some day deprived of its very life-blood by war with the United States, or some other catastrophe. India can be enabled to supply England abundantly and cheaply, with two essentials, flour and cotton; and nothing whatever prevents India doing so at this moment, but the want of Public Works. If only the country were, by means of Irrigation, enabled to produce food as cheaply and abundantly as it could easily be made to do, and if by means of communications, its produce could be cheaply conveyed to the Coast, then Manchester is safe; for its supply of the two things upon which its very existence depends, cannot fail. But while three-fourths of the people of India are employed in raising food, and an eighth in carrying their produce over the unimproved face of the country at a cost that would instantly paralyze England if subjected to such an incubus, this magnificent appendage to England must be comparatively lost to her, and the prodigious, and incalculable stimulus that it might give to her manufacturing and general prosperity, must be in a great measure lost.

The only way that I ever heard this neglect of such a country by her rulers satisfactorily accounted for, was by a shrewd friend, who said, "Sir, the fact is, that such a coun-
" try with its immense population and unbounded capabili-
" ties would, if it had been managed with the smallest degree
" of European energy and intelligence have thrown such
" amazing means into the hands of England, as totally
" to destroy the balance of power, and place her so im-
" measurably ahead of all other countries, as would have
" made her mistress of the world." Perhaps now that the United States have made such progress in population, &c., as to form a powerful counterpoise, this cause for India being kept in a state of paralysis is removed; and the time may now have arrived, when England may be safely trusted with the vast accession of power, which an active and enlightened management of India will inevitably give her. Suppose all the rest of India had been treated only as Tanjore has been, what could have prevented the same results following universally; the population being doubled, the Revenue increased 70 per cent. and the value of private property quadrupled? And suppose that instead of only the imperfect works that have been given to Tanjore in a long course of years, (half a century) all India, had as fast as it was acquired, been boldly and liberally supplied with the works which are indispensable to a state of life and prosperity; and thus been relieved from a burthen equal to the whole present taxation of the country, and at the same time provided with that powerful stimulus which free intercourse

would supply, who cannot see that the addition of such a source of supply for England's manufactures and such a market for her goods, would have placed her in such a position of power and independence as cannot be estimated? How coolly we talk of 100 millions of people and how little we think what such a population might be, if roused from their torpor and despondency, brought into a state of life and activity, and united under one intelligent government!

CHAPTER III.

VIEWS OF THE GOVERNMENT AND CIVIL SERVICE OF INDIA ON THE RELATIVE IMPORTANCE OF THE MODE OF COLLECTING THE LAND REVENUE, AND THE PROMOTION OF PUBLIC WORKS.

Views of the Civil Service.

HAVING thus examined the opinions held on these subjects by the authorities in England concerned in the Government of India, let us go on to investigate the views of the ruling body in India, the Civil Service, the actual executives who are to carry out the orders of the superior powers. Are they writhing under the system under which they are employed? Have they from seeing the practical working of these views on the spot, in the poverty, ignorance and despondency of this immense population in the provinces, and the want of every thing which should mark the country to be under a powerful, intelligent, well instructed, and energetic European people, with unbounded means at their disposal and above all with the principles of truth and righteousness taught them in the Bible—have these men generally, from seeing continually the fruit of the views of their superiors, become so deeply sensible of the utter ignorance displayed in them, as to be weary of being parties to such a system? Have they been incessantly pressing upon their notice the disgraceful results of such a mistaken system in the actual state of the people? Have they urged upon the consideration of their rulers, the measures unavoidably resorted to, to get out of the people the insignificant Revenue paid by such a multitude in such a fertile country? Have they been continually pointing out, that so long as such a system is pursued, it is impossible that the Revenue should improve, or Government be supplied with the means of improving the condition of the people, and marking the country as having been under the government of a wise, benevolent and energetic people? Have they said, "We "have now tried for 50 or 100 years what can be done, by "keeping our eyes incessantly fixed on that one point which "we at first learnt from the Native Governments who pre-"ceded us, to be *the thing* on which all national prosperity "depended, viz., the *mode of collecting the Land Revenue;* "and we have found that not one single step in advance "has been made by means of it; that the people are still "as ignorant, as poor, as inert, and as helpless as the day "they came under our power. We have done our utmost; "we have screwed out of them the last Rupee that we could "get from them, in order to try and show a good result in "the amount of Revenue, and we have utterly failed: and "we must in every respect and on every occasion press "upon your notice, that whatever may be done about *col-"lecting,* so long as nothing is done about *producing* the "sources of Revenue, we shall never have a Rupee available "for the instruction and improvement of the people."

Nothing could be more to my present purpose than the work lately published by Mr. Campbell, called "*Modern*

India;" a work intended to give a complete view of all essential points connected with the country. It is not the work of a man of former days, nor is it that of a man who though really younger, is in fact of the old school in his ideas generally; an opponent of all improvement and a worshipper of evils provided they have only been long in existence; neither has he even been associated with the old school men. On the contrary, he is evidently one of the best specimens of the Civil Service, the governing body; though not a man of unusual talent, he is evidently a sensible, active minded man, heartily interested in the country and in his duties and brought up in a new school incomparably superior to any yet seen in India; a school which has given us the first prospect of better things, and exhibited one of the best indications of honesty, in not being altogether afraid of the public knowing what it is about. A multitude of things have been introduced in the North West Provinces which are quite new, and looked upon with horror by the thorough old school men, things which beyond all doubt are calculated immensely to improve the condition of India, and indicate an awakening of the mind of the Civilians there, which compared with the torpor elsewhere, is like life from the dead. Now let us see what is the main point in the estimation of a man who is the type of the best class of the governing body; of the most enlightened, intelligent, zealous, and earnest portion of that body who really hold the welfare of India in their hands. If we search his book through and through, we shall find that this point is nothing more or less than *the mode of collecting the Land Revenue; not* the education of the people, *not* the securing to them a never-failing and abundant supply of food, or the power of transporting the produce of labour from where it is worthless to where it is valuable, *not* the free intercourse of the inhabitants, nor even the diffusion of the knowledge of that Religion in which alone the true principles of right and wrong are found; neither in one of these things, nor in all of them together does Mr. Campbell consider the great means of good government to lie, but rather in this one grand root of all good and evil, happiness and misery, wealth and poverty, safety and danger, *the mode of collecting the Land Revenue!*

Mr. Campbell states that the "Magistrate and Collector is a sort of local governor." Certainly if he be not so, if he be not the representative of Government in his district in all capacities excepting the Judicial, there is nobody else whose business it is to attend to the various interests and wants of a community such as that of India, who stand in the same relation to their present rulers, as children in a nursery to their grown up guardians. What they cannot do for themselves we must do for them. With his magisterial duties, therefore he is not merely the *Collector*, but the person who should in the fullest sense of the word superintend the district; and it is his business to attend to every thing upon which the well being of the people depends, excepting of course Judicial matters. If it be said, "No, this is never intended; his duty is solely to *collect the Revenue*, as that of the Judge is to investigate crime," then it is admitted that Government looks with perfect indifference on the sources of good and evil in the country; considering its sole duty to be, after securing peace, to hang criminals, and pay itself for so doing. But this is totally contrary to all that is said; for theoretically the Government is generally acknowledged to have the whole welfare of the people in its keeping. Even supposing however that the sole business of Government were to pay itself for keeping peace and hanging criminals, it is still a complete mistake to suppose that its officers have nothing to do but to *collect* Revenue, and that the people will without any aid, procure the means of paying the taxes. If only a thousandth part of the time and labour expended on adjusting and *collecting* the Revenue, were bestowed on the means best calculated to enable the people easily to pay it; the Government would be rolling in money.

But to return to our author. Even meeting him on his own ground, and supposing the ultimate end and object of Government to be simply to obtain a certain amount of Revenue, and that amount to be the sole test of what is done, (for Mr. Campbell winds up his statements of the management of each Presidency by a simple statement of Revenue collections designated as the "Result" of the Ryotwar system), can any thing be conceived more absurd, than to take it for granted that these results are simply the effects of a certain mode of *collecting the Revenue?* A man might almost as well conclude, on seeing his friend look unwell, that it was because he was wearing a coat of some particular colour. Mr. Campbell takes the general collections of all Madras, and gathers from them the *effects* of the Ryotwar system. And yet, amongst these districts, are some that have upon the whole made at times, or throughout our rule steady progress; others that are now in a most wretched state, and others again that had at one time sunk excessively low, but are now to a great degree restored, without these fluctuations having the least reference to the kind of settlement in the districts. But can any one who thinks at all seriously on the matter, for a moment believe that there are no more powerful agencies at work than the *mode of collecting the Revenue*, even in respect of the amount of that Revenue? I shall not attempt to go into this subject generally, nor have I the least pretension to be competent to it: the only two points which I insist upon, are; first, that the whole governing body, (of which Mr. Campbell is a type) do in fact, as a body, though of course not without individual exceptions, really act upon the principle, that *the mode of collecting the Revenue* is *the one thing* to be thought of; and secondly, that there are in reality many other points of incalculably more importance than this one; and among them the promotion of Public Works.

Let us now take a district under this so-called wretched Ryotwar management, by which every miserable victim is condemned to hold his own land, whether much or little, independent of all his neighbours, and obliged to do whatever he pleases with it, without any other ryot having the right to interfere with him; a thing which would in England be considered an advantage, but in this extraordinary country, is it seems, the greatest misfortune under which a man can labour. Let us suppose this district, though possessing a fertile soil and partial supplies of water, to be yet in a great measure liable to lose its crops from irregularity of seasons, (sometimes floods, sometimes drought) and also to be for the greater part of the year without any means of transporting its produce, owing to the soil being alluvial, and the rivers unbridged; and further let us suppose that Government immediately on taking possession, begin to expend annually a certain sum of money, either in keeping off floods, leading water in new directions, or opening communications, so as to enable the land to yield a return on the outlay of 200 per cent. Assuming that 30 lacks (£300,000) is the Revenue at first, and that by means of 40,000 Rupees (£4,000) laid out annually on improvements (besides a like amount, necessary to keep up the progress already made) a progressive increase of *income* of 80,000 Rupees (£8,000) a year is obtained; this outlay if continued for fifty years, would cause a total increase of *income* of 40 lacks (£400,000) a year. The *Revenue* taken from the district will thus have increased by 20 lacks, (from £300,000 to £500,000) and as it is actually counted into the treasury there can be no question about that. The increase of income to the people 20 lacks, (£200,000) is shown by the saleable value of the land having increased by 300 or 400 lacks of Rupees (3 to 4 millions sterling), and yielding interest to the proprietors at 5 or 6 per cent. Suppose that one of the ways in which this return for outlay has been obtained, is by supplying 7,500 cubic yards of water to each acre of land at a cost of 5 Rupees (10 shillings) of Capital, whereby an increase of produce is obtained to the extent of 10 Rupees (£1) a year per acre, more than before. Another is, by laying out 1,000 Rupees (£100) on a mile of road, by means of which 50 tons of goods per day are conveyed all the year round, at one Anna (1½*d.*) less per ton per mile than they could previously be carried in the dry season only; being a saving of 1,000 Rupees (£100) a year, besides the gain by being able to convey the goods in the wet season, and let us suppose the district to be thus provided with 1,000 miles of road, effecting a saving of 10 lacks (£100,000) a year in transit alone.* This is a correct statement of what has been done in Tanjore and will enable any person to understand, how even under a wretched Ryotwar system, a district may stand Mr. Campbell's test, and show a very comfortable increase of Revenue; and such an improvement as would if extended over five districts only, meet the average balance against India of 1 million a year, for the last 30 years.

On the other hand let us take another district, under Zemindary and Village settlement, where almost every farthing collected, (except what is expended on collection) is sent out of the district; where the old and partial means of securing a supply of food are left to go to ruin, and not a mile of road made in it; not a reservoir of water constructed; not an embankment thrown up to prevent the river drowning any extent of crop, and not a stream bridged: so that almost its produce except what can be consumed in the

* Besides these ordinary advantages let us suppose that the district were, once in 20 or 30 years, when the whole Carnatic is deprived of its usual local rains, enabled in consequence of the care taken to provide it with water, to sell nearly half its own produce at enormous prices to all the surrounding districts, thus nearly doubling its income for that year, instead of sharing in the general calamity, and having to import half its food at a high price.

village where it grows, is utterly valueless. Besides this ordinary state of things, let us suppose a failure of local rains to occur, which in consequence of its being unmitigated by a single tank of water, or a single channel leading water from an unfailing river which borders the district for 80 miles, gives rise to the utmost horrors of famine, sweeping off in a few months fully half of the population, and reducing the Revenue at once by 14 lacks (£140,000) a year; a loss which is not fully recovered for twelve years. Now this is a correct statement of what has happened in Guntoor. Does any body find it hard to understand how any kind of *settlement* would have failed to make this a flourishing district? Let any gentleman in England manage two estates in these two different ways. Let him manage one Ryotwar, letting it out to a number of small and large farmers independently, and expending a portion of the rent every year upon it in such a manner as to make it more productive to the extent of 2½ per cent. than previously, while he only raises the rent 1¼ per cent.; and let him manage the other by giving all his tenants a joint lease of it, but take the whole rent without expending one farthing on repairs or improvements; let him continue this for 50 years, and then take his friends to see the *results of his two modes of settlement* with his tenants.

Now let us suppose as regards Tanjore, that instead of the petty trifling way in which it has been improved, a really intelligent and vigorous system had been pursued. Suppose for instance that instead of 40,000 Rupees (£4,000) a year, even 1 lack (£10,000) only had been spent in irrigation improvements, so that the district had been brought into tolerable order in that respect in 20 years instead of 50; and that by continuing the expenditure, sufficient water had been stored up, to supply it throughout the dry season, and thus enable the people to grow sugar and other valuable products, instead of being as now, without water for four months, and growing rice only. Under the former system, the district might long ere this, have been exporting 100,000 tons of sugar a year, worth 200 lacks (2 millions sterling) besides various other things. Let us suppose further, that instead of merely constructing in the course of the latter 30 years of the 50, very imperfect unmetalled roads worked at 3 Annas (4½*d.*) per ton per mile, a system of steam canals, by which goods could be carried at half a Pice, (one-sixteenth of a penny) per ton per mile, had been commenced from the first. At present there are just 1,000 miles of road in the district ; and supposing the average traffic to be equal to 50 tons of goods a day, the daily cost must be 9,000 Rupees (£900) or 32 lacks (£320,000) a year. If steam canals had been provided for the great bulk of the traffic, this would have relieved the district from an expenditure of 25 lacks (£250,000) a year on the goods and passengers moved ; besides at least an equal sum being probably gained in the additional value given to goods which are now not moved or sold at all, on account of the present high rates of transit. With these improvements an additional income of at least 100 lacks (1 million) in more valuable products would have been gained, and a saving would have been effected in transit, worth 50 lacks (half a million) a year, so that the Revenue might now be 100 lacks (1 million sterling) instead of 50 lacks, (½ million sterling) and the net income of the people also 100 lacks (1 million) more than at present. And all this might have been done without a Rupee (2*s.*) being permanently withdrawn from the general treasury; for the district would itself have more than repaid the outlay for all these improvements from year to year, out of the additional Revenue it would have been yielding ; just as of late in the Rajahmundry district, where, while 20 lacks (£200,000) have been spent in 8 years, 30 lacks (£300,000) of additional Revenue have been received. No reason whatever can be assigned, why this should not have been done, and thus this one district been enabled instead of paying £200,000 a year in mere Revenue towards the late annual deficit of a million, to pay £700,000 or seven-tenths of the whole deficit ; and only two districts so improved, would have made the difference of our having for the last 30 years a surplus Revenue upon all India of half a million sterling, instead of a deficit of a million. And I think we may venture to say this would have been the case even under the Revenue system which according to Mr. Campbell is the worst in India ; that is, even if every land owner had been compelled to manage his own land in his own way, and without the interference of his neighbours.

Is it not astonishing that sensible men can be so blinded as to imagine that every thing depends upon the *mode of collection of the land Revenue* throughout India ? When a district that pays 20 lacks (£200,000) a year in Revenue, is paying the same for transit or for want of transit, who cannot see that there is at least one thing of more importance than "the Settlement ?" I have brought forward most prominently this point of Public Works ; but it is only *one* of many, all of which are of a hundred times more importance than "the Settlement." Take for instance Education. Suppose some "Collector" had taken it into his head, that an intelligent and instructed million of people would be better off in every way than a million of people raised very little above the beasts, in fact as entirely without any thing that can properly be called knowledge, as their bullocks ; and that under this idea he had everywhere established schools where all fundamental knowledge could be acquired in the vernacular languages—what would be the state of his district by the time a generation had grown up ? Suppose further, that he had been so fanciful as to think that it might even be of some use to them to know the true principles of right and wrong, of truth and falsehood, and had caused them to be instructed in the only religion where they were to be found, so that instead of falsehood being almost invariable, and truth scarcely known, his district had been brought up to the standard of England; so that when a Judge entered upon a trial, he could stand upon the ground, that it was ten to one the evidence he heard was true. Suppose a district under such a system as this, and consider whether the people might not be better off upon the whole, even under a miserable Ryotwar settlement like that which England groans under, than under a Village settlement, but without any knowledge or right principles? Nothing is more certain, than that it is quite possible, not only for an individual, but for a whole body, thus to have their attention so fixed upon some comparatively insignificant point, as altogether to lose sight of a hundred other things of incalculably greater importance; and until the governing body are driven out of this strange infatuation, the progress of India must be slow indeed.

Let any person only consider the countless volumes that have been written on this frothy question, "What is the best mode of collecting the land Revenue;" not merely by inferior men, but by our very ablest Governors and Collectors, from Sir T. Munro downwards; and can he fail to be astonished beyond measure at the way in which this matter has been treated? It was originally purely a Native idea, and is a perfect specimen of the operations of the Asiatic mind; similar to the notion of the Brahmins, that a man's eternal happiness depends upon his never having trodden upon a bit of leather, without purifying himself afterwards. Of all the sad and depressing things continually before our eyes in India, one of the worst is, to see the Anglo-Saxon who has been born and bred in an atmosphere of freedom and knowledge in which his mental vision has expanded and strengthened beyond anything before seen in the world, allowing his mind gradually to shrink and contract, until he at last comes to think the poor wretched ideas of the bookless Asiatics, the height of wisdom. Thus daily to witness the mental deterioration of fine intelligent young men, is indeed most melancholy; and yet, there is nothing surprising in it. The young lad on entering the Civil Service in India, is sent to some remote place, where he sits from morning to night surrounded by his slavish Native Cutcherry servants; and continues immersed in this poisonous atmosphere day after day, and year after year, with but very little intercourse either with Europeans or with books. Under such circumstances, how should anything better be expected than that without being in the least sensible of it himself, his mind should become more and more dwarfed, till he really sees things with Natives' eyes? Of course, a few active minded energetic men keep themselves to a considerable extent above this influence; but I can safely affirm, that until of late years, there was hardly an individual in the Civil Service, who had not been more or less grievously injured in this way, and I confidently appeal to the state of India at this moment, in proof of the assertion. Is it at this moment in an Asiatic or a European condition? How is the time of a *Collector* occupied? What portion of it in matters immediately connected with the collection of the Revenue, and how much on matters calculated to raise either physically and mentally, the state of the people?

To an Engineer in India intent on Public improvements, the thing that continually weighs him down is, that he cannot but feel at every step that he is transacting business with men, who relinquishing their English notions, are imbued with Native views of things, imbibed with the air they have breathed in Cutcherries, for 10, 20 or 30 years. Do these men think that the welfare of the people depends upon their having correct principles, and knowledge of right and wrong, books, means of intercourse, and the power of exchanging commodities, or upon a proper division of labour, whereby only a small portion of the community are employed in producing the actual necessaries of life, while the rest are thereby set free to prosecute arts, sciences, learning, &c.? Not in the least; these are matters of no importance in their estimation: *the question* is, "How is the payment of the land tax arranged?" They do not even consider it a matter of any moment, compared with the *mode of collecting*, whether by facilitating the production and transport of food and manufactures, the *income* of the *district* might not be increased tenfold; that is, whether the Revenue drawn be one-fourth, or one-fortieth of the *income* of the people. And yet, these are all Englishmen who know that our national prosperity and strength, are the results of the enormous economy of human labour by means of Public Works, whereby only a few are actually employed in providing the mere necessaries of life, (food, clothing, and shelter) thus leaving a large number of the people at liberty to promote learning, arts, &c.

Until this erroneous idea that *the one thing needful* is the *Revenue Settlement*, be given up, nothing can be done. Till the attention of the Civil Service is turned to the *sources of income*, and the circumstances of the people thus improved, we shall be met at every step as hitherto, with the invariable answer, "*we can't afford it*," and there will be no education or any thing which can really elevate the people. One of the first and fundamental things is, by means of Public Works to increase the income of the country; and this is entirely within our reach, since any amount of money can be obtained from without, for the execution of improvements which will pay 10 or 20 times the interest of the capital. There is not a shadow of ground for delaying these things one day, and they will naturally place at the disposal of Government, funds for every other purpose. If the increase of Revenue in Tanjore were not all carried off to supply the deficiencies of the districts which have been utterly neglected, there would be abundance of means there for every purpose. If it paid only its share of the current deficit, (in addition to its original Revenue of 30 lacks (£300,000) which may be taken at 1 per cent. on a million sterling, or 1 lack) (£10,000) there would still remain 19 lacks (£190,000) available. One half of this, say 9 lacks (£90,000) might be at once given up to the people, by abolishing such items of taxation as are most burthensome, and 10 lacks (£100,000) would still remain for education and such other things as could not yield a direct return in money. At the same time, all sorts of works which could conveniently provide a direct income to cover interest, should be carried on without stint by means of borrowed capital. For instance, a canal capable of bearing Steamers of 300 tons should be cut through Tanjore, and extended to Madras and the Western Coast, thus throwing the district open to both Home and Foreign trade. Such a work if executed for 20,000 Rupees (£2,000) a mile, would produce a saving of at least 30,000 Rupees (£3,000) a mile per annum, taking a traffic of 2,40,000 tons at 2 Annas (*3d.*); and hence after paying 1,000 Rupees (£100) as interest, the income of the district would still be augmented by 29,000 Rupees (£2,900) a year, for each mile, or 20 lacks (£200,000) a year on one main line. The great mass of trade being thus provided for, to be carried at an almost nominal price, Tanjore would soon be rich enough to afford to have high speed for travelling and conveyance of valuable goods, as in England. Another portion of capital might be borrowed for the purpose of providing water by storing in reservoirs, for the summer irrigation; and so on.

The district being thus enriched, its income increased from 200 lacks (2 millions sterling) a year to 300 or 400 lacks (3 or 4 millions sterling) and the Revenue reduced from 50 to 40 lacks (from half a million to £400,000) by the removal of burthensome taxation, what would then become of the great question, *the mode of collecting the land Revenue?* This would be found to be easily settled, when the amount was only 10 per cent. of the income, instead of 30 or 40 per cent., as at present.

By the way the Tanjore district affords a curious comment on the endless discussions about "*the Settlement.*" For 20 years past, one-half of it has been settled Ryotwar, and the other half Mouzawar; and there is no difference to signify between the condition of the two. The same is the case also in two divisions of Mysore. In Nuggur, the old Native system was almost entirely abrogated when the country came under British administration, the Ryotwar system introduced, and other changes of the same sort made: whilst in Chittledroog, the old village system, with division of the crop, &c., was continued. In both, the Revenue has increased very much; quite as much in the latter as in the former; and the improvement is chiefly attributable in the first place, to steady and honest government; secondly, to European superintendence, and thirdly, to the attention given to roads, tanks, &c.

A new work entitled "*India as it may be*" has recently been published by Mr. Campbell; in which he attempts the harder task of setting things to rights. Nothing is clearer to me, than that no Indian Civilian can possibly do this. The man who could write Mr. Campbell's first book, has proved that no one of his class can accomplish the object of the second. His whole head must be emptied of its present views and notions, before it can possibly find room for such as are required to enable a man to make India "*what it may be.*" Witness one single specimen of Mr. Campbell's ideas, in the opinion that gagging and secrecy are essential to good and effective government. We are to believe that he *would prefer* being compelled by his superiors to pass among his fellow countrymen and Native fellowmen, as a man of infamy, rather than run the risk of a system of publicity. And of course the man who could thus allow himself to be degraded by his superiors, would act on the same principle towards his subordinates, and prohibit them the right of justifying themselves in the sight of their fellow-men. Is it not astonishing that in our day men can be found—*Englishmen*—who dare publicly to declare, that such is their fear of publicity, that they will rather submit to the most degrading position, than have their conduct openly discussed? Rather allow any stains upon their character, than be liable to such a publication of their official acts, as will enable their fellow rulers and fellow subjects to judge of their conduct generally? Need we enquire one step further to satisfy ourselves of the utter unsoundness of a system which leads men to prefer anything to the light? "He that doeth truth cometh to the light that his deeds may be made manifest." Is it not enough to make a man ashamed of his country and service, to see such principles openly acknowledged? Any man may make great mistakes from want of judgment, &c.; but if he be honest, he will never be afraid of publicity. The system of gagging their servants, at once stamps a Government as unsound and dishonest; and those who are slaves as subordinates, are surely training for tyrants when they get into power. This secrecy is one of the blights under which India has withered hitherto, and so deeply rooted is this principle, that it can never be eradicated but by a power from without. What thousands of abominations are daily perpetrated, that could not stand one moment's exposure, if liable to it immediately after the act! A man stands up and confesses himself the author of such an atrocity as the Affghan War, after an interval of some years, but he dare not have looked his country in the face, if his agency in the matter had been discovered soon after the war had been entered upon. The grand check upon evil must be the liability to seeing it all in print the next morning; and the knowledge that all the facts will be made known to every body, before the interest of the matter is lost. How wonderful it seems then, that any body of men can be so misguided as openly to declare that they dare not have their official acts known and canvassed; thus admitting that they are bent on doing things which will not bear the light.

If we examine Mr. Campbell's system of Finance, we find it equally unsound. *If* he can get an additional million out of Oude, *if* he can reduce the Military Establishment by 2⅓ millions, &c., (observe how tenderly he deals with the Civil Service, who are only to surrender one-twelfth of what the Army is to give up) *if* he can thus obtain a surplus income of 4 millions, *then* he will put all to rights. All this is mere speculation; we know very well that there is not the slightest probability of reducing the Army or plundering Oude to this extent, or anything approaching to it, and so there is an end to the whole scheme; and he might have just as well have suggested nothing. About the *sources* of Revenue Mr. Campbell scarcely says a word; though he has, it is true, at the end of his book a few pages about Public Works, just enough to show that he totally misapprehends the whole matter, as is universally done by the Civil Service. He indeed ends his book with this notable discovery, "Without money we can do nothing;" a conclusion which a man might arrive at, without reading the volume through, and without any great genius. If after reading Mr. Campbell's book we had been rewarded by being informed, *how* this money was to be got, it would have been more satisfactory. If some body would only take up the matter where Mr. Campbell leaves it, and proceed to show how to improve the *sources* of Revenue, he would do us better service. Why are the people so poor at present? Because, being entirely without any means, excepting bullocks, which can be substituted for human labour, it is as much as they can do to feed, clothe and shelter themselves; or rather I should say, *more* than they can do, at least while they have to keep their rulers in luxury. This is the plain indisputable answer to the question. On the other hand, why is England rich? that is, why has it the means of supplying itself with a thousand things beyond the mere necessaries of life? Because, while it contains only 25 millions of people, there is as much done by the aid of Steam, Water, Roads, Canals, Railroads, Ports, Docks, &c., as could be effected by the labour of perhaps 200 millions of people; and having therefore the work of that number, while the necessaries of life are required for only one-eighth, there is of course an enormous surplus of wealth exchangeable for other things. And this is not peculiar to one country; for if besides the labour of 140 millions in India, we had the work of another 500 millions performed by means of Roads, Canals, Railways, Water, Steam, &c., there would be in India also abundance of labour available for other things beyond the necessaries of life, and consequently abundance of wealth.

Now where is the difficulty? Thousands want to lend money at 4 per cent., thousands of Europeans and Natives want employment as Superintendents of Works, &c., thousands of Iron Manufacturers and others in England want a sale for their goods, lacks of people in India want employment as labourers and artificers, millions of Ryots want water for millions of acres; tens of thousands of miles of communication and the means of carrying produce need to be constructed, and thus millions might be expended so as to yield 10, 20 or 50 times the interest paid for them. Every thing is ready except *one thing;* but here we encounter *the* difficulty which has kept India immersed in ignorance and poverty, from the day we commenced our rule up to this day. It is this; *that Englishmen instead of teaching the Natives of India the things which make us what we are, sit down to learn of the Natives the things that make them what they are.* How wonderful it is, that a man who, if he were in England, would be certainly engaged in furthering every thing in which England glories, should in India, occupy himself from morning to night with this notable subject, *the settlement of the land Revenue of his district.* He sees for instance that his district is paying 10 or 20 lacks (£200,000) a year for the transit of goods, and that it cannot find a sale for what it produces for want of the means of sending it to places where saleable ; and yet he is completely at a loss as to what can be done to relieve and improve it. He turns again to the "*Settlement,*" and tries once more what he knows has been tried a thousand times before in vain, viz., how to make a district steeped in poverty pay additional Revenue, without increasing its resources. He sees and hears of capital employed in almost every kind of Public Works yielding 50 or 100 per cent. ; he sees the people of his own district producing for themselves certain articles of food, clothing, &c., at double or treble the cost for which these could be procured from another part of the country if there were but cheap transit ; whilst other districts are wanting, and paying double or treble for things which could be got far more cheaply from his district ; and yet he cannot think of any thing to enrich the people except giving a little more time to the "*Settlement,*" or reading a few more thousand sheets of paper on that everlasting subject. Here is the real and the sole difficulty ; but to remove it, one word from our rulers is all that is required ; every thing else is ready, and has long been ready. Let them only open a Loan for 20 millions to begin with, order the expenditure of 3 lacks a year in every district, purchase a million tons of rails and such other things as can be got at once for money, and will help towards *the improvement of the resources of the country ;* and the whole difficulty is got over. This might be done to-morrow ; it is only necessary that what has been so well done by the Governor General about the Telegraph, be applied to every thing else of this kind; that is, to say "Let it be done." But like every thing else that has ever been done to promote the real welfare of India, it must come from without; for all past experience shows how little hope there is of its coming from within.

CHAPTER IV.

NECESSITY OF ANGLICIZING THE SYSTEM OF GOVERNMENT.

Old Indian ideas the destruction of India.

There is a great deal of talk now about the necessity of having the Court of Directors filled with old Indians. Old Indians are the destruction of India. A few indeed are necessary on account of their knowledge of Indian matters, but what is wanted is a great majority of untainted Englishmen; Englishmen who are not turned into Asiatics. India never can make a fair start in the race of improvement, till old Indians are in the minority among the ruling body. What is wanted is, representatives from different classes in England, who will bring their English energy and understanding to the work. They would make mistakes no doubt, but they would not make *the* mistake, of ruling India on Indian principles and notions. Hopeless must the case be while the ruling body is only recruited by Indians, and those old Indians too. Who cannot see that while we have only old men and old ideas connected with the abominable state of things which has so long existed in India, there can be nothing fresh, nothing vigorous, no life in the system of Indian Government. In looking back on the past history of India, have we so much reason to be satisfied with the results, that our grand plan should be to perpetuate old views and ideas ? To say nothing of the certain effects upon every man, of 30, 40 or 50 years of life in India, one of the great curses of Indian service is, that nobody can be in any situation of influence till he is quite past his best days. It should be considered that a man of 50 in the Indian service, is on an average quite as old as one who has passed 60 years in England ; and what would be the state of England, if no man could be in either of the Houses of Parliament, or in any important office of Government, until he was past 60 ; especially in such days as these, when the progress of things is so much more rapid than it ever was before ? Only let it be remembered that all those in Council, in the Boards, or at the head of Departments, are men of 30, 40, or 50 years' service, who have undergone the wear of an Indian climate for that time ; and that most of the Members of the Court of Directors are of the same class in age, and who can then feel surprized that we are *rather* behind hand, and that we have plenty of counsel, but very little action ? A matter comes before an old worn-out Board ; it is sent on to a still more worn-out Council, and it ends with a Court, whose chief boast is, that it is composed principally of Members a little older still. Is it surprizing that India perishes for want of *action ?* What we want is, that in every branch of the Government there should be a large proportion of men, in full possession of all their energy and activity. In England, every thing is kept alive, because men in the prime of life meet on equal terms with those who have had long experience, but have lost much of their energy ; whereas in India, a man must not speak till he is long past his best days.

What is the inevitable consequence of such a state of things ? just what we have always had ; a miserable, dwarfed system of proceeding, which makes us the contempt of the Asiatics themselves. The only counteracting thing is, that we have often had young Governors and Governors General, or at least men who though of considerable age, have come out with all their energies unimpaired by a long Indian residence, and with their fresh English notions. But when our edifice of senility has been capped with a real old worn-out Indian, the consequence has been melancholy indeed. A sprinkling of men, fresh from England, young enough to be in full possession of all their energies, would be invaluable in the Boards and Councils of India, notwithstanding their want of Indian experience; and some change of system, providing an opening for those to be heard, who though young in age and in the service, are men of talent and energy, is essential to the vigorous government of India. At present, whatever a man may be, he is kept down till his time is gone by, before he can be admitted into any place of importance in the Government. What numbers of men of talent, who would have been invaluable if they had been Heads of Departments at 30 or 40 years of age, have been kept in insignificant posts and not allowed to speak, till they were so much shaken in constitution, that they were fit for nothing, and have then taken an appointment in a Board or in Council, as a place of rest. What we want is, *action;* we have had *counsel* till India is a standing disgrace to England; now let us try another plan. Instead of Falstaff's proportion of bread to sack, let us have a little more *action* and a little less *counsel.* It would be strange indeed if any proposition however good should survive, if it has to run the gauntlet of all the "*buts,*" that it will encounter from the scores of old Indians it has to pass in the Boards, Councils, and Courts, that are arrayed against it. Any one stolid old school man among the whole, may succeed in effectually arresting and strangling the wisest project. How many undeniably essential things declared to be "excellent plans," by all the Boards and Councils, have received their quietus from a single "*but,*" from some dreaming old man, who just wakes up enough to remember that there was nothing of that sort when he was a "Collector," and thinks therefore that the only safe plan is not to run the risk of attempting it.

Thus it *has been,* thus it *is,* and thus it *ever will be,* till there is some fundamental change in the system, both in England and India ; and till people begin to consider that though "*counsel*" is a good thing, yet that "*action*" is essential. Some children were walking with their nurse, and they came to a cottage. "Oh," said the children, "where is your favourite old hen that used to sit so well." "She sat rather too well, master." "Too well, how could that be." "Why, she did nothing but sit. She had grown "so old that she had not warmth enough to hatch, so I got "a younger one. To be sure she is rather careless, and "breaks an egg now and then, but she hatches the rest." Thus India has been sat upon for 50 years, but as yet there are no signs of hatching ; not a chirp has yet been heard, and if more warmth be not applied soon, we must not be surprized some day to find that instead of life, we have under us nothing but corruption. The present state of things cannot possibly continue very long. For my part so heartily sick and ashamed am I, when I look at the present wretched state of these millions so long under the Government of a Christian and civilized nation, that I should like to have an Act passed, that no man who had been more than 15 years in India should be in Court, Council, or Board, either Governor, or Head of a Department ; and that at least half should never have been in India at all. Something however must be done to eradicate the old effete system, and to substitute in its place, an honest, manly, open, vigorous one which shall not compel men to issue orders proclaiming to the world, that they are afraid of being found out ; one which shall place the country twenty years hence in such a state that we shall be able to point boldly to it, and challenge the world to deny that its millions have been in every way immeasurably benefited by our rule. We have indeed nominally a free Press now, but the liberty to publish what nobody is at liberty to send for publication, is a very negative sort of freedom. "But," says some one, "Would not a greater "degree of freedom give too much license to the corrupt, de- "graded, insolent Indian Press?" To meet this friend on his own ground, I would say, gas and oil sometimes remind us that the town is not lighted with amber; but still honest men, when they can't have the light of the sun, prefer these imperfect substitutes, to leaving themselves entirely at the mercy of thieves and cut-throats. Monopolists would gladly cut off the supplies from the newspapers, just as London thieves would gladly cut the gas pipes; not that they are afraid of the thing itself, but of the light that it produces. An honest man even, may now and then find the gas-light inconvenient; but upon the whole as he is conscious that he has no intention of injuring his neighbour, he accounts it an inestimable benefit. At present as things are, Editors are cut off, as far as the power of the governing body goes, from all authentic sources of information, and are then reproached for misrepresentations. People do not consider to how great a degree matters are kept in a healthy state in England, by the degree of publicity which obtains; and so long as India is deprived of the incalculable advantage of a watchful intelligent public being informed every morning of whatever was done the day before, such revelations as we continually have of Indian matters, when it is too late for them to be of any use, must be expected. A certain Governor of Madras, who when something was suggested to him, said, "Oh no, that won't do, the newspapers will make such a fuss about it," showed how much more effectual a check is the fear of immediate publicity, than any organized superior authority.

It is not in fact *mis*representations that are dreaded; it is *representations*. Persons who dread publicity do not want to know the real state of things in the country; nor do they want the people to know the state of things in their offices. Who ever heard of a Collector eagerly taking advantage of the residence of European Merchants, Manufacturers, Missionaries, &c., residing in his district, and in daily contact with the Natives about the ordinary affairs of life, to obtain information from them as to the real state of the Natives, the real effect of his proceedings upon them, and the conduct of the subordinate officials? In 30 years I have never known an instance of it; whereas I have known a man give to a Collector most valuable and important information, which had not the slighest chance of ever reaching him otherwise, surrounded as he is by a phalanx of Brahmins; and the only acknowledgment the informant received was a most impertinent and over-bearing reply. On one occasion the Government were informed that some lacks of Rupees were deficient in the cash chest of a Collector. What can a Government do with such vile *mis*representations? And after the district had been some years longer under a man who could not of course check corruption of which he himself set the example, a deficiency of 8 lacks was discovered. If a man will praise every thing, declare that nothing could be improved, that the Natives are rolling in wealth, that every district is a garden, that trade is every where in a most vigorous state, that all the old Public Works are in perfect order, that no roads, bridges, tanks, channels, ports, &c., are required—then, every word he says is true and he is a most worthy man. But if he tells the real state of things, he is a vile *misrepresenter;* and if he points out how the state of things may be improved, how the treasury and the people may be enriched, how abuses, oppressions, and corruption, may be checked, he is a troubler that must be put down. In such a state of things as now exists with respect to India, how incalculably important is the present Parliamentary enquiry; when those who are so anxious to shut their ears must be compelled to hear, and to know that all England hears the truth respecting it; and with what earnestness should all the real friends of both England and India improve so inestimable an opportunity!

I cannot but hope that these papers, which though roughly and hastily written are the fruit of 30 years' experience and active practical acquaintance with the subject of Public Works in India, and of constant contact with the Natives in their villages, may with God's blessing, be of use in stirring up the friends of India to consider the point. It may be said, that Public Works are very secondary matters, and that after providing for the protection of the country, Civil and Judicial affairs are after all the great things to be attended to. The question of Public Works is however in reality a fundamental point; for upon it and upon it mainly depends the capability of the country to supply funds for every purpose, both Military and Civil. Without Public Works, the country must remain sunk in poverty and ignorance, for funds cannot possibly be produced from the country itself to provide for what is necessary to elevate and improve the state of the people; whereas, with Public Works, the most abundant funds can be obtained for any purpose. We have now proofs of the effects of capital expended in almost every kind of Public Work. The Paumbam Channel, between Ceylon and the Peninsula, has been deepened from 5 to 10½ feet, and it has reduced the freight between Tanjore and Ceylon, 6 Rupees (12 shillings) a ton, which on the 70,000 tons of grain alone, is a saving of more than 4 lacks (£40,000) per annum, while it has cost in all only 2½ lacks (£25,000). The opening of this Channel has also led to a complete change of the system of navigation, by substituting good keeled vessels that can work to windward, for the old native tub that could only sail before the wind; this is a case of Coast improvement. Tanjore has been irrigated and drained, and provided with common roads and bridges, at an outlay of 20 lacks (£200,000) in all (besides repairs); and both the Revenue and net income of the people, have increased by at least that amount *annually*. The western road from Madras cost about 12 lacks (£120,000) and the cost of transit on it has been reduced to one-third; producing a saving on 100,000 tons a year over 125 miles, of 15 or 20 lacks (£150,000 or £200,000) a year. The northern canal, which probably originally cost about 150,000 Rupees (£15,000) is now yielding a Revenue of 30,000 Rupees, (£3,000) besides the saving to the community. A set of works for the improvement of Rajahmundry are well advanced; consisting of a weir across the Godavery, with navigable and irrigating channels, &c. They have been in hand 7 years, and about 20 lacks (£200,000) have been spent up to this time, including repairs, and the Revenue has increased steadily from an average of 19 lacks to 25 lacks (£190,000 to £250,000) giving a total increase of 30 lacks (£300,000) against 20 lacks (£200,000) expended; and this besides an enormous gain to the people. So that this vast system of works, which when completed will have cost 25 lacks, (£250,000) equal, allowing for the difference in the value of money, to nearly 1½ millions sterling in England, has been carried on not only without demanding a Rupee from the general treasury, but with a clear surplus of 10 lacks (£100,000) of Revenue, besides vast benefits to nearly a million of people; and promising to yield probably within a few years a permanent increase of Revenue of 10 or 20 lacks (£100,000 or £200,000) a year; for not a quarter of the land is yet fully watered. These are undeniable facts.

I should observe that in all my calculations about returns, I keep entirely separate the two questions, what are the actual profits of a work to the community? and what may be the profit realized by the Government if they undertake a work? for it is most essential that these things should be kept perfectly distinct. Our great question is not that of a speculator or Company, "what will be the individual gain?" but "rather, what will be the total benefits to the community?" When we have formed some tolerable estimate of this, then we may proceed to consider the second point, "what pro-"portion of those profits may it be advisable to carry direct "to the treasury?" In many cases it is clearly advisable not to take any, but to trust to the indirect effects of a work upon the Revenue, to pay the interest of the money expended upon it. This I think is the policy with regard to common roads and canals, leaving them entirely free, and the traffic burthened only with the bare cost of transit. Of course it is clearly desirable that when such a work is executed, the greatest possible use should be made of it, and the smallest toll, to say nothing of the evils of interference, necessarily prevents some things being carried along it that would otherwise have the benefit of it; and there are special and palpable evils connected with levying taxes on goods while in motion. The general principle of taxation should be, to take duties only when goods are in store, or are being stored, so that the owner has time to complain or appeal. In the case of irrigation to land, on the other hand, when taxes are to be levied at all events, the additional tax causes no extra expense in collecting, or additional interference with the owner. In some cases also, it may be advisable merely to take so much as to provide for the interest of the money, and in others it may be a good opportunity to make the work a direct source of Revenue to the State. The State of New York is doing this with the Erie canal, but I must think this a very questionable policy in the case of a canal.

There is also a question as to the policy of levying a toll for the purpose of reducing the debt on the work, but I think this might perhaps be advisable where tolls are levied at all. For instance, if 4 per cent. be the rate of interest, and if by levying tolls amounting to 5 per cent. the principal would be paid off in about 35 years, then this toll might be advisable; and considering the enormous benefits yielded by most Public Works in India, it would form no very heavy charge upon them, if sufficient were levied to pay off the capital in 10 or 15 years.

One of the most important points to be kept in view in these matters, is this, that in a country so much in want of Capital as India, the real cost of a work to the Government is very far indeed from being equal to the amount involved in it: for it is impossible for Government to spend a lack of Rupees (£10,000) in a district, without the existing Revenue immediately feeling the effect of the expenditure to a great extent. So much so, that I am inclined to think from what I have seen, that such expenditure is, even at the very time, little more than nominal, so far as it is spent on the spot. The people generally, and especially the Ryots, are so paralyzed from want of Capital, that every Rupee that comes into their hands enables them to do something which shall return them 50 or even 500 per cent. in improving cultivation. So that the effects of a lack of Rupees spent on Public Works, is, first, to find work for men who would otherwise be employed in the dry season to so little purpose that their food is almost a dead weight to the community; and secondly, by providing purchasers for produce, to put it in the power of the Ryot to extend his cultivation, and pay additional land-tax. On this account there would assuredly be an immediate and most sensible relief to the Finances, by the mere expenditure of 20 millions of borrowed Capital in the country, quite independent of the direct returns.

The essential fundamental principles that should be kept in view in the matter of Public Works for India, are, in my opinion,

1st.—That on no account whatever, should money be taken

from the current Revenue, to be spent upon them; it being quite contrary to every principle of reason and justice, to make the present generation pay the principal for works, of which they only have a life use.

2nd.—That the account of all expenditure on Public Works, should be kept entirely distinct from the current disbursements of the country.

Till these two principles are acknowledged and acted upon, I can see no hope for India. The current Revenue never can provide money for great Public Works; and to make the latter wait for the former, is to put the cart to draw the horse. The Revenue can never produce Public Works; and nothing but productive Public Works can create an increase of Revenue. But how wonderful it seems, to be obliged to put such things as this on paper! Is there an Englishman, who does not know, that if the people there had waited till the Revenue provided money for Public Works, they would have waited till now? Out of the hundreds of millions that have been expended in England on roads, canals and railroads, on lighting, paving, and sewers, on docks and harbours, on lighthouses, and a hundred other things, what per centage has been paid by the generation who executed them? Is not ninety-nine-hundredths of all the capital expended on those works, a debt to this day? And is it a burthen to the country? It is a burthen which adds 5lbs. to the weight the country carries, and 50lbs. to its strength. It is like the load that a traveller carries away, when he stops at an Inn and eats a pound or two of dinner. It does not hinder him much from carrying any other burthen he may have. In fact, it is John Bull's Public Works that enable him to carry a national debt, which would break the back of any one of his friends on the Continent, who have not got so much in their stomach. Ask Tanjore how she would like a bargain obliging her to carry her own debt for Public Works together with their profit; paying only 4 per cent. 80,000 Rupees (£8,000) a year on the 20 lacks (£200,000) they have cost, and doing what she pleased with the 20 lacks (£200,000) a year of additional Revenue they have produced; and see if she would account it laying an additional burthen upon her? Call upon Rajahmundry also to pay her old Revenue, as well as the interest of the cost of her works, but at the same time allow her to keep the profits, instead of, as at present, paying an increased Revenue to Government as the produce of these Works; and see if she would not gladly make the exchange. What can be the reason then that principles which no man ever dreams of applying to England, should be applied to India by all sorts of people?

As regards the second of the above two principles, what better can be expected than utter confusion so long as the salary of the Governor General, and the cost of a canal or tank, are added together! How can any body tell what they are doing, while such absurdities are committed! A tank or canal is just as much bonâ fide property as the Rupees spent upon it; indeed much more so, for the latter while hoarded up (as millions at present are in the treasuries) are of no use to any living being. Imagine a man saying; "I was "very rich once, I had £10,000 in a box in my house, but "now I am a beggar; I spent it all on this estate which "yields me £1,000 a year." The Governor General's salary is money paid for advantages already consumed, and which will yield no direct permanent income to the State; at least the same sum must continue to be paid every year: whereas money laid out on works such as canals and tanks, creates sources of future Revenue. To treat productive Public Works executed by Government, as no longer property, because not in the form of Rupees, is preposterous. There should therefore be a Department of Public Works which should keep a complete and distinct set of accounts of its own, and every thing spent by it should be divided under two heads, 1st, current expenditure on superintendence and necessary repairs, (which should afterwards be entered in the general accounts of the State as part of its current expenditure;) and 2d, new works including improvements. A stock account should be kept, to balance against capital invested, and means should be taken to obtain a tolerable estimate of the actual total returns of all new works, so far as they could be ascertained and stated. And if at the end of five years it appeared from these accounts, that 20 millions had been spent, and that there were 20 millions worth of Public Works on hand, yielding in various ways upon a reasonable estimate 10 millions a year, we must not therefore conclude that we are 20 millions poorer than we were, and weary ourselves to discover how to get rid of this 20 millions of debt, but rather, comfort ourselves with the thought that we are paying with one hand £800,000 a year, and receiving with the other 10 millions sterling. I am afraid people will say, "we "don't require a book to tell us such things as these; they "are not discoveries." But what is to be done? as these things which every body knows, never appear either in the minds or the deeds of the Government of India, there seems no alternative but to bring them forward once more. Notwithstanding the general neglect of Public Works, there is even now something considerable in the shape of property, yielding abundant returns to balance the debt we have incurred. Perhaps in the new irrigation works in Tanjore and Rajahmundry, and in works elsewhere in this Presidency, such as the Madras Western road, the Grand Trunk road, the North West canals and other works, a stock account to the amount of two millions sterling or more, might be made up: and all this is bonâ fide property, just as much as the Rupees that were spent on the works: or rather, much more so. Perhaps on an average, these 2 millions yield 2 millions annual profit to the community; and if so, they are equivalent to a capital of 50 millions sterling, or fifty crores of Rupees, nearly equal to the whole Indian debt. If these things are taken into consideration, as most undoubtedly they ought to be, they will give a totally new aspect to the state of Indian Finance.

It must be remembered, that we are now dreadfully in arrears as to all measures tending to the improvement of the country; that we have to make up for 50 or 60 years of utter neglect of almost every thing that it was incumbent upon an English and a Christian Government to do. Proportional prompt decision and effort is therefore called for, and most richly will India repay those who will labour for her. It must not be supposed because we see her outwardly in nearly the same state of brutal ignorance, abject bondage to caste, and degraded poverty as when we conquered her, that therefore no change has taken place. A secret undermining of old ideas and principles has been going on both directly and indirectly, from the new circumstances in which she has been placed, which assuredly has greatly prepared the way for her to benefit by the means that may be used by an honest, active, energetic, open Government. The moment such a Government is substituted for the present system, assuredly India will show a change like life from the dead. What a glorious change for England, what a stimulating though awful trust! How incalculably important is the present crisis! If England should ever awake to her responsibilities and honours, and declare that the present system shall no longer be endured, that instruction shall be given both in the knowledge of the true God and in matters connected with the present life, and that things essential both to mental and physical improvement shall henceforth be provided for the millions whom it has pleased God in His providence, to place under our charge; then she will assuredly see 150 millions of people rapidly emerging from their present state, and becoming her glory and strength.

Who can bear to go through India, and see its degraded state, and think what it ought to be after 50 or 100 years of the rule of the most free, enlightened, and powerful of all the nations of the earth; the only nation that is not effectually hampered in her own progress either by a false religion, or by some form of slavery? What more can be necessary than to bring the influence of such a nation fairly to bear on the millions of India? What can have hitherto prevented the marks of her rule being seen in the instruction, liberation, and the enriching of the people of India, except a system which has in effect warded off that influence, by *Asiaticising* first, all who (called Englishmen) were to have a hand in her nursing. Nothing is more certain as a general rule, than that all men in a great measure, and most men entirely, lose their individuality, and become an intrinsic part of that system with which they are mixed up. A Kentucky slave trader would have as great an abhorrence of slavery as any of us if he had been in England from the age of 18 to 50; and any old Indian would be as much startled as any other Englishman, at the unchanged state of an Indian village or district notwithstanding our rule, if he had never before been out of England. He would probably say, "What! are there no Christians here? "Do you not instruct them in any thing? Have you no "roads or any other communications? What in the world "do you do? I do not see a single mark of an English-"man having been in the country." But as a part of this system, all this appears to the Anglo Indian the most natural thing in the world. "It is the way we do in India. In "England of course we are quite different beings. There "we never dream of discussing the mode of collecting the "land Revenue, but we take part in a thousand plans for "improving our own and our neighbour's condition."

A new race of beings, a new system, a new set of ideas are required. Publicity, light and air, the immediate exposure of every public document connected with the ordinary business of Government, for free discussion by young as well as old, all these things are essential to such a change as India requires. And who cannot but hope that in the providence of God we are on the eve of a new start for India; and that the present discussions will lead to breaking up for ever the old decrepid system, and give rise to a fresh, healthy, and vigorous one, worthy of our religion and our nation?

CHAPTER V.

THE PRESENT ENORMOUS COST OF TRANSIT AS A BURDEN ON THE COUNTRY.

Area of India with extent of Communication at present.

TAKING the whole area of India (including all between the ocean, the Himalayas and Affghanistan) at a million and a quarter square miles, we shall find, that to open out this tract, with main lines of communications 50 miles apart, would require about 50,000 miles of main road; besides all the minor roads, which if placed 5 miles apart would be 500,000 miles in length. We may now frame a very rough estimate of the actual extent of communications, with the cost of transit by them.

	Miles.	Rate per ton per mile.
1st. The sea navigation from the mouth of the Indus to that of the Ganges............	3,500	5 to 8½ Pice (⅝*d.* to 1 1/16 *d.*)
2d. River Navigation..	2,000	4 Pice or ½*d.*
3d. Complete roads.....	2,000	1 Anna or 1½*d.*
4th. Imperfectly made roads, perhaps.......	10,000	2 Annas or 3*d.*
5th. Unimproved tracks.		3 Annas or 4½*d.*
Total..	17,500 miles.	

Before we proceed further however, we must examine these prices, to see what proportion they bear to those of England or America. The actual value of 1 Anna is about 1½*d.* or 3 cents. reckoning the Rupee at 2 shillings; but we must allow first for the difference in the value of money. A pound of rice in India costs about 3 Pice or ⅜*d.* and the same quantity of the flour of other grains about 2 Pice or ¼*d.* Taking the cost of flour in England at 1½*d.* a pound, the value of money as shown by the value of food, may be taken at six times as great in India as in England; and if we try by the cost of labour, taking it in its simplest form, we find that a cubic yard of earth may be dug and carried to a bank 10 yards off, for about ¾*d.* on an average in India, against about 6*d.* in England. The same with other kinds of labour; and it will be near enough for our present purpose, to take the value of money in India at six times what it is in England, on an average, though over a great extent of country like India it is as much as 8 to 1. It is probably fully ten times greater than in America calculating from the rate of labour; but not more than perhaps five times by the cost of food, labour being better paid in America than either in India or England. We may therefore reckon the Indian rates of transit as equivalent in England, to

6*d.*	per ton	per mile	by sea.
3½*d.*	do.	do.	by river.
9*d.*	do.	do.	by good roads.
1*s.* 6*d.*	do.	do.	by imperfect roads.
2*s.* 7½*d.*	do.	do.	on unimproved tracks.

Is not this alone quite sufficient without a word more, to account for the impoverished and backward state of India? The average of all the traffic of India cannot be less than 1 shilling per ton per mile, allowing for the difference in the value of money, while in England the average cost to transit may probably be taken at 1½*d.*, or one-eighth of that of India; it must indeed certainly be at least eight times as great in India as in England, taking it only mile for mile.

The following are some of the English rates:

Liverpool to Manchester....	*3d.*	a mile per ton,		Railway.
London to Birmingham......	$\frac{4}{5}$*d.*	do.	do.	Canal.
Liverpool to Birmingham....	1$\frac{3}{4}$*d.*	do.	do.	Railway.

What would be the diminution of traffic in England, if the cost were suddenly increased eight fold? probably nine-tenths of it would be stopped.* But this calculation still does not give by any means a complete view of the case; we must compare also the comparative distances that goods must be carried in the two countries. In India the extreme distance that goods must be carried to reach the port is 1,200 miles; in England it is about 60 miles. The average distance that exports and imports are carried in India may be 250 miles; whilst in England it cannot exceed 40. We may safely allow therefore, that in general, goods are carried six times as far in India from the place of production to that of consumption or of export, as they are in England; so that combining this with the cost, there is in India thirty-six times as heavy a charge upon transit as in England. But there is yet a third consideration; that the average value of the commodities moved in India is far below that of those transported in England; by far the greater proportion of articles moved in India being coarse goods, raw produce and such things; while in England a very large proportion consists of manufactured goods and other valuable articles. If for instance we take a ton of Berar cotton at the price actually paid to the cultivator, the charge of transit compared with its value will be as follows:

* In America the cost of traffic by railway may be taken at 1$\frac{1}{3}$*d.*, and that of conveyance by the river navigation at $\frac{1}{8}$*d.* per ton per mile, the average being considerably below that of England.

Cost of 1 ton of cotton in Berar.... Rs. 120—£12
Do. of carriage 350 miles to Bombay
at 3 Annas (4½*d.*) per mile....... „ 66—£ 6 12*s.*
or 55 per cent.

Cost of do. at Liverpool at 4½*d.* a lb.... £40
Carriage of do. by Railway to Manchester
30 miles at 3*d*..................... £ 0 7*s.* 6*d.*
or nearly 1 per cent.

and in its manufactured state, the cost of transit would bear a still smaller proportion to its value.

Again, we may take a ton of sugar brought from the Upper Provinces to Calcutta.

Cost where produced.............. Rs. 120—£12
Do. of transit to the Coast by river... „ 20—£ 2
or 17 per cent.

Value of do. in London................ £40
Cost of conveying 50 miles to place of consumption...................... £ 0 8*s.*
or 1 per cent.

If we take the *average* value of goods conveyed in England, and compare it with that of India, we shall find that the per centage is even higher than the highest of these.* We shall therefore probably be safe in concluding, that the cost of transit in India, is equal to an ad valorem tax on the goods conveyed, fully fifty times that of England. We cannot form a correct judgment of the burthen to India of this rate of transit as compared with that of other countries, without taking all these things into consideration. What would England be with such an incubus upon it, as this tremendous transit tax in India!

The mere comparison of the rates per ton per mile, there-

* And to all these we must still add the extra cost in time and risk; for supposing that cotton is two months travelling to Bombay, the interest at 12 per cent. per annum would be 2 per cent., and the insurance also could not be less than 2 per cent.

fore, must give a totally false idea of the state of the case, unless we take into consideration, the following points :

1st, The relative value of money ;
2nd. The distance carried ;
3rd, The value of goods ;
4th, The time and risk.

Until these points are understood and considered, there can be no hope of any serious effort being made to relieve India from a burthen, compared with which the whole of the taxes received by Government are of little importance. How is it possible that India, notwithstanding its cheap labour, extent of rich land, powerful sun, and copious monsoons, can contend in the markets of the world with other nations, while weighed down by such a load ? There can be no mistake on the point of its immense advantages in all other respects, compared with other countries.

We may now try to form an estimate of the amount of this tax, as actually paid in money ; and although the data for this are very imperfect, yet we may easily satisfy ourselves that it cannot be less than a certain sum. We may take first some well established instances of the cost of traffic.

It has been estimated that the amount of inland traffic at Calcutta, is 2,000,000 tons per annum. If we take the average traffic between the N. W. Provinces and that port, at 1,200,000 tons, and the cost at 25 Rupees (£2 10*s.*) a ton, (4 Pice (½*d.*) a ton per mile for 1,200 miles) the total cost on this line of transit will be 300 lacks (3 millions sterling) a year, for goods only. The rate is stated much higher than this in the Railway Pamphlets, but there are evident mistakes in them. The total cost including interest and insurance, is there calculated at 9 Pice (1⅛*d.*) a ton per mile; which would give a total of 648 lacks (£6,480,000) besides the sums paid by passengers. If we allow for the river expenses 500 lacks, (5 millions sterling) including every thing, I think we shall be under the mark, and supposing these 2 millions of tons to be brought on an average 50 miles by land to the river, at 3 Annas (4½*d.*) per ton per mile, it will add 180 lacks (£1,800,000) to the above, making a total of 680 lacks or nearly 7 millions sterling; a sum equal to one-fourth of the amount of the whole Revenue of India, expended on this one single line of transit.

As regards the coasting trade, we have an instance in the case of the Paumbam Channel. The traffic through it, is at present 1,48,000 tons, including empty vessels; perhaps in all 1,20,000 tons of freight, allowing for loaded vessels, carrying more than their tonnage. This is mostly carried between Ceylon or the Western Coast and Tanjore or Madras, at about 10 Rupees (£1) a ton, and therefore costs 12 lacks, (£120,000) besides interest and insurance; perhaps 20 lacks (£200,000) in all; on a distance of about 500 miles. The traffic on the Western Coast is far greater than this; and the cost of the traffic along the whole 3,500 miles of coast round the Peninsula, cannot be less than 200 lacks, or 2 millions sterling.

Of the traffic by land in this Presidency, we have an instance in the great Western road from Madras. The traffic on the first 125 miles, is about 100,000 tons a year, at 1¼ Anna (nearly 2*d.*) per ton per mile; or in all 10 lacks (£100,000), besides passengers, and interest and insurance.

Allowing then 900 lacks (9 millions sterling) for the Ganges and the coast traffic alone, besides all the vast land traffic of the interior, we surely cannot over-estimate the sum actually paid in India for transit, by taking it at 1,500 lacks, or 15 millions sterling; and hence, if the average cost of transit could be reduced to one-fifth of what it is at present, the country would be relieved of a direct tax of 12 millions sterling; equal to a diminution of the present taxes by one-half.

But this is only a small part of the effect of opening the country generally, and giving it cheap, safe and expeditious transit. The present great loss is, *not* in what is paid for goods carried; but in what is lost, in things that are not carried at all. We have a strong proof of the immense traffic there would be, if the cost of conveyance were diminished, in the case of the Paumbam Channel; where, in consequence of the reduction of freight to one-third of what it was before, and the diminution of time and risk, the trade has actually increased nine fold, though the cotton that used to pass through that channel, is now shipped at the ports of Tinnevelly. What is the traffic of England now, compared with what it was, before there were either canals, railways, or even turnpike roads? It must certainly since then have increased a hundred fold, and I have no doubt that it would increase in India in something like the same degree, particularly considering that the proportion of cost of transit to the value of the goods is (as shown above) so much greater in India than it ever was in England, on account of the much greater distances the goods must be carried, as well as their inferior value. There can be no doubt, that a transit charge of 50 per cent. on the value of goods, must be a much greater check to traffic than one of 5; and that if it were reduced from 50 to 10 per cent., the increase of traffic would be much greater, than if reduced from 5 to 1. It is in fact absolutely beyond calculation to what extent the traffic would increase, if goods could be moved 100 miles a day at 1 Pie ($\frac{1}{8}d.$) per ton per mile, instead of 10 miles a day $1\frac{1}{2}$ Annas ($2\frac{1}{4}d$); and I have no doubt, that by due improvement of the rivers, a very large proportion of the traffic would be conveyed at 1 Pie ($\frac{1}{8}d.$) per ton per mile.

As yet, I have noticed only the loss in money from the expensive transit, or absolute non-transit of goods; but who can estimate the effect on the country, of the hinderance to personal intercourse resulting from the present state of things? What would be the state of England, if not only the cost and time of passenger transit were increased ten fold, but if also there were throughout the country no such things as relays of animals posted for conveyances; so that if a man wanted to travel, he must go by daily stages only, as long as the same animal could go, and the journey from London to Liverpool were thus to take a man who could afford to ride, seven days; the same time that such a distance takes in India. In this country, if a man wants to go a moderate journey such as 300 miles, he must be 15 to 30 days about it, besides all the inconvenience of having to take people with him to cook his food, or cook it himself wherever he stops. This country is not even in the state England was, before there were railroads or turnpike roads; because even then, there were relays of animals throughout the country. How much intercourse would there now be in England, and how would business be carried on, if a merchant of London who wanted to see a manufacturer in Birmingham must be from home a week; or, having to transact business with a Yorkshire clothier, must be absent a fortnight? It is impossible for those who have not witnessed it, to conceive the amount of disadvantage under which India labours in this respect.

Notwithstanding these difficulties, however, the passenger intercourse is even now surprisingly great, though I am aware that the general idea on the subject of travelling in India, is quite the contrary; the question having in fact been raised, whether there would be at first any considerable number of passengers on the railroads.

The following are some of the ascertained numbers.

On the high road from Negapatam to Tanjore, at a point 20 miles from a City, in 1837	1,200 adults a day.
On the bridge over the Colleroon 3 miles from the Town of Trichinopoly....	19,000 per day.
From Calcutta towards the Upper Provinces......................	1,500 ,, ,,
On one of the main roads 11 miles from Madras......................	3,000 ,, ,,

From these instances and from experience in the country, there is no doubt that if there were *cheap* transit even at the rate of 100 miles a day, there would be an immense passenger traffic on all the main lines. Between Negapatam and Trichinopoly, for instance, there can be no doubt that the present passenger traffic would be quadrupled; so that there would be 5,000 travellers a day. On the great western road from Madras, also, as soon as the railway is extended to 150 or 200 miles, there will, no doubt, provided travellers can be conveyed at a rate proportional to that in England, suppose at 1 Pie or $\frac{1}{8}$*d.* per mile, be several thousands of passengers a day.

Of the beneficial effects of free intercourse on the country, especially in weakening the system of caste, (the great curse of India) who can fully judge? But of this at least we may be certain, that with such means of intercourse, the country will in ten years make more real progress in every thing that is desirable, than in one hundred years without them.

Returning however to that part of the subject which can be shown in figures, we see that we have to deal at the very least with a matter of 15 millions sterling a year in actual payments; and if we only allow as much more, as lost in things either not produced, or wasted, because the cost of transit prevents their having a market, it will show an annual loss to the country of 30 millions sterling, or much more than the whole amount of the taxes. Could we relieve the country from five-sixths of this, it would be at least equivalent to abolishing all taxes; and it would in fact be incalculably more beneficial, because there would be all the gain of the immense stimulus thus given to industry and exertion. Of the existing hinderances to production, from high cost of transit we may judge from the following. If a ton of any produce be carried 200 miles at 3 Annas (1$\frac{1}{2}$*d.*) a mile, or a total cost of 37$\frac{1}{2}$ Rupees (£3 15*s.*) for the whole distance, a trade of the extent of 100 tons would cost 3,750 Rupees (£375) a month, or 45,000 Rupees (£4,500) a year. So that if at the present high rate of transit, an article be not worth moving; by reducing the cost of transit two-thirds, that article might yet afford a merchant a profit of £3,000 a year. Again, the cost of carriage of cotton, from the place of production to the shipping ports, is often £8 a ton; ten times as much as would afford a merchant's profit on the goods.

Seeing therefore, that articles which cannot now be carried because there would be no profit on them, might, with cheap transit, be brought to afford a profit ten times as great as would be sufficient to create a trade in them, it becomes easy to comprehend, how on every diminution of cost of transit, the amount of traffic increases so surprisingly. Again, if one part of the country be particularly favorable for the growth of some article of produce, the extension of its cultivation will depend, not only on the cost of transit, but also on the cheapness with which food and other necessaries of life, can be brought to those employed in producing that article. At present, the cultivators of a good cotton district are compelled to grow their own food on the spot, because the great cost of transit utterly precludes the conveyance of such a bulky thing as grain, from any distance; whereas, if the cost of conveyance were reduced, the whole of the land peculiarly favorable for cotton, might be given up to that culture, and food for the cultivators brought from other parts where cotton could not be grown so profitably. At present it costs ⅓*d.* to convey 1 lb. of rice 180 miles, thus doubling its original cost; so that the carriage of food for one man for a year, (720 lbs.) for that distance, would cost 10 Rupees, (£1) or nearly 1 Rupee (2 shillings) a month, about half a man's wages;* whereas, if the transit cost were reduced to one-fifth, or to one-twentieth, (as it might be where there is water-carriage), the same quantity of rice (720 lbs.) might be brought

* Which are about 2 Rupees monthly for an ordinary agricultural laborer in his own village.

that distance for 1 Anna (1½*d.*) a month; and thus the soil and climate best suited to a certain article of produce, might be wholly given up to its cultivation. How immense would the traffic thus become! Perhaps for instance, the principal part of the agricultural population of Berar would be employed in growing cotton, while their food would be grown in the irrigated lands of the Delta of the Godavery. If only two millions of people were so provided with food, there would be a traffic up the Godavery, in food alone, of 700,000 tons a year.

Not a ton of any thing except timber is now carried by the Godavery, though it is navigable for at least six months in the year. A comparatively moderate outlay would make it navigable throughout the year; and if it were navigated, goods could be carried between the Coast and Berar for from 1 to 5 Rupees (2 to 10 shillings) a ton, whereas the present difference in the value of rice, cotton, salt, and wheat, in these two places, is on an average about 100 Rupees (£10) a ton. The Berar people now grow their own rice, at four times the price they could get it for from Rajahmundry by the Godavery, and also pay four times as much for salt; while they have no sale at all for their wheat, and comparatively little for their cotton, because of the cost of transit to the coast. Under other different circumstances, Berar could supply Manchester with cotton and wheat, at 25 per cent. less than is paid to America for the same things; and if thus provided with a market for its staples, and relieved from the high cost of food and salt, it could afford to purchase the manufactures of Manchester, Birmingham, Yorkshire, and all parts of England. In this way it is easy to see what immense traffic there may be in this country, when the cost of transit is greatly reduced; and how incorrect must be all calculations based entirely on the present amount: also, the extent of traffic there may be on a proposed line of communication. It is not only that the traffic may be doubled or trebled; it may easily be increased ten or fifty fold: in fact a reduction of cost of transit, may produce any extent of traffic. A reduction of 5 Rs. (10 Shillings) a ton, may lead to the creation of a trade in some vast and bulky staple of which not a ton was moved before; and consequently give rise to a sale of goods, to the extent of 20 times the amount saved in transit. The opening of the Godavery may on the most moderate calculations, raise the sale of cotton and wheat grown in Berar, to the amount of a million sterling, and that of rice and salt produced in Rajahmundry to half that amount; and give rise to a demand for English manufactured goods, to the value of another half million. At present, only comparatively valuable things are moved, and bulky things of small value, such as articles of food, building materials, manure, &c., are scarcely moved at all; so that the population of one District are compelled to spend their labour and occupy their land in the cultivation of articles of food which are grown far more cheaply in other parts, whilst their own land would much better repay the cultivation of the particular articles best suited to its soil and climate; the towns are polluted by an accumulation of filth, for want of which the fields are barren; and the towns are without good building materials, while the country, where they are of no value is full of them.

It is most essential to keep these points in view, in planning improved communications; otherwise, we shall be deterred from attempting them, under the false idea, that the interest of the money will be a much greater charge upon the carriage, than it would be in reality. Thus, if the cost of a railway be 30,000 Rupees (£3,000) a mile, and the present amount of traffic be 100,000 tons a year, and the actual cost of working the road 2 Pice or $\frac{1}{4}d.$ a ton per mile, the following calculation might be made of the rate at which goods must be charged, to give 10 per cent. interest.

10 per cent. on 30,000 Rs. (£3,000) = 3,000 Rs. (£300)
Which divided among 100,000 tons
would be........................ 6 Pice or $\frac{3}{4}$*d.* per ton.
Add cost of transit................ 2 ,, or $\frac{1}{4}$*d.* ,, ,,
Total.. 8 ,, or 1*d.* ,, ,,

about one-half or two-thirds, of what it would be on a good common road; which would perhaps more than quadruple the present traffic. But if a great reduction of cost took place, so that the traffic were increased five fold, the calculation would then be

10 per cent. on 30,000 Rs. (£3,000) = 3,000 Rs. (£300)
Which divided by $\frac{1}{2}$ million tons
would give per ton........... $1\frac{1}{5}$ Pice or $\frac{6}{10}$ farthing.
Add for cost of transit per ton.. $1\frac{2}{5}$,, or $\frac{7}{10}$,,
Total.. $2\frac{3}{5}$ Pice or $1\frac{3}{10}$ farthings

or one-fifth of the present cost on good common road, which would probably at the very least increase the traffic five fold, and necessitate the addition of a second line of rails, as soon as the first was in operation. In the second calculation I allow a lower cost of transit, because that of management and other things would be distributed over a greater surface. In England the actual cost of working the railways is 2 Pice or $\frac{1}{4}$*d.* per ton per mile; and it will certainly be less in this country, at the same velocity.

Let us again take the example of the Calcutta Railway; supposing it to cost 1,20,000 Rupees (£12,000) a mile, that 10 per cent. profit is to be allowed for, and that it were capable of conveying the whole of the present traffic.

10 per cent. on 1,20,000 Rs. = 12,000 Rs. (£1,200)
Divided over present traffic of 2
million tons................. $1\frac{1}{5}$ Pice or $\frac{6}{10}$ of a farthing.
Add for cost of transit......... $1\frac{2}{5}$,, or $\frac{7}{10}$ of a ,,
Total.. $2\frac{3}{5}$ Pice or $1\frac{3}{10}$ of a ,,

which is perhaps three-fourths of the present cost by the river, allowing for interest and insurance in the present mode of transit. This would no doubt cause a large increase of traffic; but if the interest were paid entirely by passengers, (which it may probably be) the transit of goods would cost only $1\frac{2}{5}$ Pice $\frac{7}{10}$ of a farthing per mile, about one-fourth of the present rate; which would probably double the existing traffic; though it could not of course have by any means so great an effect on the traffic, as a change from a common road to a Railroad, where the railway would take off 1 Anna ($1\frac{1}{2}d.$) a ton from the cost, whereas in the above case it might take off only 2 Pice ($\frac{1}{4}d.$) It must be observed, that the above calculation is made only on the ground assumed by the railway projectors, viz. that a double line of railway could carry 2 million tons a year besides passengers: it is not intended to imply that such a thing is possible.

The case will be still clearer, if we take an imperfect road, and substitute for it a good steam canal, which could be executed, in a great part of this Presidency, at a cost of 15,000 Rupees (£1,500) a mile, the interest of which would be paid by the passengers, thus,

10 per cent. on 15,000 Rs. = 1,500 Rs. (£150)

which with 1,000 passengers a day, would only be 1 Pice or $\frac{1}{8}d.$ per mile, for each person. The charge on goods would then be about $\frac{1}{2}$ P. or $\frac{1}{16}d.$ per ton per mile for a considerable distance; the same rate at which goods are now carried on the Mississipi, and one-thirtieth of the present cost of transit on the ordinary roads. At this rate, almost anything could be moved, and it will be curious to see the effect of it upon an important line of communication. In investigating the subject of a proposed line of traffic in a country so entirely without communications, the question is, *not* "what is the present traffic," but "what are the comparative prices of any great staples at different points on the line." In India it will often happen, that the main traffic on a new line of cheap transit, is one entirely created by the new work.

The most important point proved by the above considerations of the present cost of transit, is, the absolute necessity of a very great reduction in it: since no trifling reduction will at all answer the purpose, and much less will the plan of the railway projectors to convey at a rate as high, or higher than the present, answer any useful purpose. The present rate is utterly destructive and ruinous; so much so, that the country cannot thrive under anything approaching to it. The above statement of the proportion of the cost of transit to the value of the principal goods moved, shows that no small reduction will effectually relieve the country; and much less would an increase of speed without any reduction of price, be beneficial. No greater mistake can be made, than to suppose that an increase of speed is the main thing required. If the grand railways effect nothing more than what their advocates state, they will do nothing to any purpose. In the Pamphlets and Reports about the Bengal and Bombay Railroads, they talk of a charge of from 8 Pice to 2 As. (1*d.* to 3*d.*) per ton per mile. If this be all that the most perfect railways can do for India, and if there were no other means by which something could be accomplished, our case would be hopeless indeed. If India is to advance in any thing, *it must have cheap transit, really cheap transit, at one-tenth or one-twentieth part of the present rates.* In planning the great railways, the real points to be attended to have been entirely lost sight of; and this first one especially. When the projectors talk of charging 1*d.* to 3*d.* per ton per mile, they do not consider the fact, that a good common road will carry at 1½*d.*; and that the imperfect unimproved natural water transit where it exists, costs only ½*d.* In the Bengal Reports they make out that the river transit costs 9 Pice (1⅛*d.*) per ton; but this is more than double the real cost. One of the fallacies in the calculation is, that interest is charged on all goods, as being worth £40 a ton; whereas the great bulk of the traffic is, either grain value £3 a ton, salt £3, sugar £12 or £15, saltpetre £18, and iron £10; so that probably not one-twentieth part of the goods is worth £40 a ton.

What we have now to do, is to discover means whereby the cost of transit may be materially reduced, so as to give a real relief to the country, and enable it to compete with other countries. Till this is accomplished nothing is done. All our immense advantages of soil and climate, and cheapness and abundance of labour, are lost; or at least the greater part of them. This is well shown in the state of the Berar cotton trade, in regard to which it is stated by those who have the best means of knowing, that cotton is actually grown and sold on the spot at ⅘ Anna (or 1¼*d.*) a lb. To this about ¾*d.* (half an Anna) is added in bringing it into the great cotton marts of the district where it is cultivated; fully 1*d.* or ⅔ Anna more in conveying it to Bombay, and still more in taking it to Calcutta. Another penny is added to the cost in bringing it into the English markets; and thus it arrives at Manchester, at a cost that only puts it on a par with American cotton, grown by slave labour at an enormous expense. At least 1 Anna (1½*d.*) per lb. could be taken off by improving the communications, and throwing open that part of the country where so favourable a climate and soil are found for the growth of cotton. It is not merely, that for want of cheap transit a direct charge of a penny or more is added to the cost of the cotton; but for the same reason, food, salt, &c., are three or four times the price they need otherwise be. This is only one of many ways that the price of cotton is indirectly augmented. At present the purchasing of the cotton from the cultivators, is entirely in the hands of the ignorant, short-sighted, oppressive Native merchants. The Natives begin to be very sensible of the advantage that it would be to deal directly with Europeans; but nothing can deliver them from the present system, but an open communication with the ports, giving

Europeans free access to the districts, and gradually removing the absurd fancies that mercantile men have about living in the interior of the Peninsula; as if they could not do it without great risk to their lives. The extent to which the cost of the produce of India may thus in different ways be reduced in foreign markets, is beyond calculation; for the mere reduction of the charge of transit, is by no means the total amount of the diminution of cost that may be effected.

But it must specially be borne in mind, that where the distances are so great, the value of produce so small, and the present cost of carriage per mile so enormous, it is not a trifling reduction that will do. Till this point is understood, nothing effective will be done towards the real improvement of India. I am satisfied, as I have stated, that the money now paid for transit, and lost for want of it in India, is in fact equal to the whole amount of taxation.

It is not surprising that this essential fundamental point of the necessity of a great diminution of the cost of traffic, should have been treated as a matter of no consequence by the Engineers and others concerned in projecting the great railways; for their views were naturally contracted to this comparatively insignificant question, viz. "Will such a railway pay to the shareholders;" but that this really important point should have been so lost sight of, by the public and the authorities, is indeed surprising! The question for the Government to consider, is, "What does the country really "require in the way of transit, and by what means can the "greatest advantage be obtained for the whole community?" The interest of the shareholders, and that of the community in a line of rail, may be diametrically opposed. If a railway on an important line be constructed on so expensive a plan, as to require a high rate of charge to enable it to pay a good interest, an irreparable evil will have been done; and the whole power of an influential body (influential and powerful just in proportion to the amount of capital expended) will be brought to bear on that line; *not* in order to secure cheap transit, but to prevent cheap transit ever being obtained on it.

If the proprietors of the Bengal railway for instance, charge (as proposed in the Pamphlets) 1*d.* per ton per mile; there seems no hope that that line will be ever favoured with a cheaper communication, than it has at present by the river. Though other parts of the country might be favoured with this essential advantage, probably no power could be found sufficient to prevent this, the most important line by far in all India, from being sealed up against the use of any means by which cheap carriage could be obtained. Of the various means that could be used for this purpose, and there are several, (for I am certain that on this line, goods could be carried at the rate of 1 Pice (⅛*d.*) per ton per mile, as well as on the Mississipi), there would be no probability of any being adopted; so long as the owners of the 4 millions sterling invested in the railway, felt that the whole of their property depended, upon their successfully resisting all improvements.

Happily however, the matter is very far indeed from standing as it is stated in the railway Pamphlets: for even with all its present imperfections, the river transit will provide for the conveyance of goods at a much lower rate than 1*d.* per ton per mile. But as to the railway accomplishing the main object, that of materially reducing the charge, I see no prospect of it; so that whatever may be effected elsewhere, the probability is at present, that no material improvement will take place in the rates to be charged on this most important line, which ought to be the line of greatest traffic in India.

CHAPTER VI.

ON THE IMPROVEMENT OF THE LARGE RIVERS FOR NAVIGATION.

How to lighten the burden of high transit.

WHAT means can be found then, to relieve the country from the intolerable burden of cost of transit, supposing it to amount at this moment to 15 millions a year in actual payments, besides the loss of as much more in things which will not bear the present charges, and cannot therefore be moved at all? Is the case really hopeless? have we indeed no alternative but to lay out a lack of Rupees (£200,000) a mile, or 200 millions sterling on the whole 20,000 miles of main line required, and then to go on paying for ever, nearly as much as we do now?

Hopeless indeed would the state of India be, if this were really the case; but nothing can be farther from the fact. On almost every line in India, the cost can be reduced to one-fifth or one-tenth, of what is at present contemplated by the great railways.

We have first the natural water communications, and the question is, What may be done by means of them? The following paper (written some time ago) may be properly introduced here, as showing more fully what extraordinary openings we have in India, for improving the country by means of the rivers.

"By no means the least important part of the present project (the Godavery Delta works) is, its helping to open the navigation of the Godavery. That part of the river between the hills and the sea, was in the dry season exceedingly shallow in places; sometimes only a few inches deep. The annicut greatly diminishes the hinderance to the navigation of the river. Below the annicut there will be a constant deep channel to tidal-water. Through the hills the water is of a great depth, and the first serious obstacle occurs at Badrachellum, 130 miles from the coast. From thence (300 miles) to Woonie on the Wurda, which is 80 miles from Nagpore, there are (by Captain Fenwick's account), six obstructions from rock; all which might be removed or diminished at a moderate expense. That gentleman, when employed in connection with Messrs. Palmer's houses, repeatedly navigated the river with timber and loaded boats; and cut through one rocky obstruction, at a cost of only 400 Rupees (£40). In connection with the Delta works, it seems of the highest importance to open this most valuable line of communication through a country, a great part of which has hitherto been almost beyond the reach of commercial enterprize. By Captain Fenwick's account, there seems no doubt, that the cotton of Berar, and many other things, might be conveyed to a port by water, at one-tenth of what is now paid for land carriage to Bombay.

"It is highly probable that the Kistnah also may be navigated to a great extent; but I have no positive information on this point.

"In the present great question of the cotton supply, there seems to be scarcely any point more worth investigation, than this opening of the fine cotton countries of Nagpore, to the coast. No doubt the cultivation would extend rapidly along the whole line of the Godavery. It seems now to be generally acknowledged, that Berar is naturally the most suitable climate and soil, for cotton for the English market, and therefore we should make it our grand effort to open a cheap line of communication with it; and it is certain, that no other line can possibly compare with that of the Godavery, for bringing cotton to the coast. Captain Fenwick tells me, that during the three years Palmer's house brought their capital to bear on this tract, the cultivation of cotton, and the general welfare of the people increased surprisingly. There is thus a line of 500 miles of the cheapest communication, leading into the very heart of the country, to be had almost for nothing: for even if 5 lacks (£50,000) were spent in improving it, it would still only cost 1,000 Rupees (£100) a mile.

" In the paper on the Berar cotton by Mr. Ashburner, read before the Asiatic Society in 1837, the importance of this subject is shown on the very best authority. He states that this cotton can be cultivated at 30 Rupees (£3) per Bombay candy (less than 1*d.* a lb.) and that the only obstacle to its unlimited production, is the cost of transport; that it is sent to Bombay on bullocks at 24 Rupees (£2 4*s.*) a candy (less than 3 farthings a lb.) taking 70 days on the journey; and that large quantities which cannot reach Bombay before the monsoon, are consequently liable to be damaged or destroyed. That there was at that time a traffic of 20,000 tons a year, in salt and Berar cotton; and that if a good bandy road were made, there would be a saving of 16 lacks (£160,000) a year. He then goes on say. " It may be as " well, however, to show the productive powers of the " country more clearly, to instance the increase which has " lately taken place in the amount of cotton exported from " Bombay. From 1828 to 1835 the exports averaged " 178,000 bales a year, and remained nearly stationary. But " the high prices of the latter year led to more extensive " cultivation, and notwithstanding numerous obstacles to

" production, the Presidency of Bombay last year produced " and exported no less than 290,000 bales of cotton, being " an increase of 112,000 bales within the year. Some por- " tion of this increase no doubt is attributable to an unusu- " ally good season, but by far the largest share arose, as the " reports of the Revenue Collectors show, from extension of " cultivation alone." Here is a specimen of what India is capable of doing under favorable circumstances; and there can be no question but that the cotton trade would, with good roads to the interior, go on increasing as rapidly as during the year mentioned by Mr. Ashburner: for the stimulus to cultivation would then be as great from decreased expenses, as it has lately been from increased prices.

" " Thus with proper management, we might reasonably " expect to see the exports of the country in this staple " alone, swelling at the rate of 100,000 bales per annum, " and amounting probably at no distant period to a million " of bales. And what would be the consequence in other re- " spects, besides benefiting the Revenue, and improving the " condition of the people of India? Such a trade would " give employment to a vast amount of British shipping " (400,000 tons), at the same time that it created a greater " demand for the manufactures of the mother country."

" Now if this cotton, instead of being carried (as Mr. Ashburner proposes) by a bandy road, were conveyed down the Godavery at the rate at which goods are carried on the Missisipi, viz., 1 Pie (¼*d.*) per ton per mile, or about 2½ Rupees (5 shillings) per ton for the whole distance, there would be a saving of 70 Rupees (£7) a ton, or of 21 lacks (£210,000) on the whole annual traffic of 20,000 tons, besides saving the interest, insurance, waste, &c.

" Think of a great portion of this cotton being at present carried from the banks of the Godavery (500 miles from the sea) by land 500 miles to Mirzapoor, to be embarked on the Ganges at a point 550 miles from Calcutta. But the important point in Mr. Ashburner's paper is his testimony to the astonishing increase of production, consequent on an increase of price; showing clearly the grand fact, that every thing within that tract of country is in a complete state of preparation; and that nothing is wanting but a relief in the cost of transit, to make cultivation increase to almost any extent. We have in Berar, climate and soil specially adapted for producing a good marketable cotton for England; people ready to cultivate it, cattle, latent enterprize only requiring to be developed, and all requisites except communications. This line of cheap river transit would probably cause a reduction of full $1\frac{1}{8}d.$ a lb., in the price of cotton; five times as much as would be sufficient to give a material stimulus to the trade.

" But the comparative prices in this central tract with those on the coast, will strikingly illustrate the effect of communications, and show what the state of a country must continue to be, notwithstanding every other natural advantage, if not opened out by cheap transit.

	COST PER TON.		Difference.	Per centage of the difference.
	In Berar.	At Coringa.		
Rice......	124 Rs.	45 Rs.	79 Rs.	175
Cotton....	186*	325	139	75
Wheat....	31	66	35	113
Salt.......	105	30	70	200

" From this comparison some idea may be formed, of the extent to which property would be created, by opening a communication on this line of 500 miles. At the rate of 1 Pie ($\frac{1}{8}d.$) per ton per mile by the river; the cost of transport would be only $2\frac{1}{4}$ Rupees (4*s*. 6*d.*) a ton for the water carriage; and allowing on an average, a land carriage of 50 miles by railway at 4 Pice ($\frac{1}{2}d.$) per ton per mile, and 10 miles by common roads at 3 Annas ($4\frac{1}{2}d.$), the total cost of conveying a ton of cotton to and from the port, would be about as follows.

* Including the local Merchant's profit.

500 miles of river transit at 1 Pie ($\frac{1}{8}d.$)..	$2\frac{1}{2}$ Rs.	(5 shillings)
50 of railway at 4 Pice ($\frac{1}{2}d.$)..........	1 „	(2 „)
10 of common road at 3 Annas ($4\frac{1}{2}d.$)..	2 „	(4 „)
Total..	$5\frac{1}{2}$ „	(11 shillings)

"There would then be a creation of property as below, by the reduction in the cost of transport.

A ton of	Rice..............	74 Rs.	(£ 7 8*s.*)
„	Cotton..............	134 „	(£13 8*s.*)
„	Wheat.............	30 „	(£ 3 0*s.*)
„	Salt...............	70 „	(£ 7 0*s.*)

"If the Rajahmundry rice and salt were thus placed fully within reach of the inhabitants of these districts, and the wheat and cotton of Berar again, placed within reach of the manufacturers of England, it is impossible to say what the traffic on this line might become. The wheat especially, might be cheaply made into flour by the abundant water power of Rajahmundry, and conveyed to England by hundreds of thousands of tons. As wheat, it could certainly be landed in England at 4*s.* a bushel; and as flour, at a still cheaper proportional rate.

"The saving or production of property by opening the Godavery, might thus be something near this:

2,00,000 tons Rice at 74 Rupees (£7 8*s.*)....................	148 lacks,	(£1,480,000)
1,00,000 tons Cotton at 134 Rupees (£13 8*s.*)....................	144 do.	(£1,440,000)
2,00,000 tons Wheat at 30 Rs. (£3)	60 do.	(£ 600,000)
90,000 tons Salt at 70 Rs. (£7)..	63 do.	(£ 630,000)
Total...	405 do.	(£4,050,000)

The outlay to produce this trade might be as below.

For river improvements.........	10 lacks		(£100,000)
For 200 miles of railway at 10,000 Rs. (£1,000) per mile	20	do.	(£200,000)
Total..	30	do.	(£300,000)

"Of course the traffic might extend far beyond this; for the tendency of the whole thing would be, for Rajahmundry to supply a large proportion of Berar with food, while that district in its turn could feed an immense population in England, and also supply them with materials for industry. It is thus that almost any amount of property may be produced, by an outlay on communications however small.

"How immense might be the effect of thus supplying Manchester at once with cheap cotton; and how powerfully would it certainly affect the trade of that city! Who can possibly estimate the effect of thus giving to that great manufacturing city, such an immense additional advantage in its competition with other countries? In our race with America, this lowering of the cost of flour and cotton, would produce results far beyond any possible calculation.

"If the gain by the reduction of cost of these products, were equally divided between the two parties, (the buyer and seller,) it would make the following difference of prices.

Cotton in Manchester..	4*d.* per lb. instead of 4½*d.*				
Wheat in Manchester..	4*s.* 9*d.* a bushel instead of 5*s.* 6*d.*				
Rice in Berar	85 Rs. a ton	„	„		Rs. 124
Salt in do.	67½	„	„	„	„ 105

"It is well known however, that the real division of profits, is much more in favor of the purchaser than the seller, in such cases, when trade is open; but a very small addition of profit to the people, in a country already full of population and with an unlimited extent of suitable soil, would be a sufficient stimulus to an immensely extended production, and this is expressly stated by Mr. Ashburner, who is perfectly acquainted with the state of things in Berar. The increase of produce would be so great, as very soon to ensure a supply to the consumer, without any excessive profit to the producer. Nay more, if the people of Berar were supplied with rice, salt and many other things at a much lower cost than they now pay, they could afford to supply cotton at a price actually lower than at present; and yet with an increased profit to themselves.

" But with respect to the effects of such a communication, whoever may divide the profit, the facts are certain, that the people of Berar are at present paying 124 Rupees (£12 8*s.*) per ton for rice grown on the spot, whilst with easy communications, they might supply themselves with it from Rajahmundry, for 30 Rupees (£3) ; that they are paying 90 Rupees (£9) per ton for salt, while they might get it for 35 Rupees (£3 10*s.*) ; and that the Manchester manufacturers are paying £40 a ton for Berar cotton, while it could be supplied to them for £30 ; and £10 a ton for wheat, while it could be supplied to them for £6.

" The things that I have enumerated above, are only a portion of the various products which would be interchanged. Besides numerous smaller articles of food, such as chillies, cocoanuts, onions, &c., produced so very cheaply in the irrigated lands of the Delta of the Godavery, (but which are scarce and dear in Berar), who can doubt, but that, if these countries instead of being in the paralyzed state they now are, were carrying on a most extensive and profitable trade with other parts of the world, they would immediately demand vast quantities of English manufactured goods, and thus again in another way, produce an immense effect on England ?

" There seems thus to be no reason, why the Godavery may not become the line of trade of a million tons a year, when once the pent up treasures of its basin, effect a breach in the barriers, by which it has hitherto been closed.

" Respecting the nature of the navigation of the Godavery, I should state the following points.

" The fall of the river from near Chandah to the sea, averages about one and quarter feet per mile ; but this is not quite equally distributed. Captain Fenwick states, that there are six rocky barriers in its bed, which could be removed by blasting, at no great expense. The fall of one and quarter feet per mile is very moderate for steam navigation ; with a depth of 10 feet it would give a current of about 3 miles an hour. In Mr. Ellet's remarkable report on the Mississipi, he states that the Alleghany has been navigated, as high as where the fall is four and one-third feet per mile ; and the Ohio at Pittsburgh, where steamers are innumerable, has a fall of about one and half feet a mile. He says, " by " observing the descent of the Alleghany from Franklin to " Pittsburgh, we may conclude, that rivers, of which the fall " does not exceed two feet per mile, are navigable for steam " boats, unless there be great irregularity in the distribution " of that fall. In the event of such irregularity existing, " rivers having an average descent not exceeding 2 feet per " mile, if well supplied with water, must afford exceedingly " good navigation between the rapids, which must be very " remote and easily overcome."

" We learn also from these tables, that a descent of nearly 4 feet per mile is not incompatible with the existence of steam boat navigation, if the supply of water be well maintained ; for a steam boat has ascended the Alleghany as far as Olean point, overcoming, in places, a slope of nearly 5 feet per mile. In this report Mr. Ellet shows, how easily the summer navigation of the Ohio might be improved by storing water in tanks, to be discharged when the river is low ; and this is perfectly applicable to the Godavery. For instance, an additional depth of 1 foot, at a ford 200 yards broad where the current was 2 miles an hour, could be obtained by the supply of 5½ millions of cubic yards per day, or 330 millions for 2 months; and as this quantity could probably be stored for 1½ lacks of Rupees (£15,000) (perhaps much less), a sum equivalent to not more than 300 Rupees (£30) a mile on the whole length of the navigation, or perhaps a two hundredth part of the cost of a complete railroad, some idea may be formed from this, of the facility with which an additional depth of water might be given, if necessary.

"We reckon, that we can easily find situations in the Carnatic, where water can be stored for 1 Rupee per 1,000 cubic yards; and I have reason to believe, that the country in Berar is much more favorable for storing water than here, because the country there has a less fall, and consequently a bund of a certain height will retain a greater breadth of water. Captain Fenwick talks of the Godavery being now navigable for 8 months in the year, meaning as I believe, that there will be not less than 3 or 4 feet of water during that time. Supposing the quantity of water flowing, to be 500,000 cubic yards per hour at the most in those 8 months, and that it diminishes during the other 4 to 100,000 cubic yards, it would on an average require an additional 200,000 cubic yards an hour for 4 months, to keep the river in that state which Captain Fenwick calls navigable. The amount required for this purpose, would then be, 200,000 × 24 hours × 122 days = 600 million cubic yards; and I have no doubt this quantity could be stored for 3 lacks of Rupees, (£300,000) which divided over 500 miles of navigation, would be equal to 600 Rupees (£60) a mile. The great advantage of this mode of improving the navigation, is, that no works would be required in the bed of the river demanding such skill in construction, and care and attention in management, or involving such risk of injury, as to stop the navigation even for a time. No doubt some trifling work such as blasting rock, &c., might be performed in the bed of the river, which would greatly improve the navigation also; but this would be simple and of trifling cost, and by these means I have no doubt that a depth of at least 3 feet could be retained in the river throughout the year, at a fiftieth part of the cost of a double railway, and that goods could be conveyed by it at one-fifth of the cost of railway transit; and this with a speed of 150 miles a day up the river, and 200 miles down the stream, a speed that would certainly answer all present purposes. Some years ago, when some reports on the navigation of the Severn were sent me by a Civil Engineer at home, I suggested to him this mode of effecting his object, the Welch Lakes affording him peculiar advantages for storing water; but I have not heard whether any thing was done about it. Had this plan been adopted in the Ganges, it is literally incalculable what the advantages of it would have been. The cost of 10 miles of railway would have given a fine navigation of probably 3 or 4 feet, and doubtless have reduced the cost of transit in the dry season by one-half. A reduction of 2 Pice ($\frac{1}{4}$*d.*) a ton per mile, on 1$\frac{1}{2}$ million tons carried 1,000 miles, would have been a total saving of 150 lacks (1$\frac{1}{2}$ millions sterling) a year, besides the saving of time and risk; and it would have made a total change in the steam navigation of the river.

"Of course the water, besides being used for the navigation of the Godavery, would, on its arrival at the annicut, be distributed for irrigation, for which it would be worth 40 times what it cost to store it; so that if necessary, no part of its cost need be charged to the navigation. But the river is even in its present state available for navigation with vessels of small draft, for 8 months in the year at least; and it must be remembered, that the canals in Canada and New York, which have produced such prodigious results, are only open 6 or 7 months in the year. The only reasons why the Godavery is not at present used, are, want of enterprize in the Natives, and the interferences of petty Zemindars on its banks; and Government can remove the latter in a moment, and give the necessary stimulus to get over the former, by themselves setting the example of navigating it.

" This matter of the upper Godavery navigation, is worthy of a far more particular and careful report, than would be suitable in this paper; and I would only mention, as favoring highly the advisableness of undertaking such a work, the astonishing success that has attended the Paumbam works. When I was sent there in 1822, the whole amount of traffic was 17,000 tons a year, though the whole of the cotton from Tinnevelly was then carried through the Channel to Madras; whereas now, the traffic is sometimes more than that in one month (though the cotton is almost all shipped at once from Tuticorin); and the annual traffic is 168,000 tons, or ten-fold the former quantity. Such has been the effect of deepening that passage from 4½ to 10½ feet. Such an instance is an unanswerable proof of the fact, that traffic is waiting for communications, and not that communications have to wait for the traffic; as some still suppose. How strangely the state of the question of communications in India is misapprehended, has been singularly shown in this case, as before stated, by the perfect indifference with which the opening of the Godavery was treated by the Government of India.

" 1st. The Company's Government, who are so deeply interested in every thing that concerns the whole of India, would certainly gain a Revenue of many lacks, by the increased demand for salt.

" 2nd. The Government of Nagpore and Hyderabad would undoubtedly feel in numerous ways, the effect of such an increased demand for their produce.

" 3rd. The manufacturers at home are most deeply interested in this, which I feel confident is the best opening yet discovered, for obtaining for them an increased supply of cotton on the one hand, and an increased market for all English manufactured goods on the other.

" 4th. The anti-slavery body are nearly concerned in it, since nothing, so far as yet appears, would so much tend to weaken the slavery system of the United States ; the enormous profit now realized from their partial monopoly of the cotton trade, being one of the chief incentives to it.*

" 5th. The shipping interests are concerned in it. An addition of 50,000 tons of cotton alone a year, would give employment to 150 large ships; more than would be required to bring the same quantity from America.

" Further I would remark, that though undoubtedly the efforts that have been made to introduce the American varieties of cotton into India, are most commendable; yet, it seems certain now, that had a tenth part of the same money and pains been expended on opening out this magnificent cotton country by cheap communications, immensely superior results would have been obtained. Let the reader refer to Mr. Bonynge's " Future Wealth of America," the production of a practical planter ; and though we may not admire the blustering style in which it is written, we cannot but admit its force; and we have the means, in some instances, of testing the accuracy of the statistics. Its general object is to show, that cotton cultivation in America, though it has contributed so powerfully in times past to its wealth, is now irrecoverably on the decline, and must be abandoned for the cultivation of tea, coffee, indigo, and other plants. From the statistics furnished, it appears that cotton has for twelve years, declined in price 30 per cent. yearly ; rice during 9 years, in quantity and quality, 15 per cent. ; tobacco in quantity the last 5 years, $2\frac{2}{3}$ per cent. ; that bread stuffs are returning to the same amount of exports that they were, prior to the failure of the potato

* " Well, said St. Clare, suppose that something should bring down the price of cotton, once and for ever, and make the whole slave property a drug in the market."—*Uncle Tom's Cabin.*

crop in Europe; and that sugar cultivation is not advancing. With the present prices of labour in America, there is no possibility of extending the cultivation of these articles; and, except tobacco, it is feared that they will all greatly decline. Cotton cannot be cultivated in America under 5½ cents per lb.; whereas India can produce it and land it in Liverpool, at 7 cents per lb. After a fourteen years' residence (as a planter) in the East, and after a tour through South Carolina and Georgia, Mr. Bonynge is constrained to admit, that India has every means of producing as good cotton, and much cheaper than America; and he further asserts, that had it not been for the potato failure, and the timely aid of California, America could never have borne the decay of her principal staple for the last 10 years.

"What then ought the Godavery Delta to become, as the outlet of the whole trade of the basin of the Godavery containing 1,30,000 square miles, when it supplies that immense region with rice, salt, tobacco, sugar, chillies, and numerous other things, which can only be produced in inland districts at four times the price? Is it too much to expect, that an immense mercantile city will spring up on the coast, near the harbour of Coringa, from which millions of tons of wheat, cotton, oil seeds, sugar, rice, tobacco, hemp, &c., will annually be exported, and into which English manufactured articles to an immense amount, will be imported for the use of the 12 millions of people who will thus be so enriched, as to become extensive consumers of such things? I cannot see any thing to prevent this, if the country continues to be blessed with peace; unless, which is scarcely conceivable, it be insanely determined, not to take the first step towards opening the navigation of the Godavery. Probably little more than the first step is required; for in such a case, when once the trade begins, it must go on; nothing can stop it."

Upon the whole, there seems to be no possible means of

transit that can surpass steam communication by water in point of cheapness; and that too at a speed which will certainly abundantly answer all our present purposes. The rivers that may be easily improved, are, the Ganges, Jumna, Gogra, Chumbul, Gunduck, Soane, Bhugirutty, Mahanuddee, Nerbudda, Godavery, Kistnah, Wurdah, Munjera; and no doubt several minor rivers.

Perhaps in all, there may be found 5,000 miles of river navigation, which may be made thoroughly convenient. All rivers, which have not a greater fall than two feet a mile, will be quite available. Such a fall, with a depth of twenty feet, will give a current of about 5½ miles an hour, and with a depth of five feet, of 3 miles an hour; and it must be remembered that the number of days in the year in which Indian rivers are nearly full, is very small indeed, since for eight or nine months in the year they are very low. If on these lines, which it must be particularly observed will bear by far the greater portion of all the traffic of India, transit can be effected at 1 Pice or one-eighth of a Penny per ton per mile, our main object will be already gained. We know that on the Ganges there is now a traffic of upwards of a million tons a year; and if this river were greatly improved by keeping the quantity of water always up to a certain height, there can be no question, but that the amount of traffic would be prodigiously increased; probably at least doubled, and more likely increased four-fold. Perhaps the greatest improvement in the way of communication, that could be made in all India in comparison of its cost, would be by the construction of a weir across the Ganges below the head of the Bhugirutty, to turn the whole stream into that river in the dry season. This weir would keep the Bhugirutty navigable throughout the year, and give rise to an immense traffic. The weir across the Godavery (twelve feet high with a clear water way of 4,000 yards) has cost 8½ lacks (£85,000) including 6 sets of sluices, 3 locks, &c. If the Ganges weir, six feet high, cost 5 lacks (£50,000) the interest, 25,000 Rupees (£2,500) would be equivalent to a charge of 3½ Pice (nearly ½*d.*) per ton on the present traffic; or taking the distance from the head of the Bhugirutty to Calcutta at 150 miles, one-tenth Pie per ton per mile, besides the benefit to travellers. The Godavery would undoubtedly convey the whole traffic of the basin of that river, which cannot at present be less than 150,000 tons a year, and would increase in a far greater proportion than that on the Ganges; for this obvious reason, that there is at present no water carriage on the former. All goods are now carried at about 3 Annas (4½*d.*) a ton per mile; and if the cost were reduced to 1 Pie (⅛*d.*) it is impossible to say what the traffic would be, but there can be little doubt that it would be increased five or six-fold, or to a million tons per annum. If, as before suggested, two millions of people, employed in cotton cultivation, were fed from the irrigated Delta at the mouth of the river, that alone would call for a traffic of 700,000 tons a year. In the same way, the Indus, the Nerbudda, and the Kistnah, would undoubtedly convey the whole trade of their basins; though what the probable amount of it would be, I have no means of judging.

We should thus at once provide for the really cheap conveyance, of probably half of the whole traffic of the country; and if the cost of transit by the Ganges were thus reduced to half of what it now is, with a similar reduction on the Indus, and if the change of water for land carriage, on the lines of the other rivers named, were to reduce the cost there from 3 Annas (4½*d.*) a ton per mile to 2 Pice (¼*d.*), there would be a saving to the country of many millions sterling.

The following calculation, though not given even as an approximation to the actual saving, will at least give some idea of the amount of direct saving.

Saving on 1,200,000 tons conveyed 1,200 miles on the Ganges, at 2 Pice (¼*d.*) per ton per mile.............	1½ million sterling.
Ditto on 500,000 tons carried 450 miles by the Godavery, at 3 Annas (4½*d.*)..	4 do. do.
Ditto on 50,000 tons carried 500 miles on the Indus, at 2 Pice (¼*d.*).........	$0\frac{1}{40}$ do. do.
Ditto on 50,000 carried 400 miles on the Kistnah, at 2½ Annas (3¾*d.*).....	0⅓ do. do.
Total....	6 millions sterling.

besides the amount saved on the Nerbudda, Soane, &c. But besides this, there would be a profit on all the additional traffic on the Ganges, which we may safely reckon at as much more; so that a saving of ten millions might thus be effected, entirely exclusive of the saving on the transit of passengers, and of all those immense effects (which cannot be calculated in money), of such improved lines of transit.

The following Extract from the Professional Papers of the Corps of Royal Engineers, on the Halifax and Quebec Railway, contains many things bearing upon the point under consideration:—

In the United States they are well aware of the increased value, which internal improvements and communications give to property of every kind.

In those countries works have been undertaken for that object alone, not for the mere return which the work—whether railway, road, or canal—would make of itself.

The indebtedness of the several States has been incurred almost entirely in making great internal improvements; and in the boldness and unhesitating way in which they have incurred debts and responsibilities, for the purpose of developing their resources, may be seen the secret of their unrivalled prosperity.

The State is in debt, but its citizens have been enriched beyond all proportion.

Most unfavorable comparisons are made by travellers who visit the British provinces and the United States; and some have gone so far as to state, that travelling along, where the boundary is a mere conventional line, they could at once tell whether they were in the States or not.

On the one side the State Governments become shareholders to a large amount in great public works, lead the way, and do not hesitate to incur debt, for making what has been termed "war upon the wilderness;" employment is given, and by the time the improvement is completed, property has been created, and the employed become proprietors.

On the other side the provincial Governments do not take the initiative in the same manner, and hence in the settlements, and in the provinces generally, may be seen this marked difference in the progress of people who are identically the same in every respect.

Until the British provinces boldly imitate the policy of the States in this regard, and make "war upon the wilderness," their progress will continue to present the same unfavorable contrast.*

The creative or productive power of canals, railways, &c., may be traced in the history and progress of the State of New York.

The Erie canal was commenced in 1817, and completed in 1825, at a cost of 7,143,789 dollars, or £1,400,000 sterling. In 1817 the value of real and personal property in the city of New York was, from official documents, estimated at £16,436,000 sterling. In 1825 it was estimated at £21,075,000 sterling. In 1820 the population of the State was £1,372,000 and in 1830 the population of the State was £1,918,000.

The canal was found so inadequate to the traffic, that between the years 1825 and 1835, a farther sum of £2,700,000 was to be expended in enlarging it.†

Making the total cost to that date £4,100,000 sterling.

It has been seen that in the city of New York

In 1817 the official value of real and personal property was £16,436,000
1835 ditto ditto ditto £45,567,000

Being an increase of $2\frac{3}{4}$ times in 18 years.

For the State of New York.

In 1817 the official value of real and personal property was £63,368,000
1835 ditto ditto ditto £110,120,000

Or an increase of nearly £47,000,000 sterling in the value of property; attributed chiefly, if not entirely, to the formation of the canals.

In 1836, the amount conveyed to tide-water by the canal was 697,357 tons.

* In one remarkable case however, our Engineers have taught the people of the States a lesson; the magnificent Steam Canals on the line of the St. Lawrence have effectually drawn the traffic of the upper Missisipi valley from the Erie Canal fitted up for animal draft. (Note by Ed.)

† It is to be again enlarged.

And on the 1st of July of that year there had accumulated in the hands of the Commissioners, an amount sufficient to extinguish the whole of the outstanding debt incurred in its construction.

The net receipts from all the State canals, after deducting the expenses of collection and superintendence, for the year 1847, was £449,270. Villages, towns, and cities have sprung up along its course.

The population of the State, which was

In 1810, - - - -	959,949
Was in 1845, - -	2,604,495

In 1846 the value of real and personal property was estimated at £128,500,000.

It will be seen from the above, therefore, that in addition to the wealth created for individuals, the canals produce a large annual revenue to the State.

The following Extracts from the financial affairs and statistics of some of the States may be quoted in illustration of this part of the subject:—

1847.

MASSACHUSETTS.

	Dollars.
Total indebtedness of the State, 1st January 1847 -	999,654
Credit of the State, lent to railroads, - - - - -	5,049,555
Total liabilities of the State,..	6,049,209

As security for the redemption of the scrip lent to railroads, the commonwealth hold a mortgage on all the roads, and also 3,000 shares in the Norwich and Worcester, and 1,000 in the Andover and Haverhill.

PENNSYLVANIA.

	Dollars.
Public property, canals, and railroads, at original cost,	28,657,402

MARYLAND.

	Dollars.
Receipts from Baltimore and Ohio railroad, - -	42,402
Ditto from canal Companies, - - - - - -	11,550

NORTH CAROLINA.

	Dollars.
Debt of the State, on account of railroad Companies, -	1,110,000

OHIO.

	Dollars.
Debt contracted for the sole purpose of the construction of Public Works within the State, - - - -	19,246,000
Canals, 820 miles in length, cost - - - - -	15,122,503
Net receipts in 1846, after paying repairs and expenses -	408,916

In 1810 the population of this State was			45,865
In 1820	ditto	ditto	581,434
In 1840	ditto	ditto	1,519,467

Or tripled nearly in 20 years, during the progress of her canals.

Michigan.

	Dollars.
Debt on 30th November, 1845	4,394,510

Total length of railroads finished and belonging to the State, 222 miles.

This State was authorized to raise a loan of 5,000,000 dollars for internal improvements.

For the same purpose, Congress granted to the State 500,000 acres of land.

In 1840 the population was	212,267
In 1845	304,278

Or an increase of 50 per cent. nearly, in five years.

Indiana.

	Dollars.
In January 1847, the public debt was	14,394,940

By the terms of the Act adjusting this debt, it is to be equally divided between the State and the Wabash and Erie canal. Of this canal, which is to be 458 miles long, 374 miles are in Indiana; 174 of this portion are finished, and in operation. There remain 200 miles to be completed, upon which part, about 1,200,000 dollars have been expended by the State. It is estimated to cost the farther sum of 2,000,000 dollars to complete the entire canal. To cover this amount the State is to transfer to trustees 963,126 acres of land adjoining to or in the neighbourhood of the canal.

The population of this State, in 1811 was			24,520
Ditto	ditto	1830	343,031
Ditto	ditto	1840	685,086

Or doubled in ten years.

Illinois.

		Dollars.
1847	Total internal improvement debt,	8,165,081
	Total canal debt,	6,009,187
		13,174,268

The population in 1830 was		157,455
Ditto	1840	476,183

Or tripled in ten years.

The sales of the public lands during one year (1845)
In the United States amounted to - - 1,843,527 acres.
Producing - - - - - - - - 2,470,298 dollars.

Or an average of 5*s.* 7*d.* sterling per acre.

But to show the effect produced by a canal or railway passing through property, the following Extract may be quoted, from the Report of a Board of Directors of the New York and Erie Railroad company, in February, 1844:

"The Board find that they have omitted one description of property, which has heretofore been considered of great value, but the right to most of which has been lost to the Company, by failure to complete the road within a certain period; the most valuable of which consisted of 50,000 acres of wild land in Cattaraguas country, near Lake Erie, and one-fourth part of the village of Dunkirk."

"An offer in writing was made in 1837 by responsible parties to take these donations, and pay further the sum of 400,000 dollars, provided certain portions of the railroad were completed within a specified time."

That is, about 8 dollars, or 33 shillings 4 pence sterling per acre.

In Michigan 461,000 acres were granted by Congress for the endowment of a University. These lands were selected, in sections from the most valuable of the State. The price of these was at one time 20 dollars or £4 6*s.* 8*d.* sterling per acre, but became lower afterwards; 17,142 acres, the quantity sold up to 30th November, 1845, brought £2 9*s.* per acre; 69,000 acres, devoted to Schools, were sold per £1 7*s.* per acre.

Such then, are some of the results of making "war upon the wilderness."*

Upon the whole, the opening and improvement of the rivers of India, would provide perhaps the cheapest possible carriage for half the traffic of India, with a fair speed; and produce a saving in money of at least 10 millions sterling, and more likely to a much greater amount. Reckoning that so large a sum as 2,000 Rupees (£200) a mile were expend-

* In fact the sole reason why England has hitherto bought its millions of bushels of wheat, and hundred thousand tons of cotton from America, is, because both the States and Canada have at an enormous expense formed water communications from the valley of the Mississipi, and made a proper use of their rivers, which we in India have not done, excepting in the case of the Ganges, which has only been used because the Natives used it before we came. The United States spent 8 millions sterling on the Erie Canal, without which (or the St. Lawrence navigation) not a bushel of wheat could have gone from the upper Mississipi to England; while if we had spent £70,000 on the Godavery, we could have supplied all England with both wheat and cotton.

ed upon these improvements (chiefly in storing water as above described) the total expense for every 5,000 miles, would be 100 lacks, or 1 million sterling. What other means of improving the country could possibly be compared with this? Excepting in irrigation, no opening for the employment of capital equal to this could possibly be found; nor one that would produce one quarter of these results. If four-fifths of this outlay be employed in storing water, it would give for the Ganges, 1,200 miles at 2,000 Rupees (£200) per mile total 24 lacks (£240,000); which, at 2,000 cubic yards stored per Rupee, would supply 4,800 millions of cubic yards, or an average of 24 millions a day for 200 days; and this would be equal to a gradually increasing supply from nothing, to 48 millions per day, or 26 millions per hour when the river was at its lowest. That is, an average of 24 millions of cubic yards per day for the whole 200 days, would provide a supply of 48 millions when the river was at the lowest if it fell gradually: equivalent to raising the water 3 feet where it was 600 yards broad, with a current of 1½ miles an hour. But so utterly insignificant is such an outlay compared with the object to be attained, that if necessary, five times as much water as is here calculated, could be stored. If this water were divided between different reservoirs, placed in the upper parts of the basins of the Ganges and its several feeders, the Jumna, Chumbul, &c., the total length of navigation improved would be perhaps 2,400 miles, and the cost would then be 1,000 Rupees (£100) a mile; or, there would be an annual charge of 50 Rupees (£5) in interest, which divided between 800,000 tons average traffic, would form a charge of one-eightieth Pice per ton per mile. Let this only be compared with the effects of 100,000 Rupees spent on a mile of railway!

CHAPTER VII.

NAVIGABLE CANALS.

Good Steam Canals better in some respects than Rivers.

WHEN the rivers are thus turned to account, the next question is, whether on any lines, canals could not be constructed, so as to give the cheapest possible lines of transit? Whenever good steam canals can be obtained, they will of course be preferable in some respects to rivers; the principal reason being, that they can be worked day and night, so as to give a speed of 300 miles a day with fast steamers. For a chiefly down trade, as that of India is on all the lines of the rivers, there will of course be an advantage in the current, if not too great, which still-water canals would not have; but still, the transit on steam canals would be exceedingly cheap; certainly not exceeding half Pice ($\frac{1}{16}$*d.*) per ton per mile. On the channels in Rajahmundry in their present incomplete state, 3 Pice ($\frac{3}{8}$*d.*) a ton per mile is paid for short trips of 10 or 20 miles; and the rate would certainly be very much lower, for long voyages of 100 to 500 miles, in canals completed in every way, and with suitable boats; for the boats now in use on the Rajahmundry channels are those formerly used for the river navigation, and by no means the most suitable ones for canals. The cargo boats used on the Godavery works, cost, including the aid of two small steam tugs, half Anna ($\frac{3}{4}$*d.*) per ton per day for all expenses; which, supposing they pass over 20 miles a day, would give one-third Pie ($\frac{1}{24}$*d.*) per ton per mile per day; and these boats carry twice the crew they would, if working only on canals. For the carriage of the coarsest goods, such as building materials, &c., for which a very low speed would be sufficient, the cost of transit would be still lower.

It must be observed also, that the transit on Government canals, would be greatly more extensive in this country, than in England, for two reasons;

1st. On private canals, it is not for the interest of the owners that an extremely low rate of transit should be charged; the fear of crowding the canal and consuming water, prevents their reducing the tolls beyond a certain point; whereas, it would be the interest of Government to encourage the utmost possible use of the canals, and it would be advisable to let all goods go free, rather than in the least diminish the traffic. When the Government have executed such a work, it is for their interest that the greatest possible use be made of it, and it would probably be best not to levy any toll; as there can be no doubt that the indirect returns from it, in increase of taxes from land and other things already taxed, would much more than yield to Government the interest for money so expended.

2d. Canals made expressly for steam navigation would of course be used for many purposes, for which canals in England often cannot be used. With capacious locks, so made as to be rapidly filled and emptied, and the canal itself both broad and deep, they will be admirable passenger lines. The locks on the Rajahmundry channel will admit vessels of more than 100 tons; and if ultimately kept six feet deep, as intended) they will admit iron vessels of 140 tons, and thus allow of the highest speed. (Steamers on the Hudson draw only four feet, with a speed of 18 or 20 miles an hour.) But passenger traffic at slow speed would be immense, as travellers could be carried at an expense much below that of walking. The 20 H. P. steamer on the Godavery worked at low speed, (6 miles an hour) costs 2 Annas (3*d.*) per mile, and including wear and tear, &c., 4 Annas (6*d.*); but when tugging with 100 passengers, would cost less per mile, as she would go faster, and the charge would thus be only ½ P. ($\frac{1}{16}$*d.*) per man per mile, even if there were no first class passengers on board, to pay a larger share of the expenses. Such canals could undoubtedly be navigated in this country at 8 miles an hour, and at a charge of 1 Rupee (2 shillings) per 400 miles, for the lowest class of passengers. How great the number of passengers would be on such a line, is curiously shown in the case of the Pulicat canal, on which—though it forms at present no part of any great line of communication, but merely extends 30 or 40 miles from Madras, to a part of the country where there are no great towns—there are more than 100 travellers a day paying about 1 P. (⅛*d.*) per mile, though they actually travel slower than a man walks. Were this line extended to the Northward, so as to form part of the main Northern approach to Madras by land, connecting that city with Hyderabad, Nagpore, and the Northern Circars, there could not be less than 1,000 passengers a day, and there would probably be several thousands; with steamers moving at a moderate speed, and charging from ⅓ Anna (½*d.*) down to ½ P. ($\frac{1}{16}$*d.*) per head per mile.

As for the lines on which canals might be cut with advantage, and would upon the whole be the most suitable kind of works, we have first, the Ganges canal, already well advanced. Of the value of this work as a means of irrigation, I need not here speak particularly; it will no doubt be a work of incalculable value in that respect, though the effects of such works in that part of the country, seem to be unaccountably small as compared with those of similar works in the Madras Presidency; and though accompanied with the terrible drawback which attends irrigation in all moderately hot countries, viz., fever. As a work of communication too, there can be no question, but that it will also be of incalculable value. Such a magnificent canal, extending nearly in a straight line 450 miles, (besides its branches of 400 miles) passing through a most populous and fertile country, and terminating at the point where the Ganges, even in its present state is navigable for steamers all the year round, will, if I mistake not, be the most important work yet executed or commenced in India. If it cost, (as now estimated) 160 lacks (£1,600,000) for 850 miles, (including the heavy works of the first 15 miles) its cost will be under 20,000 Rupees (£2,000) a mile, for a canal 50 yards broad and 10 feet deep at its head; and gradually diminishing to its lower end, though still a good navigation. Such a work in this country at such a price, even if intended merely for navigation, would surely be one of the greatest bargains ever made. If 8 per cent. covers interest and management, the annual cost would be 1,600 Rupees (£160) a year per mile, amounting, on a trade of one million tons a year, to a charge of only one-third Pice ($\frac{1}{24}d.$) per ton per mile; and if the interest, &c., were paid entirely by passengers, (as it might very well be,) it would provide that vast tract of country with a transit for goods at a rate not exceeding half Pice ($\frac{1}{16}d.$) per ton per mile, free from all risks, and navigable day and night, at any speed that each kind of freight might require. Having also a current in the direction of the trade, the cost of transit will probably be the lowest that has ever yet been seen in internal transit; if not even lower than sea transit, which for long voyages does not now exceed ½ P. ($\frac{1}{16}d.$) per ton per land mile; (£3 a ton from India to England, 12,000 land miles measured on the shortest route). The importance of this canal at the present moment is beyond calculation; it will show in the strongest light the difference between steam canal communication, and grand railways: for if interest and insurance are charged to irrigation, (as they may well be in this case,) it will be very nearly equivalent to the total abolition of the cost of transit; as the actual expense will be so small, as scarcely to be felt in any articles of produce. Indeed, the contrast between this and the Bengal railway, will be very curious; the one, costing only 20,000 Rupees (£2,000) a mile, providing for the interest, &c. by its use for irrigation, and conveying goods at certainly ½ P. ($\frac{1}{16}$*d.*) per ton per mile, and first class passengers at perhaps 2 P. (¼*d.*); and the other, costing Rupees 100,000 or 1,20,000 (£10,000 or £12,000) a mile, and charging, (according to the reports) 8 P. (1*d.*) per ton, and probably at least 4 P. (½*d.*) It is true, that while the canal is worked at 300 miles a day for passengers, the railway may be worked at 700; but the advantage of speed in this country, is at present, utterly insignificant in comparison with that of reducing the *cost* of transit.

Supposing 500,000 tons of goods carried 450 miles by canal and railway, at the above rates, the account would stand thus:

500,000 tons by Railway 450 miles at 4 P. (½*d.*) per ton per mile...	47	lacks	(£470,000)
Interest 5 per cent. on 450 miles of Rail at 1¼ lacks per mile....	28	„	(£280,000)
Total cost by Railway.....	75	„	(£750,000)
On the other hand:			
500,000 tons by Canal, 450 miles, at ½ P. ($\frac{1}{16}$*d.*) per ton per mile....	6	„	(£ 60,000)
Annual saving, by Canal..	69	lacks	(£690,000)

or ½ million sterling.

But this calculation does not include the benefits from increased traffic; for the cost of transit on the canal being $\frac{1}{8}$ of that by Railway, the traffic by the former might be ten times that on the latter.

Had the canal been continued on to Calcutta, and at the same cost, viz. 20,000 Rupees (£2,000) a mile, the valley of the Ganges would have had the greatest advantage in the way of transit that could be desired or indeed that could be found in the world; and probably at the cheapest rate.

We have already however, 850 miles of noble canal in a considerable state of forwardness; and there cannot be a doubt, that even now, it ought to be continued on to Calcutta; giving 500 miles more. We have not yet seen what a double railroad is capable of conveying, but it certainly cannot accommodate a trade of two million tons a year, (about 7,000 tons a day) unless the passenger trains be restricted to the same speed as goods; and if so, the advantages of very high speed (for which so much has been sacrificed,) will be lost, and the railway would even in this respect have no advantage over a canal: *so that the railway does not in reality lessen the necessity for a canal.* It is still generally, but erroneously supposed, that railways and canals are directly antagonistic works; though the contrary has been fully proved both in England and America. For instance, far from the railway between New York and Buffaloe having superseded the canal on the same line, 20 millions of dollars have within a few years, been expended on the enlargement of the latter; and it now carries the great mass of traffic, although closed by frost for five months in the year. Even if the railway could accommodate 7,000 tons a day, probably as much more would be conveyed by a canal, if worked at $\frac{1}{8}$ P. ($\frac{1}{16}$*d.*) per ton per mile. Between Manchester and Liverpool, where there is a much smaller traffic than there would be here, there are no less than four lines of communication, all in full use; and 2 millions of tons a year are carried by two of the canals, while only 180,000 are carried by the railway.

There is yet another point showing how narrow a view has been taken of the subject. Even with respect to this one particular line, the question "How can this actual amount of traffic be best provided for?"—the proper question for the Government and the public—has never yet been asked. There can be no doubt I think, that the great mass of the traffic will remain untouched by the railway; it will continue to come down the river just as it does now; and there is little probability that the railway will convey more than 2,000 tons a day, at the utmost.

The necessity of providing for the remainder of this traffic, brings us to the question, which would be best; to form a canal? or, as before suggested, to throw water into the river? I think there can be no doubt that the canal will be in every way superior to the river, however much the latter may be improved; and the cost of transit, including interest, will still be much less on the canal, than on the river. But on the other hand, there is this strong argument in favor of first improving the river, viz., that it can be done at one-tenth the cost, of a canal, and probably in one-tenth of the time; and this brings us to the second fundamental point in the general enquiry about communications in India: viz., *the time in which extensive lines can be opened throughout India.* In my opinion, the grand evil arising out of this unfortunate mania for English railways in India, has been, that in following the illusion of *high speed of transit,* we have been effectually turned off from the great object of all, viz., *speed in executing communications.* No man can be more sensible than myself of the advantages of speed of transit, which in England was a vital point; but it is utterly insignificant in this country, in comparison with the importance of quickly laying open the whole country. In this respect then, high speed railways are in fact what the Australians called their bullock waggons "*crawling nuisances;*" crawling across the country at the rate of 10 miles a year, while we ought to be getting over 5,000 miles in that time. It is exactly like a catamaran man spending a gold mohur on a bracelet, but leaving his 10 square inches of clothing as it was; or like a starving beggar spending on an Ice, what would have given him bread for a month. What will be the results, even in respect of speed, of this mode of proceeding? that at the end of ten years we shall be able to travel at thirty or forty miles an hour from Calcutta towards Lahore some one or two hundred miles, and to creep over the other 20,000 miles of main lines, as we do now. And in the meantime, what are we spending on transit throughout the country? Perhaps fifteen millions sterling a year.

Suppose we spend 100 lacks (1 million sterling) a year on railways, and accomplish 100 miles, what will be our position at the end of twenty years?

Expenditure.

20 years at 100 lacks (1 million).	£20 millions sterling.
Extent of railway opened	2,000 miles.
Main lines required	20,000
Remaining unexecuted........	18,000 miles.

Estimate of Results.

Traffic on 500 miles by road from Calcutta......................	500,000 tons a year.	
Saving on do. as compared with river transit.....................	Nothing.	
Average traffic on 1,500 miles of other lines....................	50,000 tons.	
Annual saving on do. as compared with land carriage at 2 Annas (3*d.*) per ton per mile	90 lacks	(£900,000)
Saving in 20 years, allowing half that amount for the whole period....	900 lacks	(£9,000,000)

Now if, instead of expending 100 lacks (1 million) a year for 20 years, on complete railways, the same time and money be spent in other ways, the following might be accomplished.

5,000 miles improved river navigation at Rs. 2,000 (£200) a mile..	100	lacks	(£ 1,000,000)
2,000 miles of coast canal at Rs. 3,000 (£300) a mile.........	60	„	(£ 600,000)
3,000 miles of canal on other favorable lines at Rs. 5,000 (£500)...	150	„	(£ 1,500,000)
14,000 miles cheap single railway, at Rs. 12,000 (£1,200) a mile.	1,680	„	(£16,800,000)
Total..	1,990	lacks	(£19,900,000)

So that we should have,

Good river navigation.....	5,000	miles.
Coast canal...........	2,000	do.
Other canal...........	3,000	do.
Cheap railway..........	14,000	do.
Total..	24,000	do.

Results.

Saving on 500 miles of Ganges at 2 P. ($\frac{1}{4}d.$) a ton on 1 million tons...	50	lacks	(£ 500,000)
Do. on 800 miles of Indus, at 2 P. ($\frac{1}{4}d.$) on 50,000 tons..........	4	„	(£ 40,000)
Do. on 2,700 miles of other rivers, at $2\frac{1}{2}$ Annas ($3\frac{3}{4}d.$) on 50,000 tons	216	„	(£ 2,160,000)
Do. on 2,000 miles of coast canal at 3 P. ($\frac{3}{8}d.$) on 50,000 tons....	15	„	(£ 150,000)
Do. on 3,000 miles of other canals at $2\frac{1}{2}$ Annas ($3\frac{3}{4}d.$) on 50,000 tons	240	„	(£ 2,400,000)
Do. on 14,000 miles of railway at 2 Annas ($3d.$) on 20,000 tons..	700	„	(£ 7,000,000)
Total saving..	1,225	lacks	(£12,250,000)

or $12\frac{1}{4}$ millions sterling.

Or in 20 years, (taking half of this for the average of the whole period)... 122 millions sterling.

That is, if grand railways are carried on, we shall at the end of 20 years, have 2,000 miles of main communications, or *one-tenth* of the main lines the country requires, and have saved 9 millions sterling; whereas if we follow another system, first turning to account the facilities we have for water communication, and then proceeding with cheap railways, we shall at the end of the same period have *the whole* of the main lines opened, and have saved 122 millions sterling. In calculating the saving upon each line, I have of course compared it with the kind of transit for which it will be substituted, whether river, coast, or land carriage; and though this must necessarily be a very rude kind of estimate, yet there can be no doubt that it gives in the main, a true representation of the case. In its simplest form, the question is, " Shall we first have 80 miles of fine " double railway, or 4,000 miles of good river navigation; " and when we have done what we can with water, shall we " have 1,200 miles of fine double railway, or 14,000 miles " of cheap single railway?"

If instead of taking a little strip of the country, and setting ourselves to ascertain whether a railway will pay, we take the whole country from the Himalaya to Cape Comorin, and consider what it most requires, and how the greatest advantage may be obtained in the shortest time, we shall have no doubt as to the main point, viz., that grand railways will not answer our purpose. No body is more sensible than I am, that complete railways are the most perfect communications, and invaluable in an advanced country where there is a vast number of people whose time is extremely valuable; and to this state we may hope India will come in time; but what is most wise in a rich man, is utter ruin to a poor one, and to lay 100 miles of railway, and leave 10,000 miles of trunk lines unimproved, is as great a mistake as could be made. If we want fine railways as soon as possible, the best way to obtain them, is, to take the shortest course to throw open the country; and by thus removing the insufferable burthen under which it groans, enable it to put forth its energies. Every mile of railway costs not only what is expended on it, but also what is expended on the 50 miles of land transit, for which with the same money, as much river navigation might be substituted. Thus, if instead of spending 10 lacks (£100,000) on the Godavery, the improvement of that line be delayed for 20 years, and 10 miles of fine railway executed instead, there will be, on a traffic of 50,000 tons carried by land from the basin of that river (400 miles at Rs. 60 (£6) per ton per mile), a loss of 30 lacks (£300,000) a year, or 600 lacks (6 millions) for the whole period of 20 years; so that the actual cost of the railway, great as it may be, is a mere trifle in comparison of the loss that it causes. Further this sum of 600 lacks (6 millions) in money, is trifling compared with the full amount of loss to this vast tract, thus remaining closed against all the refreshing influences that a free communication through it, would inevitably bring in. Who can form an estimate of the mischief thus done?

During the 20 years that it took to throw a net-work of railways over England, that country had the advantage of a complete system of canals and good turnpike roads. How totally different is the state of India, and what will it do during the 200 years that will be required at the present rate of progress, to provide it with railways! But the fact is, that this will never be done; people delude themselves with these railways, and fancy they are actually supplying the wants of India, while they are in reality doing nothing in comparison of what it wants.

But to return to the question of a canal, or river improvements, for the line from Allahabad to Calcutta. On the principle already advanced, of *speed in making communications*, I would certainly advocate the latter rather than the former, because the work could be completed in one-tenth of the time. Supposing we throw more water into the river, at a cost of Rs. 2,000 (£200) a mile, then, the cost of the whole, 12 lacks (£120,000) would be realised in three months, if a saving of only 1 P. (⅛*d.*) per ton per mile, were produced on 1½ million tons per annum; or, if the canal were begun at the same time and finished in five years, the cost of the river improvements would be saved 20 times over before the canal was opened, without taking into account the greater cost of the canal, viz. Rs. 20,000 (£2,000) per mile.

If the money and labour already expended on railways had been spent on river improvements, we should already have 1,200 miles of very fair navigation, and be saving at the very least 1 P. (⅛*d.*) per ton; or on 1,200,000 tons for the whole 1,200 miles, 72 lacks (£720,000) a year. Such is the price we are now paying for our finery, because beggars as we are, we will be as great men in one point, as our wealthy neighbours. Let us first get rid of our incubus by the readiest means, and let in the air and light to the dark interior regions of the country; and then we may sit down, and consider how to provide ourselves with the greatest luxuries in the way of transit.

I do not at all mean to insist on the kind of work above advocated as the only possible works; on the contrary, what I desire, is to see many minds exercised on this point; looking fairly at the whole subject, and considering what India requires as she now is, and how it may best be obtained. I am satisfied, that the means I propose, are incomparably more to the purpose than those now in progress; and that by their means we shall in a tenth part of the time attain the very objects we are now grasping at, viz., rapid and luxurious travelling; but if any one can propose still better means, so much the better.

There seems to me, however, very little hope at present of any plan, by which a greater extent of very cheap transit can be obtained in a short time, than by improving the rivers. When

I speak of the works costing little, it is chiefly with reference to time. The saving effected by speedily getting rid of the present cost of transit, is, (as shown above,) enormously greater than any saving in the execution of the works. On a line of land carriage of 100,000 tons a year, the present expenditure is about Rs. 20,000 (£2,000) a year per mile; and if this be continued for 10 years, 2 lacks of Rs. (£20,000) a mile will be lost; while the substitution of a cheap railway for it, would only cost perhaps Rs. 12,000 (£1,200) a mile, and the improvement of a river not more than Rs. 2,000 (£200)

As I have already said, something may be done in improving the beds of the rivers, but in general the first point is to throw more water into them; and I calculate that water can be stored at 2,000 cubic yards per Rupee (2 shillings) an estimate which is the result of long experience among the tanks of the Carnatic. Without any remarkable advantage in the site, a bund may be made almost any where at this rate; but in many situations where the form of the ground favours it, thrice this amount may be stored for a Rupee (2 shillings). A bund ten yards high, would cost in the Carnatic 14 Rupees (£1 8*s.*) a yard, and if the fall of the country were ten feet a mile, and the water stood eight yards deep at the bund, it would retain 17,000 cubic yards of water for every yard length of bund, with little assistance from the form of the ground. If the fall of the country were less, the quantity of water retained would be proportionably greater; and it is to be observed that in India generally, the slope of the country is much less than in the Carnatic.

It must also be remembered, that in choosing sites for tanks to store water for the rivers, we should have the choice of the whole of the upper part of the basins of those rivers. It would not signify where they were situated; in some cases no doubt, it would be necessary to purchase land: but the wildest and most uncultivated parts would generally be chosen.

There are many tanks in the Madras Presidency, each of which contain water enough, alone materially to improve the navigation of the Godavery; and were our Government to take such a matter in hand, no doubt sites could be found to contain a much larger body of water, than any existing tank holds.

What quantity of water it might be desirable to throw into other rivers, such as the Ganges, I do not know; but of this I have no doubt, that the cost would bear no comparison with the benefits, if such an immense traffic as that on the Ganges were facilitated. If the water at a shallow be 1,000 yards broad, and the current two miles an hour, it would require thirty million cubic yards a day, or 3,000 million cubic yards for 100 days, to keep it a foot deeper. This might cost about 30 lacks (£300,000); a very small sum to benefit a navigation of suppose 700 miles, on which a million tons pass annually. The interest of it would be equivalent to about $\frac{1}{10}$ P. ($\frac{1}{80}$*d.*) per ton per mile for those 100 days; and probably it would save 20 times as much in the cost of transit. But what is now doing on this line? It is proposed to spend 1 lack (£10,000) a mile on 500 miles of railway; a sum that would supply 250 million cubic yards of water a day for 200 days, sufficient to provide a stream 2,000 yards wide, and three feet deep, flowing at 3 miles an hour, which would make the Ganges throughout the year a perfect navigation for Steamers drawing 5 or 6 feet, besides effectually protecting the country from floods. But there is not the least occasion to go to any expense approaching to this; the cost of 50 miles of railway will certainly give 700 of excellent river navigation. As I have said before, on the Ganges line something more *must* be done besides laying a railroad; for I suppose it will not be expected that even a double line of railroad will convey 2 million tons a year, or on *an average* about 7,000 tons a day, besides passengers; in which case it might on some days be required to convey 14,000 tons and 5,000 passengers. The traffic which cannot be carried on the railroad, must be provided for in some other way. Is it finally determined to leave the greater part of the traffic with all the present disadvantages? This is out of the question. Suppose that only half a million tons are left to go by the river from Allahabad to Calcutta, on an average of the whole distance, the cost of the traffic by river (according to the railway advocates' calculations) will be as follows: 500,000 tons × 9 Pice × 600 miles = 140 lacks (£1,400,000) a year. Is this to be allowed, while at least 100 lacks (1 million) a year, might be saved by improving the river, at a capital cost of perhaps 30 or 50 lacks (£300,000 to £500,000) or an annual expense of 1½ or 2½ lacks (£15,000 to £25,000.)

I am not aware what the cost of the projected canal from Calcutta to the Ganges, was estimated at; but whatever it might be, it would not affect my position, because what we want, is *immediate* relief. We have to deal with a loss of 100 lacks (1 million) a year; and if we take in hand a work which will require 5 years to execute, we ensure a loss of 5 millions sterling.

CHAPTER VIII.

CHEAP RAILWAYS FOR LOW SPEED, AND RAPIDLY CONSTRUCTED.

Time in forming communications, the fundamental point.

In the question of supplying India with the means of transport, the fundamental point is, *time—the time in which the communication can be formed, and brought into operation.*

Let us first take some line,—not one on which there is such an extraordinary amount of traffic as on the Ganges but yet one of considerable traffic, which may be considered a fair specimen of the ordinary main lines of the country, such as the line between Madras and Bombay (760 miles). The present traffic on this line has been ascertained near each end. The total cost of traffic on the Thull and Bhore Ghauts together, (as given in the published reports,) is about Rs. 22,000 (£2,200) per mile per annum; and the average rate near Madras is about Rs. 12,000 (£1,200) a mile, for goods only. The mean of these two is about Rs. 17,000 (£1,700) a mile; and if this diminishes from the Ports towards the interior, till at the centre of the line it becomes scarcely any thing, then, the average of the whole will be about Rs. 8,500 (£850) per mile. But it is quite certain, that if very cheap and expeditious communications were opened along this line, a vast quantity of traffic *now existing*, which at present makes for the Ports by the shortest routes, would be brought by the nearest way to each point of it; and hence we may safely conclude, that of the present traffic, much more than the above average would pass along the new communication; perhaps nearly double, suppose to the amount in all, of Rs. 15,000 (£1,500) per mile. If then the actual cost of transit, (including interest,) were reduced from 2½ Annas (3¾*d.*) to one-fourth, viz. ⅝ Anna (1*d.*,) there would be a clear saving of Rs. 12,000 (£1,200) a mile, on existing traffic. But as before argued, in the case of such a diminution of cost, there will be at least as much property saved, by the conveyance of goods which could not be moved before, on account of the expense; so that we may reckon, that on the average, there would be a saving of Rs. 24,000 (£2,400) a mile, or on the whole line (24,000 Rupees × 760 miles) a saving of 180 lacks or £1,800,000 sterling per annum. Now if a new road be carried across this space, at the rate that the Bombay railroad is going on, (about 12 miles a year,) beginning at both ends at once, the distance will not be accomplished in less than 30 years; and even allowing that the parts on which is the greatest traffic are executed first, still, taking 180 lacks on 760 miles for 30 years = 5,400 lacks, about one-third of that sum, viz., 1,800 lacks, (18 millions sterling) would be lost during the 30 years. But of course we must reckon upon the traffic greatly increasing, during that time, owing to the general improvement of the country, if as we hope a new order of things prevails; and on this account we may fairly reckon the loss from the delay of the work, at 25 millions sterling, or £33,000 a mile (Rs. 3,30,000) for the whole period; so that to the cost of a railroad, we ought to add this sum, with its accumulations of interest; making in all, about 5 lacks of Rupees, (£50,000.) If therefore the railroad cost only half a lack (£5,000) a mile, it will thus appear, that the time in which the work can be executed, is ten times as much importance, as the cost of the work itself.

We shall thus find it better to spend double or treble on any work, than to delay its execution; and supposing it were necessary, in order to get the communication completed in half the time, to lay out double the money upon it, the account would stand thus. On the one hand,

Cost of constructing 760 miles at ½ lack (£5,000)..........	380 lacks.	(£ 3,800,000)
Interest and working at Rs.4,000 (£400) (¼ of present cost) a mile per annum, for ½ of 30 years (15 years)...........	456 do.	(£ 4,560,000)
Expenditure for 15 years transit on common roads as above Rs. 16,000 × 760 × 15 years...	1,824 do.	(£18,240,000)
Total expended in 30 years on Railroad slowly constructed...	2,660 do.	(£26,600,000)

On the other hand:

760 miles at 1 lack (£10,000)..	760 lacks.	(£ 7,600,000)
Interest and working at Rs.4,000 (£400) a mile for ½ of 15 years (7½ years)..........	228 do.	(£ 2,280,000)
Do. do. for last 15 years of the 30 years.............	456 do.	(£ 4,560,000)
Expenditure in transit on common roads, for ½ of first 15 years (7½ years)..........	912 do.	(£ 9,120,000)
Total expended in 15 years on Railroad speedily constructed..	2,356 do.	(£23,560,000)
Saving by speedy execution..	304 lacks.	(£ 3,040,000)

Or, there would be a saving in the 30 years, of three millions sterling, by laying a railway in half the time at double cost; but even this does not allow for the gradually increasing traffic, nor for the amount lost in interest, which would tell very greatly in favour of the second calculation.

The real question is then, What is the kind of work that can be most rapidly carried across? Supposing that it were a cheap railway which could be executed in two years, at an expense of Rs. 20,000 (£2,000) a mile, and could be worked as cheaply as the other, (the additional cost of draft on a less perfect road being counter-balanced by the diminished interest), the calculation would then stand as follows:

760 miles at Rs. 20,000 (£2,000)	152	lacks.	(£ 1,520,000)
Working &c., at Rs. 4,000 (£400) a mile for 30 years..	912	do.	(£ 9,120,000)
Expended on transit by common roads, during the execution of the work..........	62	do.	(£ 620,000)
Total for cheap Railway..	1,126	do.	(£11,260,000)
Total expenditure on expensive railway made in 30 years as above shown..............	2,660	do.	(£26,600,000)
Do. on cheap Railway completed in 2 years..........	1,126	do.	(£11,260,000)
Saving by cheap Railway..	1,534	lacks.	(£15,340,000)

or 15½ millions sterling nearly.

In other words, if the cost of transit of the present traffic, including what is brought on to the line in consequence of its improvement, be Rs. 24,000 (£2,400) a mile, and it could be reduced to a quarter of that sum by a railroad, there will be, for every year the work is delayed, a loss of Rs. 18,000 (£1,800) a mile, or 137 lacks (£1,370,000) on the whole line; and it would be as cheap, if necessary, to spend a lack of Rupees (£10,000) a mile on it, and do it in 1 year, as it would be to spend Rs. 10,000 a mile on it, and do it in 10 years. Thus,

Cost of 1 mile of road............	Rs. 10,000	(£ 1,000)
Loss by excess of expenditure on 1 mile of common road during time of execution (10 years) allowing ½ of the whole length for the average..	Rs. 90,000	(£ 9,000)
Total expenditure..	1 lack.	(£10,000)

The immediate question then seems to be; *By what means can the greatest extent of line be opened in a certain time?* which leaves entirely open the final question, *What may be the best ultimate kind of communication?* This simplifies the matter exceedingly; and under this view of the case, there can be no doubt, that while such a railroad as that now under execution at Bombay, is creeping across the country at suppose 12 miles a year as at present, or even allow 100, it is advisable at all events in the meantime to execute another more rapid though less perfect work, which would have the important effect of at once giving full value to whatever portion of the superior work is executed, by bringing the whole traffic down to it, just as if the main line were completed. What we want then, is a ready made railroad that we can buy out of hand, and which will require little work to put it on the ground; and it is evident that with such means we might at once have a railway wherever a line would pay the interest of the money; and this on any number of lines.

When this point is once acknowledged, and the minds of many are turned to discover what will be the best kind for our purpose, no doubt many suitable ones will be found. The one I should propose, (for the low tracts at least), is simply a series of wrought iron beams supported on cast iron posts, screwed into the ground with Mitchell's Patent Screw. The beams might be from 12 to 20 feet long; and such beams are now being rolled without difficulty. They should be very deep of course; and the upper surface need not be more than 1¼ inch broad, for I would not think of working these roads at very high speed, or with heavy waggons. They would not have to bear a twentieth of the weights used on the English roads; and consequently need not have a surface of half the breadth. On the higher tracts and where low embankments are required, I would lay down one of the new forms of rails, with a broad base, requiring neither chairs nor sleepers. I would allow considerable slopes on these lines, and if, as is generally the case in India, there be a decided preponderance of traffic in one direction, there should be greater slopes in that direction than in the other. It would probably be quite sufficient to have gradients of 1 in 100 one way, and one in 70 or 80 the other. *Cuttings* to a small extent might be made, but I would have no embankments of any height in the first instance; and as the drainage of the country would not be interfered with, no masonry works would be required. The rivers would be crossed by high screw piles; or it might be worth while in some places, to have narrow masonry piers, involving but little work. The iron beams must be stayed across at intervals, to secure the gauge. It would be a question on some lines, whether cast iron or teak posts should be used; but as the former could be got in any quantities, and could always be used in another place, when they had done their work where first erected, they would be preferable in general. From the general state of the surface of the country in India, a very great extent of line could be formed with the above slopes, without any excessive height of posts; and where the country was not so favourable, one of the following plans might be adopted. High posts, (either cast iron or teak,) might be screwed in to a good depth, and if necessary supported by being placed at a small angle towards each other, (instead of perpendicular,) which with the screw, would give immense stability; or else, a series of masonry piers might be raised, or a regular embankment be formed, or greater gradients might be allowed for that division of the road, and additional horses or engines used. It must also be particularly observed, that the more difficult country will generally be about the watersheds and furthest from the coast, where the traffic will be the least, perhaps not more than a tenth of that nearer the coasts; so that it is by no means essential to have such moderate gradients there, as in the lower parts of the country.

I have supposed that these lines will be worked at a moderate speed; as our choice at present is, not between a high speed and a low speed, but between a low speed and none at all. *One thing is certain, we cannot have the complete railroads laid at once all over the country.* The present question is, not, whether at the end of 15 years we are to have 15,000 miles of high speed railway, or 15,000 miles of low speed lines; but rather, whether we are then to have 1,500 miles of high speed line and 13,500 of common roads, or 1,500 of high speed, and 13,500 of low speed railway. What an absurdity it is then, to insist on either high speed, or nothing; to travel 100 miles out of a 1,000 at 40 miles an hour, and the remaining 900 at 3 miles an hour! The point of speedy travelling, is altogether insignificant in the present state of things in India, in comparison with cheap transit generally; and further, this plan for quickly covering the country with cheap communications does not in the least interfere with the question of speedy transit, but on the contrary will immensely assist it, by completing the lines though imperfectly, years before they could otherwise be completed at all.

I am of opinion, that Mitchell's Screws will give immense stability to the posts, by enabling us to insert them into undisturbed ground; and the question will be, what depth it may be necessary to insert them and whether one or two lines of posts will be required. Probably a single post with a cross hand beam to support the two rails would be sufficient. How very little height will be required in some parts of the country, is shown by the levels for the Madras and Arcot railway, which only requires an average height of bank of 4½ feet, with gentle gradients. Such a screw-pile railway would not be very expensive; but even if it were, the rapidity with which it could be put up, would compensate for a very great cost, if necessary; for, as shown above, no less than Rs. 24,000 a mile are every year lost in cost of transit for want of a proper line. The estimate for a mile of this proposed railway, may be something like the following, supposing that two-thirds are over low ground: and that two lines of posts are used.

176 cast iron posts averaging 8 feet in length, and weighing 4 cwt. each (in all 35 tons, at £8)................	Rs. 2,800	(£ 280)
176 rolled iron beams 20 feet long, 80lbs. per yard, or 5 cwt. each, (44 tons at £10 a ton)................	„ 4,400	(£ 440)
2,400 yards of broad flanged rail at 40lbs. (44 tons at £10)...........	„ 4,400	(£ 440)
Excavation 16,000 c. yds. at 1 Anna..	„ 1,000	(£ 100)
Sundries......................	„ 3,000	(£ 300)
Total Rs...	15,000	(£1,560)
Say at the utmost, Rs...	20,000	(£2,000)

Such a road should be furnished with very cheap buildings; and if worked with light loads, and at low speed, with cattle or very light engines, ought scarcely to require any repair; what I would particularly insist upon, being, that the loads should be so light as not in the least to affect the way. One of the most essential points in such works is, if possible to have no masonry at all, because that most retards their execution; whereas, if there be only a little earthwork to be executed on the road, and the rest of the expenditure is on rails and other things that can be obtained at once, 1,000 miles of line could be executed in a single season.

With respect to the cost of working such a road, we have the following data.

The actual expense of draft in England at high velocities, is about $\frac{1}{5}d.$ or $1\frac{1}{2}$ P. per ton per mile, and allowing for these roads having steeper gradients on the one hand, and on the other being worked at a lower speed, we might take the expense at the same rate as at home; but as labour and materials are so much cheaper in this country, we may on this account reckon that the cost will certainly be less than in England, suppose $\frac{1}{8}d.$ or 1 P. per ton per mile.

Again, the cost of conveyance by bullock carts on a good made road here, is about 1 Anna ($1\frac{1}{2}d.$) per ton per mile, (exclusive of carrier's profit); but the cost of bullock-draft on such a railway, would be reduced to about one-sixth, on account of the diminution of resistance, and this would give only about 2 P. ($\frac{1}{4}d.$) per ton. Again, from results already obtained in this country, we may safely calculate steam power on a railway, to be only half the cost of that of bullocks; which would reduce the cost to 1 P. ($\frac{1}{8}d.$) per ton per mile, the same as obtained by the former calculation. Upon the whole therefore, I think we may take 1 P. ($\frac{1}{8}d.$) per ton per mile, as the cost of draft.

The calculation for working this kind of railway, might then be as follows:

10 per cent. interest, on say Rs. 20,000	Rs.	2,000 (£200)
Management......................	,,	100 (£ 10)
Repairs........................	,,	100 (£ 10)
Sundries.......................	,,	300 (£ 30)
	Total Rs..	2,500 (£250)

which, divided between 144,000 tons, gives

General charges per ton .... $3\frac{1}{3}$ P. ($\frac{1}{2}d.$)

Cost of draft per ton .... 1 P. ($\frac{1}{8}d.$)

Total charge per ton per mile.. $4\frac{1}{3}$ P. ($\frac{9}{16}d.$)

or about one-seventh of the present cost of transit.

In previous calculations, I estimated the charge at one-fourth of the present rates. Here, it comes to only one-seventh, even reckoning the whole of the charges of the railroad as paid nearly equally by travellers and goods; whereas, probably almost all the charges would be paid by travellers, and goods charged with *little* more than the bare actual expenses, thus enabling us to get the utmost advantage from the line, and reducing the charge for goods, to a very small item.

Thus, if the present number of travellers be only 1,000 per day, and if cheap and comparatively rapid conveyance increase them four-fold, the total number of persons conveyed per annum, would then be 1,460,000; and the charge for each on account of interest, (even if paid entirely by travellers,) would be only $\frac{1}{3}$ P. ($\frac{1}{24}d.$) per man per mile, so that the total charge for the poorest class of passengers, (all expenses included,) might thus still be under 1 P., ($\frac{1}{8}d.$) per mile.

Respecting the present number of travellers, we have the following data.

On the Bhore Ghaut .... 2,84,000 per annum
or 800 per day.

We have no other statistics of passenger traffic on this line; but the following shows how enormous it is, in the country generally.

On one main road in Tanjore (1837).. 1,289 per day.

On another .... 1,550 do.

and these not in the immediate neighbourhood of any great town. Now if men travel in these numbers without any one facility,—having to walk, and therefore only able to travel at the rate of 20 miles a day, so that on a journey of 200 miles and back, they must be absent from their work and their families at least three weeks,—we cannot doubt, that if the same could be done in two days, and at less expense than it would cost a man to walk, the intercourse would be immense; probably more than quadrupled.

I have myself no doubt that passengers will abundantly pay the interest, &c. for the railway; so that goods may be carried at the bare cost of transit. In England, even at the comparatively high speed there, some goods are now carried at ½*d.* or 4 P. per ton per mile, still allowing some profit; and if in this country, goods could be carried at even 2 P. (¼*d.*) (one-fifteenth of the present cost) it is difficult to estimate what the increase of traffic will be. When a ton can be carried 100 miles for a Rupee (2 shillings) a very trifling difference in the market price at two points, will be sufficient to cause a thing to be transferred from one to the other. Thus, if grain be worth Rs. 30 (£3) a ton in one place, a small difference in value, say 6 per cent., or 2½ in 40 seers per Rupee (2 shillings), might be sufficient to give rise to a trade between that and another place 200 miles off. The coarsest goods, such as fire wood, building materials, straw, &c. would be carried hundreds of miles; and we need not be surprised if the goods-traffic increased nearly ten-fold, like that through the Paumbam Channel since its improvement.

If we allow the total cost of draft, interest, &c., on such a road as this executed in 2 years, to be (as first assumed) one-fourth of the present cost, then, the comparative results of this, and a complete railway begun at both ends at once, and executed at the rate of 50 miles a year, (or four times the rate they have been working at Bombay,) may be thus calculated.

760 miles at Rs. 20,000 (£2,000)..	152 lacks	(£ 1,520,000)
Transit (at ¼ present rate) Rs. 4,000 (£400) a mile for 14 years.....	425½ ,,	(£ 4,255,000)
Cost of working one half, (380 miles) as common road, for 2 years, at present rate Rs. 16,000........	121½ ,,	(£ 1,215,000)
Total Expense..	699 ,,	(£ 6,990,000)

Again,

760 miles at Rs. 100,000 (£10,000).	760 lacks	(£ 7,600,000)
Cost of working one half (380 miles) at ¼ present rate, Rs. 4,000 (£400) a mile for 15 years...........	228 ,,	(£ 2,280,000)
Do. of ½ at present rate. (Rs. 16,000)	912 ,,	(£ 9,120,000)
Total Expense..	1,900 ,,	(£19,000,000)
Loss by waiting for complete road...	1,201 lacks	(£12,010,000)

or 12 millions sterling.

If we suppose that traffic would be increased four-fold by improved communications, we must add to the above difference the loss occasioned by non-transport for 15, instead of 2 years, of three-quarters of the goods; and further take into account, the incalculable loss from postponement of passenger traffic; besides loss of interest.

This will help to give us some notion, of what we are now paying for high-speed complete railroads; for, (as shown above) these roads would, on account of delay in executing, cost 2 lacks (£20,000) a mile more, in point of fact at least 4 lacks (£40,000) a mile or more, in money, considering the delay in the additional traffic; and besides this, all the loss that cannot be shown in money. Even supposing that the above calculations require great correction, they will still leave no possible room for question as to the main point, viz., *that nothing can compensate for loss of time in opening the country;*

and therefore I repeat, that although a railroad that could be laid in a year, should cost four or even ten times what I have calculated, there can still be no question but that it ought to be done at once, rather than wait.

I do not pretend to say that these railways are the best possible means of accomplishing our object ; on the contrary there may be much better. What I *chiefly* wish to show, is first, that what is most wanted is, *speed, not in travelling on the railways or canals when executed*, but *in executing them ;* and secondly, that it is quite possible to have a kind of communication, that can be quickly executed.

The railway proposed above, would have the following advantages.

1st. It could be executed at any rate of speed, since England could provide rolled and cast iron in any quantities; and at the rate of 100,000 tons of cast iron and 130,000 tons of rolled iron supplied per annum, 3,000 miles a year could be executed, and the whole extent of main road required (15,000 miles) thus easily completed in 5 years ; (at the rate of 3,000 miles a year.) Supposing then, that Rs. 1,000 (£100) a mile were spent on the ground, it would only require an expenditure of 30 lacks (£300,000) a year ; which, if fifteen main lines were begun at once at both ends, could easily be managed so that 1 lack (£10,000) would be spent annually on each portion of the undertaking. Thus, about 200 miles of the most important part of each main line would be finished each year ; or, else, only five of the most important lines might be begun at once, and 600 miles of each would be finished every year.*

2d. As soon as any portion of the line was laid with more

* We have happily already some instances, showing the rapidity with which works can be executed in India. The two masonry weirs across the Colleroon, (one 800 yards long, and the other 680,) were both completed in the same three months. One branch of the Godavery weir (960 yards long) was carried in one fortnight across to such a state of completion as to allow of the water going over it. The Nuggaram aqueduct over a branch of the Godavery, (800 yards long, and containing 49 arches of

complete work, the former could be taken up and placed on another line, at a trifling cost. If worked with light loads it would last for ever; or at least for so many years as would amount to much the same.

3d. By laying down these lines, we should leave ourselves quite at liberty to pursue further plans at leisure; and we should have the great advantage of thus feeling our way, and in laying permanent lines have the experience of these temporary ones, to help us to judge whether they were quite the best that could be adopted.

4th. These lines would be of the greatest use in the execution of more complete works, by the conveyance of materials.

5th. Even if any sections of the lines contained very heavy works, that need not delay the opening of the other parts of the ultimate line, as these might be worked in the meantime; and such a work therefore as the ascent of a ghaut, or a long tunnel, might be executed on the best plan, even though it took many years to finish it.

6th. Such a line might be put up any where, where it would be of use for the present, although it were probable or even certain, that it would not ultimately form a portion of any permanent line.

40 feet,) built in a tideway, had the last arch keyed within four months from the time of commencing to make bricks. This work is 28 feet broad; and it was ready for the water to go over it in about 7 months from the same time. It is built with the crowns of the arches 7 feet below the surface of the water in the river; and before the side walls could be finished, a tremendous flood occurred, which went 2 or 3 feet over all and entirely submerged the work for 5 days, but without injuring it. Great precautions had of course been necessary to secure the foundation under such circumstances, in the bed of a river consisting wholly of loose sand; and under Providence these precautions were completely successful. It is highly encouraging also to find, that far from these sandy rivers being almost insuperable obstacles, (as has been supposed,) works can be constructed there, which will allow of the river going over the parapet walls, without injuring the work. This, as well as hundreds of other works of various kinds, bridges, aqueducts, rivers, sluices of all descriptions, &c., have been built in rivers in the Madras Presidency where there was not a vestige of anything but loose sand, to an unknown depth; and have been standing for many years; probably not one of them has foundations 10 feet deep, and in general they are not more than 6 or 8 feet.

7th. If it were found to increase the traffic very greatly, there could be no objection to adding a second line; though both were to be eventually superseded.

8th. It must be remembered, that it is hardly possible for us to judge what changes may take place, in consequence of these powerful agents being brought to act upon a country hitherto so neglected. As yet, every thing has been cramped, and forced into certain places and lines by natural obstacles; but when the natural resources of the country are set at liberty by the opening of the country generally, so as in fact to remove natural obstacles, most unexpected changes may take place. One change is almost certain, viz., that all the minor ports will become places of extensive foreign trade, by the settlement of European merchants; and thus, much more of the trade will go from the interior to the nearest ports, than at present. Certain spots which are the most suitable for certain kinds of produce, but are at present unavailable on account of the cost of transit and their inacessibility to the European merchant or manufacturer, will then be applied to the purpose for which they are naturally suited. For instance, many places 200 miles from a port, now not available for sugar cultivation on account of the transit costing £3 a ton, would be highly profitable plantations, if the transit cost only 10 shillings a ton. These temporary lines would soon bring such things into view, and might materially modify the decisions upon the permanent lines.

9th. By no means an insignificant result of this plan, would be the considerable demand that it would make on England, for one of its most important products and manufactures; and an annual consumption of 230,000 tons of iron for many years, would have a very perceptible effect on the Iron trade.

We may now consider some objections that may be made to this kind of road. Probably the first will be, that a raised road will be more dangerous than an ordinary one. There is no doubt that there will be some little additional danger to travellers; but it will be very little. In the first place, I propose that these lines be worked at a much lower speed than the complete roads; and it is certain that with low speed, there would be scarcely any accidents, since almost all that now occur, are caused by high speed. Secondly, I would work goods and passenger traffic at the same speed, so that the chances of collision would be almost entirely removed. Thirdly, I cannot but think, that upon the whole in this country, there would be less danger of loss of life, on a road of which a great part was raised on posts above the level of the country, than on one which men would be frequently crossing, or even walking along. Considering the apathy of the Natives, we must expect many accidents to happen to stragglers on the roads, if made accessible; and thus the raised lines would remove some sources of danger to passengers. At the Godavery works, one man actually walked straight up against a loaded waggon coming towards him at three miles an hour, and was knocked down backwards, the carriage passing over him as he lay between the rails. At any rate however, the danger on such roads worked at 8 miles an hour, would be much less than that on the present railroads in England, worked as they are at 30 or 40 miles an hour, and with trains running at different speeds; and as people do not object to run the risk there, the smaller risk cannot surely be an obstacle here. If thought desirable, planks might be laid between the rails, resting on the cross stays which connect the rails, in order to enable persons to stand on the road in safety; but probably it would be better so to arrange that persons could not pass on foot along the line of the road, excepting on the ground along which a path might be made. At rivers and channels, a line of planks supported on brackets below the level of the rails could be placed outside the posts, so as to form a foot bridge; but all such minor points would easily be settled when once such a line is laid. In other respects this kind of road would be exceedingly secure; the beams would be fixed in a deep *notch* cast in the post, and secured by a horizontal stay, the ends of which should pass through both the beams and the posts; having nuts screwed on outside the *latter*, to hold them against shoulders on the stay. I do not see what further objections could be made to such a structure.

I have before spoken of the breadth of the top of the rail. On the present rails only 2½ inches broad, engines of 30 tons and waggons of 7 tons are run; so that there can be no sort of question, but that a bearing surface of 1 or 1¼ inches, would be sufficient for such a road as this, with loads of only 1 ton.

If thought advisable, both posts and beams might be made of teak instead of iron, which would cost probably about Rs. 8,000 (£800) a mile less; and a plain square bar of 1¼ inch iron might be laid on the timber, and secured by deep screws, (as in America,) only with the difference of a square bar, instead of the broad thin one used there. The difference between a bar of ⅝ inch and one of 1¼ inch thickness is immense; and the trial on the screws would be nothing with the latter, as compared with the former. A great mistake was made at the Godavery works, in making all the railroads with bars only ½ inch thick and two inches broad, for 5 ton gross loads. Square bars of the same weight would have been much better, as they give sufficient height for the *flange*, without cutting away the wood. Probably the broad thin bar was used in America, for the same reason as it was at the Godavery, by mistake; it not being considered, that if engines of 30 tons could run on a surface of only 2½ inches in breadth, there could be no necessity for so great a breadth for light engines.

If it be still urged "we *must* have high speed," the answer so far as the present question is concerned, is "Have it by all means, as soon as you can;" but this does not affect the present proposition; which is, for something to supply the place of common roads, whilst high speed railways are under construction. Because you insist upon going along the first 100 miles at 40 miles an hour, there is no necessity for our going along the next 500 at 3 miles an hour.

The present high speed railways are most important works; but like every thing else they may be proportionately mischievous, if injudiciously used. Assuredly, up to this time they have done nothing but mischief in this country, by making people suppose that they were doing something, whilst they really were doing almost nothing; and have thus occasioned many years delay, and prevented any thing being done which would really throw open India. It is just as if a man took wheat out of a bushel grain by grain to eat, and so died of starvation, while constantly employed in eating. Suppose that in ten years from the commencement of these high speed railways, there were in all 500 miles finished (and one of them too on the present cheapest line of transit in India) still, only half a million a year would be saved to the country, out of the 20 or 30 millions that *general want of communications* now costs her; whereas, within the same ten years, the whole of India might with the greatest ease have been pervaded by lines of cheap transit, and an enormous saving thus effected.

CHAPTER IX.

CONSIDERATIONS AS TO THE TRUE VALUE AND COST OF HIGH SPEED OF TRANSIT.

Cost of high speed disproportionate to gain in time.

One of the fundamental points to be settled before determining on a system of communication, is *the value of time in the transport of goods and passengers.* Speed like every thing else may be bought too dear; and one thing is certain, viz., that *increase of speed whether by land or by water, by railways or roads, involves an increase of expense much more than proportional to the gain of time.* In fact the increase of cost in high speeds, is enormous; and both poor individuals and poor communities will find rapid transit so much beyond their means, that in order to purchase it, they must impoverish themselves so as greatly to retard their progress. They may obtain rapid travelling in an isolated case, but it must be at the cost of greatly delaying the attainment of this object generally. If a poor man aims at having the means of keeping his carriage and travelling fast whenever he likes, he must not while he is still poor, spend his spare money in buying a carriage.

The question therefore stands, "What the cost of speed is?" and in the case of any particular country, "whether it can be afforded?" The cost of speed in water transit can be pretty well calculated, as a double velocity through the water produces a four-fold resistance, and therefore four times as much power is required to convey a thing a certain distance at a double speed; and there is a further consumption of money, in consequence of the necessity of having in operation a power proportioned to the additional speed, as well as to the additional resistance. A boat going at a double speed, meets with a four-fold resistance; and if it be necessary, that the power to overcome this four-fold resistance should pass through a double space in a certain time, it then requires eight times the power to be in operation, though for only half the time. Further, the machine which produces this power must itself be carried; and its weight and bulk must increase with the increase of power. Besides this, there are various other minor sources of waste in using high speed; so that we may reckon, that a double speed afloat requires at least a six-fold expense; besides the inconvenience of having to provide a greater capital. That is, a man may travel at the rate of 5 miles an hour, for one-sixth of the cost at which he can travel at 10 miles an hour; taking into calculation, interest, consumption of materials, and every thing else. He would also have to raise about a six-fold capital, or perhaps much more; but that is of course a separate question; he might be able to afford the additional current expense, but yet be quite unable to raise the required additional capital at all, or at least not without so crippling himself in other ways, as to render it upon the whole unadvisable. If a merchant has credit, he of course considers how he may apply that amount of credit so as to produce the greatest profit.

As regards land transit, it is now clearly ascertained that the increase of cost for increased speed follows much the same law as afloat. On a common road, horses require so much of their power for moving themselves at higher speeds, as rapidly to absorb the greater part of it; thus leaving only a small portion to produce useful effect, and at the same time the resistance rapidly increases. The same also is the case with railroads; the resistance increases, and a large portion of the power of the engine is absorbed in moving itself. But besides this, there is in the case of railroads an enormous increase of *first* cost in constructing the road. For high speeds a most perfect apparatus is required, enormously heavy engines, and consequently rails of immense weight; most secure fastenings, &c., and also gentle slopes and easy curves, at a cost in excavation almost incalculable in some instances. It is well known, that the effect of a blow on the rails, increases as the square of the velocity; and hence, an engine of double weight moving at a double speed, strikes the rails with eight times the force. There is also another source of increased expense in the case of a railroad. If a high speed be required where the traffic is considerable, a double line is unavoidable: for if there be only a single line, either the quick trains must start at long intervals, or all trains must travel at the same speed, (and that a moderate one,) because the great bulk of goods being of small value, are not worth the cost of transit at high speed. Thus, the capital required for high speed by railway, would be immensely increased; and the high interest consequent thereon, would also greatly increase the actual cost of transit; and therefore, whatever means we use, *we must pay very high for speed.*

The question is then reduced to this, "Are our circumstances in India such, as to render it advisable for us at present to enter upon a general system of communication, that will afford a very high speed?"

Let us first try and form some judgment of the actual cost of high speed on a railway, as compared with low speed by the same means of transit. It is said, that the present Calcutta railway will cost $1\frac{1}{4}$ lacks (£12,500) per mile, for a double line; the interest of which, at a little above the present Government interest, suppose 6 per cent., will be Rs. 7,500 (£750) a mile per annum, or Rs. 24 (£2 8*s.*) a day, excluding Sundays. The goods traffic on this line is immense; some accounts say 2 million tons a year. We have no means of ascertaining what amount of goods the railway would convey, if worked at lower cost than river navigation; but if we suppose, that while worked at high speeds for passengers, it would convey 2,000 tons a day, then the interest, (if borne entirely by goods) would come to $2\frac{3}{4}$ P. (nearly $\frac{3}{8}$*d.*) per ton; and if to this be added the English rate of cost for working the roads, viz., 2 P. ($\frac{1}{4}$*d.*) per ton, it would make the total charge $4\frac{3}{4}$ P. (nearly $\frac{5}{8}$*d.*) per ton per mile. The prices by river are at present about 4 P. ($\frac{1}{2}$*d.*) (including interest and insurance;) by a perfect common road 8 P. (1*d.*); by a less perfect metalled road 14 P. ($1\frac{3}{4}$*d.*); by a common unmade road 3 Annas ($4\frac{1}{2}$*d.*), and by canal $\frac{1}{2}$ P. ($\frac{1}{16}$*d.*) Supposing however, half the interest were paid by passengers, the portion still chargeable on goods, would be Rs. 12 (£1-4*s.*) a day, or $1\frac{3}{8}$ P. (nearly $\frac{3}{16}$*d.*) per ton; and the total charge would then be $3\frac{3}{8}$ P. ($\frac{1}{2}$*d.* nearly) or perhaps, (allowing cost of draft, &c., to be less than in England, say $1\frac{5}{8}$ P. about $\frac{3}{16}$*d.*) not more than 3 P. ($\frac{3}{8}$*d.*) Let us now suppose the railway worked at low speed,—say 8 miles an hour—in which case all trains would travel at the same rate, so that a single line of rails would be sufficient; and as only very light engines would be necessary, light rails might be laid, and a vast reduction would be made both in cost of construction, and in wear and tear, &c. Such a line might no doubt be laid at $\frac{1}{10}$ the cost of the other, or Rs. 12,500 (£1,250); and the interest viz., Rs. $2\frac{1}{2}$ (5 shillings) a day, being divided (as before) between travellers and goods, would be only $\frac{1}{8}$ P. ($\frac{1}{64}$*d.*) per ton, and the cost of transit, including wear and tear, would probably thus be reduced to 1 P. (⅛*d.*): the total charge being 1⅛ P. ($\frac{9}{64}$*d.*) per ton, or about Rs. 3 (6 shillings) per ton for 500 miles; whereas, the charge at high speed (as calculated above) would amount to Rs. 8 or 10 (16 to 20 shillings) per ton, for the same distance. This is calculating on an amount of traffic, three times as great as that on any railway in England; but with only 300 tons a day, which would still be a large traffic, the difference in amount of interest alone would be 8⅓ P. (a trifle more than 1*d.*); or as much as the whole cost of carriage on a good common road, and probably fifteen times the cost of carriage on a canal.

But we must now see what the charge for travellers must be, in order to make up half the interest, (Rs. 12 (£1 4*s.*) a day,) as the cost of high speed; and this brings us to the main point of difference between this country and England as respects quick transit, viz. the insignificant proportion of rich travellers here. Throughout India generally, the number of first class travellers, (that is, of Europeans and Natives who can afford to pay very high rates,) is extremely small; and the number who travel in Bengal and the N. W. by steamers and horse carriages, is perfectly insignificant in respect to giving employment to a railway. We may form some idea of what number of first class travellers at certain rates there would be, by considering the comparative state of things in India and England in this respect. The cost of travelling in England to first class passengers, is about 2½*d.* or 1⅔ Annas per mile; and allowing the value of money to be six times as great in this country (by the comparative cost of food and labour) this will be equivalent here to about ⅓ Anna or 4 P. (½*d.*) If this rate were charged, would there be as many first class passengers as in England? In order to ascertain this, we must consider first, that the proportion of rich to the whole population is immensely less in India than in England; where we see more wealth in travelling one mile, than in travelling a hundred miles in this country. On this account, the number of first class passengers would be perhaps scarcely one hundredth of the number in England, which (according to Dr. Lardner's statement,) was in 1847, 157 a day on the average of some of the principal railways, and 360 on the line of greatest traffic. This however was not the number travelling over the whole length of the roads, but the total number of travellers over any part; the average distance travelled was 40 miles, and the total length of road and branches being 438 miles, the average number of first class passengers for the whole length of the roads, was only 33 per day. The greatest amount of travelling of this class was on the Eastern counties railway, where it was equal to 68 per day, passing over the whole length.

It must be remembered secondly however, that the number of travellers in India generally, will be greater in proportion than in England; because each great line of railway will affect a much larger population. Thus, each of the 6 lines of railway radiating from London, accommodates on an average one-sixth of the population of the United Kingdom, or nearly 4 millions; whereas the Ganges line will connect about 60 millions with Calcutta. This is a most material point to be considered in comparing traffic in India with that of England; where any particular line of road connects only a comparatively small number of people with a port or a market. Thus, notwithstanding the present imperfect communication on the Ganges, it has even now, an amount of traffic in goods far exceeding any line in England; and we may therefore reckon, that other things being the same, the number of first class passengers would be perhaps ten times as great as in England. At present, the total number of travellers in India to be called first class passengers, that is (those travelling by steamers, and by palanquin or carriages,) appears (by the railway pamphlets) to be daily, about 9 by the former, and 33 by the latter; in all 42 per day, or two-thirds of the number of first class passengers, on the greatest passenger line in England. But then it must be remembered, that they pay at present about 5 Annas ($7\frac{1}{2}$*d.*) per mile; 3 times what is paid in England, or, proportionally to the different value of money in the two countries, 18 times as much. The great reduction of time and cost of travelling resulting from a railway, would undoubtedly increase the number very greatly; but the main question is, not, how many *could* pay first class fares, but, how many would *prefer* them to second class ones. If there were first class trains travelling at 30 miles an hour, at a charge of 2 Annas (3*d.*) per mile, and second class trains at 10 miles an hour, charging 3 P. ($\frac{3}{8}$*d.*), I believe the number travelling by the first class trains, would be found to bear a very small proportion to the number going by the others.

Let us consider what would be the consequence even in England, if first class passengers were carried at 1*s.* 6*d.* a mile (which would be in due proportion to 3*d.* in this country,) although the proportion of wealthy people there is at least 100 times what it is in India; and although (from the different state of things there) people so much better understand the value of time. Perhaps 99 out of 100 Natives would rather pay Rs. 8 (16 shillings) for travelling 400 miles at 10 miles an hour, than Rs. 50 (£5) for a speed of 30 miles an hour. And in order to obtain this high speed for so very small a proportion of the traffic, the whole road must be constructed at such an enormous expense, as to entail a high rate of charge for all goods and $\frac{99}{100}$ of the passengers, and a low profit to the shareholders. In this country, the loss in time both to the great body of travellers and goods, that is, the loss arising from the difference between travelling 5 and 40 miles an hour, is most insignificant. A ton of cotton, sugar, salt and grain, is of the value of £15, £12, £3 and £3, respectively; and these would form the great bulk of the traffic. Taking the average value at £10, the interest (at 10 per cent.) in a journey of four days, (500 miles at 5 miles an hour) would be only 5 P. or ($\frac{5}{8}$*d.*,) and the saving by going 40 miles an hour would be only $\frac{7}{8}$ of that, say 4 P. (about $\frac{1}{2}$*d.*); while the difference between the cost of conveying goods on a first class railway and a cheaper one, would perhaps amount to as much as from 1 to 8 P. ($\frac{1}{8}$*d* to 1*d.*) per ton per mile. And so with passengers; taking their time as worth Rs. 50 (£5) a month, (corresponding with £360 a year in England) —and only a very small portion of the population have incomes approaching to that—3$\frac{1}{2}$ days would be worth to them Rs. 6 (12 shillings) which, saved in a journey of 500 miles, would be equal to 2$\frac{1}{2}$ P. ($\frac{5}{16}$*d.*) per mile.

The great difference between England and India in this respect, has certainly not been considered in planning the railways. Not only is the proportion of wealthy people whose time is of considerable value, prodigiously less in India than in England; but also, the average value of goods carried, is very much less here. The fact is, that while a very high speed is, in a country so wealthy and so far advanced as England, of the greatest importance, it is in a poor country like India, entirely secondary to cheapness. It is just the same with individuals; if a poor man insists upon travelling quickly and consequently expensively, before his circumstances admit of it, he may remain a poor man all his life; whereas, if he will but be content to economize in this as well as other things at first, he may in time be able to travel as quickly as he likes.

But even this is comparatively a very insignificant part of the question; the main point being, that in thus aiming at a very high speed at once, we are completely deluding ourselves and losing the very thing we are aiming at. The advocates for high speed say "Let us have a thoroughly good speed *at once;*" and then they proceed to attain their end, by laying down in one corner of India, a few miles of grand railroad, along which you may travel for the first stage at 30 miles an hour, and then continue along the remaining 1,000 miles of your journey at 3 miles an hour; if indeed the monsoon permits you to move at all. At Bombay only 10 miles have been laid in one year; so that ten years hence, a traveller going from thence to Calcutta, might go the first 100 miles in 3 hours, but must take 17 days (travelling day and night), for the remaining 1,200 miles; his average speed being only 3¼ miles per hour.

The fact is, *the extent of the spaces for which we have to provide communications has been totally lost sight of, and in consequence, the whole system is without a foundation;* but this no doubt is greatly owing to the system having been planned chiefly by men full of English ideas. In England, by the time 50 miles of railroad are laid in any direction from a port, it has arrived at what may be called the traffic-shed of the country, the point from which traffic moves to the opposite coast of the island; but from Calcutta to Lahore is a distance of 1,300 miles; and even from Bombay to the centre of the Peninsula is 400 miles. In England, there are 5,000 miles of railway, or about 1 to 12 square miles; and taking the area of India at 1¼ million of square miles, it would require in the same proportion 120,000 miles of railway. Even taking only one-sixth of this, there will be at least 20,000 miles of main communication required to open India; 4,000 merely to connect Lahore, Calcutta, Bombay, and Madras, (without a line from Madras to Calcutta direct;) so that if railroads were commenced at all four points at once, and carried on, (as at Bombay) at the rate of 10 miles a year, it would still take 100 years to lay these few lines, which would after all have but a very small effect upon the whole traffic of India. Only two of these lines are yet begun; and as to really and effectually opening India, we are in reality doing nothing: or rather, worse than nothing, since this delusion makes people imagine that they are doing what has to be done, and thus prevents them setting in earnest about the right means. If the construction of a few hundred miles of grand railroad in the course of 20 years, so blinds people, as to prevent any thing effectual being done to open India; it will, instead of a blessing, be the greatest curse which in the present state of things, the country could suffer.

Supposing however, that *speed, and nothing but speed,* were really our sole object, which would most effectually promote it? To lay down in 5 years, 1,000 miles of railway at Rs. 5,000 (£500) a mile; or else, 170 miles at Rs. 120,000 (£12,000) a mile? In the latter case, we might at the end of 5 years travel 170 miles in less than 5 hours, (at the rate of 34 miles an hour) and the other 830 miles in 12 days, (at the rate of only 3 miles an hour); whereas in the former case, we might at the end of the same period, travel over the whole distance (1,000 miles) in 4 days, at the rate of 10 miles an hour. Even if our object be therefore, to obtain speed alone, the first question is, *how most rapidly to throw open the country;* and for this purpose, 20,000 miles of good common road to be travelled at 7 miles an hour, and costing only Rs. 5,000 (£500) a mile (in all 1,000 lacks (£10,000,000), would be of immeasurably greater value than 800 miles of first class railway at Rs. 120,000 (£12,000) a mile, with a speed of 34 miles an hour: since the former could give an average speed through the country, of more than double the latter. *Speed* is indeed what is most urgently wanted; but *speed in forming communications,* not *speed in travelling upon them.* If indeed it were possible to lay first class railways at the rate of 2,000 miles a year, this part of the question would be altered; but I suppose every body will acknowledge that this cannot, or at least will not be done; and even if it were, still, 50,000 miles of cheap railway, which could be laid with the same means in the same time, would be of incalculably more value.

Nothing therefore can be more delusive, than when thus carrying on a work which will take hundreds of years to accomplish, to imagine that we are really gaining our object. What is the use of going a hundred miles at the rate of 34 miles an hour, if we must then go on at 3 miles an hour over thousands of miles? Surely it is evident, that even if our only object were speed, another plan must be pursued; and how much more so, then, when speed is not our main object by any means, but cheapness is of incomparably more importance. It must be remembered that in this matter, almost all who are engaged in planning such works, are liable to be under a bias; for they cannot help feeling how agreeable it would be to themselves to travel at high speed, and thus give a very undue importance to this point. Even a merchant will be very apt to think more of his own travelling quickly, than of obtaining his thousands of tons of goods at a lower price; and therefore to misjudge the relative importance of those two things. I do not mean to deny that high speed is a very desirable thing, or that it should be kept in view; but I do say, that if it be purchased for a few hundred miles, at the cost of keeping the great body of the country without improved communications for an indefinite period of years, it is manifestly purchased too dearly; and that those who are pursuing such a system, are undoubtedly defeating even their own object.

Let us now see further, how this system affects the welfare of the country as regards cost of transit, and stoppage of intercourse; comparing it first, with common roads. The ordinary cost of transit, where there are no made roads, is, in the practicable season, from 2 to 3 Annas (3*d.* to 4½*d.*) a ton per mile; with the incalculable disadvantage of traffic being almost completely stopped during three or four months of the year; and allowing only a trifle for this latter, we may fairly reckon the average cost of transit at 3 Annas (4½*d.*) Of the effect of good common roads in cheapening transit, we have proofs in different parts of the country; for instance, on the grand Trunk road of Bengal, the cost of transit has been reduced to 8 P. (1*d.*) per ton per mile, and on the great western road from Madras, it is even now little more than 1 Anna (1½*d.*;) but the latter is not yet by any means in complete order, and the price will undoubtedly fall still lower. From these examples, we may take the average cost of transit on a thoroughly good common road, at 9 P. (1⅛*d.*) or one-fourth of the present cost; showing a saving of 2¼ Annas (about 3¼*d.*) per ton per mile; and as regards the cost of such a road, the grand Trunk road in Bengal having cost about Rs. 8,000 (£800) a mile, the western road from Madras (a badly planned road,) about Rs. 7,000 (£700), and others in Madras from Rs. 3,000 to Rs. 4,000 (£300 to £400) a mile, we may therefore take the average cost throughout the country generally, at about Rs. 5,000 (£500) per mile, the grand Trunk road being a wider and more complete work than would be necessary in general. And on the other hand, the average cost of a mile of first class railroad, may be taken at Rs. 120,000 (£12,000); a sum that would make 24 miles of first class common road.

The cost of working complete railroads, seems to be strangely estimated for in this country; Mr. Chapman hopes they may be worked at 2¾*d.* a ton (including interest,) or 2½ times as much as good common roads are now worked at; a strange sort of improvement by the way, and perhaps scarcely worth paying Rs. 120,000 (£12,000) a mile for. In England, the actual cost of working at considerable speed, is ⅕*d.* or 1⅗ P. a ton; but in this country it would certainly be less; suppose 1 P. or ⅛*d.* To this must be added the cost of management, which in this country however, will be very moderate; but still, the whole cost (inclusive of interest) will probably be 4 P. (½*d.*) per ton per mile; it cannot be very much less, and the railway men estimate it much higher. Calculating then the comparative effects on the country, of Rs. 120,000 (£12,000) spent either on 1 mile of railway, or on 24 miles of common road, with a traffic of about 200 tons a day, and taking interest at 10 per cent., we have the following results:

Present cost of Transit on existing common unmade road.

60,000 tons 24 miles at 3 As. (4½*d*)	Rs. 2,70,000	(£27,000)

Present cost of transit on good common made road.

60,000 tons 24 miles at 9 P. (1⅛*d.*)	Rs.	68,000	(£ 6,800)
10 per cent. on Rs. 1,20,000 (£12,000) (the cost of the road.)	,,	12,000	(£ 1,200)
	,,	80,000	(£ 8,000)
Repairs and management at Rs. 500 (£50) a mile (24 miles)..	,,	12,000	(£ 1,200)
Total cost on 24 miles good common made road..........	Rs.	92,000	(£ 9,200)
Annual saving on 24 miles, by a good road..............	Rs.	1,78,000	(£ 17,800)

Cost of transit on 1 mile of railway, and 23 of unmade road.

60,000 tons 1 mile at 4 P. (½*d.*)	Rs.	1,250	(£ 125)
60,000 tons 23 miles at 3 Annas (4½*d.*)..............	,,	2,58,750	(£ 25,875)
10 per cent. on Rs. 1,20,000 cost of railway (£12,000)...	,,	12,000	(£ 1,200)
Total cost of 1 mile of Railway, and 23 of unmade road.....	Rs.	2,72,000	(£ 27,200)
Annual loss by railway compared with present unmade road.	Rs.	2,000	(£ 200)
Annual loss by Railway compared with good common road	Rs.	1,80,000	(£ 18,000)

This is only a fair representation of the different effects on the country, as regards most of the main lines, of spending Rs. 1,20,000 (£12,000) on 1 mile of railway, or on 24 miles of common road; and to counter-balance this enormous loss, we have the following difference in speed. Of course, there is no reason why a common road should not be worked constantly by relays of bullocks, in the same way as a railway is worked continuously; and if worked day and night by relays, we might have a speed of at least 50 miles a day for goods, and for passengers 8 miles an hour, or 200 miles a day. By the railway on the other hand, goods would be carried at the rate of 400 instead of 50 miles a day, thus saving 9 days in a journey of 500 miles; and the saving in time to first class passengers, would be about 1½ days for the same length of journey; but as before stated, the value of the great mass of goods is so low, and the proportion of travellers in this country to whom time is any great object, is, and will for some years to come, be so exceedingly small, that this cannot be considered a point of any great importance. Now the question is, whether this speed be worth purchasing at the enormous cost of about Rs. 8,000 (£800) a mile per annum, where there is a traffic of 200 tons a day; or on the 20,000 miles of main road supposed to be required in India, a cost of 1,600 lacks or 16 millions sterling a year. Can any body who knows any thing of India, or indeed of the subject of communications generally, doubt for a moment which would be most beneficial? 800 miles of railway, or 20,000 miles of common road? The same capital that would suffice for the one would serve for the other, and who can question which would be preferable to do at *present*, whatever might be done *ultimately*?

Having thus considered the matter with reference to the benefits to the country, we may next examine it in regard to the investment of capital. Let us suppose a Company with a capital of 1 million sterling, with which they may form in 5 years, either 80 miles of high speed railway, or 2,000 miles of common road; and compare the respective cost.

60,000 tons conveyed 2,000 miles on present roads, at 3 Annas ($4\frac{1}{2}d.$) per ton per mile......	225 lacks.	(£2,250,000)
Do. do. same distance on good common road, at 8 P. (1*d.*) per ton per mile............	50 „	(£ 500,000)
Saving by good road..	175 lacks.	(£1,750,000)

If only one-fourth (about 43 lacks (£430,000) were taken as toll, leaving three-fourths (132 lacks (£1,320,000) clear benefit to the community, this would still give the shareholders 43 per cent. on their capital; and the community would further have the immense advantage of a regularly organized system of conveyance by a Company; goods being carried 50, and first class passengers 200 miles a day, instead of 10 and 70 miles respectively, as at present.

With 80 miles of railway, the comparative results would be as follows:

60,000 tons conveyed 80 miles by Rail, at 4 P. ($\frac{1}{2}d.$) per ton per mile.......	1 lack.	(£10,000)
Do. do. same distance on present roads at 3 Annas ($4\frac{1}{2}d$) per ton per mile....	9 lacks.	(£90,000)
Saving by Railway..	8 lacks.	(£80,000)

If one-fourth of this (2 lacks (£20,000) were taken as profit, the return on the capital (100 lacks (1 million sterling), would be 2 per cent.; and the saving in transit to the community, 6 lacks (£60,000). Or, the comparative results of the investment on the two works, would be as follows:

Profit to shareholders on 100 lacks (1 million sterling) expended on 80 miles of railway..........	2 lacks.	(£ 20,000)
	or 2 per cent.	
Profit on same sum spent on 2,000 miles of good road...........	43 lacks.	(£ 430,000)
	or 43 per cent.	
Annual saving to people by railway	6 lacks.	(£ 60,000)
Do. do. do. do. by good road.	132 ,,	(£1,320,000)
Greater saving by good road.....	126 lacks	(£1,260,000)

Such would be the result so far as goods are concerned, and the number of first class travellers is at present so utterly insignificant, as clearly to show, that unless the rates be greatly lowered, very few indeed of that class will travel by railway. There will be a vast number of other passengers if carried at very low rates, but certainly not otherwise. Perhaps the payments from passengers might be,

50—1st class a day (15,000 a year) at 2 Annas (3*d.*) per head per mile.....	Rs. 1,875	(£ 187½)
200—2nd class (60,000 a year) at ½ A. (¾*d.*)	,, 1,875	(£ 187½)
2,000—3rd class (600,000 a year) at 2P. (¼*d.*)	,, 6,250	(£ 625)
Gross receipts per mile	Rs. 10,000	(£1,000)

It must be observed, that these rates (1st class 3*d.*, 2nd class ¾*d.*, and 3rd class ¼*d.*) are equivalent respectively to 18*d.*, 4½*d.*, and 1½*d.* in England; which supposes a proportionally much higher rate of charge, in a much poorer country. And yet the profit from even this, would not be great; for if the cost of transit amounted to one-half (Rs. 5,000 (£500) a mile,) there would only remain the other half or 5 per cent., as profit on passengers; but I will not go further here, because this is enough to show, that the profits could never approach to those on the same money, invested in common roads. Even if the whole of the money paid by passengers on a railway, could be taken as profit to the shareholders, it would still be trifling compared with that on a common road, as has I think been clearly shown; and thus, the return of capital invested on first class railways, as compared with that laid out on common road, cannot stand five minutes' calculation.

We now proceed to compare a very cheap railway, with a first-class one. A cheap railway—with a gauge of 3 or 4 feet, light rails, without sleepers, sharp curves, considerable gradients, and timber viaducts,—fit for working at very low speeds, by horses and bullocks or with light engines, may be constructed throughout India generally for Rs. 6,000 (£600) a mile; and could probably be worked at 2 P. (¼*d.*) a ton per mile, or one-fourth the cost of working a first rate common road. Mr. Chapman indeed in his book, estimates the cost of working such a road, at 3 Annas (4½*d.*) per ton per mile; but I suppose few readers would require me to confute step by step, several pages of argument which end in the conclusion, that a cattle railroad cannot be worked under 3 Annas (4½*d.*), or four times the cost at which the grand Trunk common road is now actually worked. We cannot be far wrong in estimating the actual cost, at one-fourth of that of the best common road.

Supposing therefore 1 million sterling to be expended on 1,700 miles of such cheap railway, then, the saving of cost in conveyance by it, as compared with a high speed railway, would be as follows:

60,000 tons conveyed 1,700 miles at 3 Annas (4½*d.*) per ton......	192	lacks	(£1,920,000)
Do. do. same distance by cheap railway at 2 P. (¼*d.*)..........	11	,,	(£ 110,000)
Annual saving by cheap railway..	181	lacks	(£1,810,000)

If one-fourth of this (45 lacks (£450,000) were taken as profit to the shareholders, it would give 45 per cent.

and the community would have a clear gain of 136 lacks (£1,360,000) a year; against (as shown above) a profit by the high speed railway, of only 2 per cent. to the shareholders, and of 6 lacks (£60,000) to the community, on the same capital (1 million sterling.)

In the same way, this sum might be expended in greatly improving 10,000 miles of river navigation (if we had so much capable of improvement) at the cost of Rs. 1,000 (£100) a mile, which would perhaps reduce the cost of transit, where the rivers are already navigated, by 1 P. ($\frac{1}{8}$*d.*) a ton; and this, on the Ganges for instance, where the traffic is estimated at 2 million tons, would amount to Rs. 10,000 (£1,000) per mile, or 1,000 per cent. on the outlay. Or, if the same capital were expended in making navigable a river not at present available (as the Godavery,) it would create an immense traffic, at 1 or 2 P. ($\frac{1}{8}$*d.* or $\frac{1}{4}$*d.*) per ton, in a tract of country where there is at present scarcely any traffic, and where the cost of transit is about 3 Annas (4$\frac{1}{2}$*d.*) per ton. Again, it might be laid out in establishing (by means of weirs), perfect steam navigation on the Ganges for an extent of 1,200 miles, at a cost of Rs. 8,000 (£800) a mile; thus reducing the cost of transit of a ton of goods, from 4 P. to $\frac{1}{2}$ P. ($\frac{1}{2}$*d.* to $\frac{1}{16}$*d.*) and saving 3$\frac{1}{2}$ P. per ton; which, on an average of 1$\frac{1}{4}$ million of tons for the whole distance, would be a saving of Rs. 22,000 (£2,200) a mile, or 350 per cent.

These rough calculations show undoubtedly, that whether our object be the improvement of the country, or the profitable investment of capital, there can be no shadow of question that what is most wanted at present, is *a system of works that will materially reduce the cost of transit over a large extent of country;* rather than one requiring a large expenditure for a very small extent of communication, however perfect that small extent might be made. I am certain it cannot require five minutes' consideration, to show to any person who is willing to learn the real state of the case, that to expend on communications of any kind, so large a sum as a lack of Rupees, (£10,000) per mile, or even ¼ of that sum, is a complete mistake. If it be said, that in these calculations no account is taken of the passenger traffic, I answer, "because that does not materially affect the question." If goods can be carried cheaply at low speeds, travellers can also; and the number who could afford to pay high for a speed above 150 miles a day, is so insignificant as not to stand a moment's comparison with the benefits of *cheap* carriage. And further, by cheap communications, higher rates of speed will on the whole be obtained; for a man will pass quicker over a distance of 2,000 miles by means of a low speed railway alone, than by means of 80 miles of high speed railway, and 1,920 of unmade road.

There are certainly not less than 5,000 miles of river navigation that can be made very good, so as to be worked at 2 P. (¼*d.*) per ton per mile; and for this, a capital of only 50 lacks (half a million sterling) would be required. If any one thinks, that it would be either more profitable to shareholders, or more beneficial to the community, to have 50 miles of high speed railroad for the same money, he must have a mode of coming to that conclusion, different from any I am acquainted with.

But let us now suppose, that besides 5,000 miles of river transit, we require (as I have said) 15,000 miles of main line of land communications. What will be the result of refusing to have any thing but complete railroads on those lines? Even if carried on in all the four Presidencies at once, at the rate of 50 miles a year, (of which, however, there is little enough prospect at present,) it will take 75 years to complete the whole. In all probability, the greater part of these lines would in fact continue bare tracks for ever; but if they were made railways, the consequences would be something like this. If the present average tonnage on all these lines, be equal to 100 tons a day or 36,000 tons a year, the cost of traffic may be taken at Rs. 7,000 (£700) a mile, or 1,050 lacks (£10,500,000) a year. If the cost of transit were reduced to one-fourth on the railroads, then, as far as the rails extended, it would be Rs. 1,750 (£175) a mile; and on the rest, it would continue at Rs. 7,000 (£700) a mile. On the average of the 75 years, half would be worked at the former, and half at the latter rate; and the total cost would then be,

15,000 miles at 1 lack (£10,000) per mile....	15,000 lacks	(150 millions sterling)
7,500 miles worked for 75 years at Rs. 1,750 (£175) per mile......	10,000 ,,	(100 ,, ,,)
7,500 miles worked for 75 years at Rs. 7,000 (£700) per mile......	40,000 ,,	(400 ,, ,,)
Total	65,000 lacks	(650 millions sterling)

And the comparative cost on the proposed cheap railways to be completed in 15 years, would be,

15,000 miles at Rs. 6,000 (£600) per mile.....	900 lacks	(9 millions sterling)
7,500 miles worked for 15 years at Rs. 1,750 (£175)............	2,000 ,,	(20 ,, ,,)
7,500 miles for 15 years at Rs. 7,000 (£700)..	8,000 ,,	(80 ,, ,,)
15,000 miles for 60 years at Rs. 1,750 (£175)..	15,750 ,,	(137½ ,, ,,)
Total	26,650 lacks	(266½ millions sterling)
Total for complete Railway (as above)	65,000 ,,	(650 ,, ,,)
Saving by cheap railway	38,350 lacks	(383½ millions sterling)

or about 5 millions sterling annually, for the 75 years; exclusive of all that would be saved by the increase of trade, and all the effects of the passenger traffic.

In point of fact, every 100 miles costs the country in transit at least 10 lacks of Rupees (£100,000), for every year that the country is kept deprived of improved communications; and supposing the traffic to be (exclusive of passengers) on the average 100 tons a day, (an estimate which is far exceeded on many lines) then, on the whole 15,000 miles, the loss to the country may be estimated at about 1,500 lacks, or 15 millions sterling a year.

It is particularly to be observed, that as respects the main point, viz., *time of completing a system of communications*, cheap railways have an enormous advantage over common roads; and as regards outlay, the former would cost little more than the latter, while five-sixths of their cost would be for iron, &c., which would be brought from England, and obtained just as fast as wanted. The preparation of a line of country for the rails, with a narrow gauge, would cost perhaps one-fifth of the outlay for a good road; and could therefore be done in about a fifth of the time. No doubt Rs. 1,000 (£100) a mile, would be sufficient to prepare the line for the rail; and hence, 100 miles a year might with the greatest ease be laid down in every district, expending only 1 lack (£10,000) a year on the spot. At the Godavery works in the Rajahmundry district, from 2 to 4 lacks (£20,000 to £40,000) a year have been spent; and allowing time for the purchase of materials for bridges, it would only require 3,000 men for ten months, to prepare 100 miles for the rails.

Thus, the time saved in laying such a railway, as compared with making a road, would on all main lines much more than pay for the railway; and this shows in a striking manner, the mistake of going on with common roads on main lines. On the great lines, for instance those entering Madras, where

Rs. 30,000 (£3,000) a year are now spent on transit, the whole cost of such a railway would be saved in three months; and if it took 5 years to make a certain length of common road, instead of 1 year to lay a railway, the cost of the latter would be saved twenty times over, in the time the former would require for its execution.

We have thus shown, that there are lines, where, independently of the saving in working the railways when laid, it would be as cheap to construct railways at Rs. 30,000 (£3,000) per mile in one year, as to make a common road in two years at Rs. 5,000 (£500) per mile; or, if one kind of railway could be laid in two years, at a cost of Rs. 6,000 (£600) per mile, it would still be worth while (if necessary) to pay Rs. 30,000 (£3,000) per mile for another kind of railway, which, by entailing less labour in preparing the line, would be capable of completion in one year. So important and pressing is the subject of opening lines of cheap communication in India, that we feel safe in saying, that there is a loss of two millions sterling to the country, for every month that the general opening of India is delayed. If a railway were made, entirely composed of wrought iron beams supported on cast iron screw piles of different lengths, so as to render unnecessary all work in the ground, beyond screwing in the piles, and fixing the beams; it would, in consequence of the great saving of time, be the cheapest communication that could be executed, even though it cost five times as much as a common road or another kind of railway, that took longer to complete. Thus, in continuing to make common roads instead of cheap railways, we not only incur a cost of transit five times as great, but also a much greater first cost, taking into account not only the actual expenditure, but also the loss in cost of transit incurred by the country during the time of construction; and in making high speed railways, there is added thereto, the loss in the additional cost of construction. If a railway costing Rs. 80,000 (£8,000) a mile, be laid over 100 miles in five years, and one composed of beams and screw piles, and costing Rs. 20,000 (£2,000) per mile, were laid over the same extent in one month, both on lines where Rs. 30,000 (£3,000) a year are at present paid for transit; then, the accounts at the end of 5 years, would stand thus:

High speed Railway.

Cost of 100 miles at Rs. 80,000 (£8,000)	80 lacks	(£	800,000)
Working half of the 100 miles for 5 years at Rs. 30,000 (£3,000) a mile.	75	„ (£	750,000)
Working the other half, same time, at 4 P. (½d.) per ton, or ⅑ of present rate.	8	„ (£	80,000)
Total expenditure..	163 lacks	(£	1,630,000)

Cheap Railway.

Cost of 100 miles at Rs. 20,000 (£2,000)	20 lacks	(£	200,000)
Working do. for 5 years at 2 P. (¼d.) or $\frac{1}{18}$ of present rate...........	4	„ (£	40,000)
Total on cheap Railway..........	24	„ (£	240,000)
Total on high speed do	163	„ (£	1,630,000)
Saving by Cheap Railway..	139 lacks	(£	1,390,000)

The difference in the cost of working the two railways, (allowing for interest on the additional capital of Rs. 60,000 (£6,000) per mile, required for the high speed railway) would then be 8 P. (1*d.*) per ton per mile, on a traffic of 160,000 tons a year.

From this it appears, that the high speed railway would in a year, actually cost six times as much as the cheap railway; and the cost of transit would be permanently more than doubled, even though interest be only allowed at 4 per cent.; and if a larger profit were allowed, the difference would of course be much greater.

No wonder however that false conclusions have been universally reached, when the chief element in the question, viz., *the annual loss on the different lines by the present defective means of transit,* has been left out of the calculation.

I have before said that I do not think lightly of the value of high speed Railroads ; on the contrary, I think them of incalculable value, and would have them in every country as soon as possible. I would have the transit from Cape Comorin to Peshawar 2,000 miles, accomplished in 40 hours if I could; but, if as at present, that were only worth to the community, suppose £100,000 a year, while the same time and money would give us what was worth 20 millions a year, even though there were not a mile of communication in all India along which we could travel at the rate of 20 miles an hour, I should think we had made a fool's bargain by preferring the former to the latter. I trust indeed that the time is not far distant, when there will be quick as well as cheap travelling throughout India ; but I am sure that the way to accomplish this, is not the one hitherto pursued, which may indeed give us a few hundred miles of quick transit in the course of years, but cannot possibly give us an *even speed* throughout the country ; and even if it could, we should still have to set about providing ourselves with what is of immeasurably more importance, *cheap* transit. If we were presented with a complete system of high speed Railways embracing all India, "*at once,*" we should still be just where we are with respect to the main point ; viz., the conveyance of the great mass of passengers and goods. It was very excusable in the original projectors of the Manchester and Liverpool Railway, to plan it for the carriage of goods, as a competitor or substitute for the canals, and not surprising, that a suggestion to use it for travelling should have been received with a general laugh by the Committee ; because they had not then actually tried such a means : But for us to start upon this idea, after it has been proved by a 20 years' trial that the projectors were totally mistaken, and after the actual result has been, that the canals although worked at only two miles an hour and without steam power, continue to carry 2 million tons of goods, while the Railway carries the travellers and a small portion only of the more valuable goods (not $\frac{1}{15}$ of the whole)—for us to set about the opening of an entirely new country under the influence of the same ideas held 20 years ago, as though we had no such an example before us, is indeed a most strange infatuation. The high speed Railways in England do not, and never can, carry the great mass of the goods-traffic of England, small as it is compared with what there would be in an immense country like India; and even if they could, it would only be at a cost at least four times as great, as the same traffic could be carried by steam canals.

Nothing can be more certain, than that these Railways will not accomplish that for which they were intended, even on the great lines of communication; that is, to convey the whole of the passengers and goods requiring carriage on those lines. They cannot convey the whole at any cost, much less at the small cost that is absolutely necessary; and therefore, we have still to consider the whole subject from its foundations, just as if nothing had yet been said or done.

Imagine the manufacturers of Manchester, and the merchants of Liverpool, deprived of their water communications *wretched as these are,* and left to the mercy of the Railway to carry all their passengers and at the same time their 2,200,000 tons of goods; and, suppose that without a competitor, the Railway could carry perhaps at the utmost, one-fifth part, at its own price. Who cannot see, *that Manchester could not exist under these circumstances?* And yet this is exactly what is now proposed, as the grand remedy for all the evils of India.

WATER.

Water of India more valuable than gold of Australia.

THE savages of Australia trod upon gold for hundreds of years, while they were often in want of food, and always without a rag of clothing. Very similar has hitherto been the state of things in India ; with an unlimited supply of water within reach, which would more than provide for every possible want, the people of India have been generally barely supplied with the necessaries of life, and often so entirely without them as to perish by hundreds of thousands : whilst their European rulers though possessed of this treasure, of far greater value in proportion to the cost of obtaining it than the richest gold mine in the world, have been unable to make their income equal their expenditure.

It seems as if in India, men had universally jumped to the conclusion, that because water is immensely *valuable*, it must therefore be immensely *costly ;* without stopping to calculate what its cost really is. A person in India in the midst of the hot season, naturally forms in his mind an idea of the immense value of water ; and it does not readily occur to him, that what is so valuable may at the same time be the cheapest thing in the world ; just as it was at Port Phillip, where the last thing that men were inclined to suppose, was that many tons of so valuable a thing as gold, should be under their feet.

Our present question then is, What is the comparative *value* and *cost* of water in India ? We will not stop now to enquire its value for drinking; that is of course inestimable, and the same in so far as it is required to prevent famine; but we must content ourselves here, with a calculation of its value for those purposes which come within reach of a money valuation.

These purposes are 1st, Irrigation. 2nd, Navigation.

Irrigation.

Water may be used in three ways for irrigation.

1st. For the complete irrigation of a crop which requires to be constantly and abundantly supplied, beyond what the ordinary monsoons afford.

2nd. To enable us to grow, at seasons when no rain at all can be expected, things that require only a trifling quantity of water.

3rd. As in the case of sugar, to enable us to grow what requires so long a time to nurture, that the monsoon is not of sufficient duration.

The first kind of irrigation, is in this part of the country chiefly applicable to rice, of which there are innumerable kinds, requiring from four to six months to nurture; but as it is usually in the seedbeds for the first month, and needs no water for the last month or six weeks, water is required only during the intervening period of from two to four months; excepting indeed a small quantity for the seedbeds, which are only one-thirtieth part of the extent of the transplanted crops. As regards rice grown in the height of the hot season, the evaporation in the Madras Presidency generally, being nearly half an inch a day, it follows, that about 70 cubic yards a day would be evaporated from an acre of rice land, if fully exposed to the action of the wind. From experience, this does in fact seem to be about the extreme quantity required for rice; and the average required during the whole crop, appears to be considerably under this, even in the hot season. Supposing a six months crop; then, at the rate of 70 cubic yards a day, an acre of rice land would require for a four months supply, 8,400 cubic yards. It never actually consumes this quantity, it is true; but it is very important that the water should occasionally be changed; and allowing for this and for great waste, we commonly reckon 7,500 cubic yards as the extreme quantity required for an acre. The four months crop of course requires less; only about 4,000 cubic yards; but it is proportionably less valuable. If grown in the monsoon, a large proportion is of course supplied by the rains; for instance, if 30 inches of rain fall, this is equal to 4,000 cubic yards per acre; but much of this is lost, because it falls in too large quantities at a time, and therefore runs off to waste. Supposing therefore only one-half of this quantity (2,000 cubic yards) to remain available, then, reckoning 7,500 cubic yards per acre, there will remain 5,500 cubic yards to be supplied artificially, for a six months crop; or, we may allow on an average, 5,000 cubic yards per acre for the four and six months crops grown during the monsoon, and 7,000 for those raised in the hot season.

The value of an acre of rice land must vary very much, according to the nature of the soil and the market price of rice; but in the Madras Presidency, where the average weight of produce is about 1,200 lbs., we may take the average value at Rs. 15 (£1-10*s.*) per acre.

The produce of unirrigated land is of course much more variable, on account of the precarious nature of the rains, a large portion of the crop being constantly lost either from excess or deficiency of moisture; but we may take the average value of dry crops grown in the rainy season, at Rs. 6 (12*s.*) per acre; leaving Rs. 9 (18*s.*) as the difference due to irrigation. The additional expenses of rice cultivation above that of dry cultivation, are not easily averaged, because they consist partly of the interest of money invested in the preparation of the land, and partly in the transplanting, &c.,

but we may at least safely allow an increase of Rs. 6 (12*s.*) per acre, as due solely to the water; which gives 5,000 cubic yards for Rs. 6 (12*s.*) or 800 cubic yards for 1 Rupee (2*s.*) In the hot season more water is consumed, but the crop is proportionably more valuable; and if we allow water for rice to be worth 1 Rupee (2*s.*) per 1,000 cubic yards *when so used,* we shall certainly not overvalue it at least as regards this part of India.

The second way in which water may be used, is for the cultivation of what we call dry grains, in the dry season. For this purpose very little water is required; sometimes little more than the moistening of the soil at first, to enable the ryots to plough, and to make the seed germinate. One of the principal dry grains, cholum, cannot bear heavy rains at all, after it is one or two feet high; so that if rain continues two or three days, the whole crop rots as it stands, which frequently happens; but often, it does not get a drop of rain after it is a foot high, and then there is an abundant harvest. One of the great uses of having water at command, is, to enable the ryot to grow his grains at whatever season he pleases, and thus secure a good crop: for instance, if the cholum crop could be sown after the heavy rains are entirely over, it would never be lost, and the very little water required for it, would easily be provided. Again, in the height of the hot season, when the agricultural population is scarcely at all employed to any good purpose, a very small quantity of water is sufficient to enable them to grow a crop of some dry grain. Tens of thousands of acres in the delta of the Godavery (where nobody until lately thought of attempting to grow any thing in the hot season) are now, in consequence of a supply of water being at command, covered with crops of oilseeds and other things; for with these crops, a first watering of about 4 inches, or 500 cubic yards per acre, with perhaps as much more during the growth of the crop, secures the harvest. Then, the difference between the cost of cultivation, and the selling price of the produce, is the value of 1,000 cubic yards of water; this of course varies greatly, but reckoning it at Rs. 3 (6*s.*) we find that water is worth in the hot weather, about 1 Rupee (2*s.*) per 330 cubic yards.

The third kind of irrigation applies chiefly to the cultivation of sugar, chillies, &c.; which require water for a greater length of time than the monsoon lasts. Sugar is of course a thing of first importance. In the Presidency of Madras it is a 10 or 11 months crop, requires water until within a month of being cut, and consumes a very large quantity. In the height of the hot weather when quite young, and only 2 or 3 feet high, it takes 70 cubic yards a day per acre; during the monsoon, when 10 or 12 feet high, it probably consumes much more; and in the cold season when approaching to ripeness, it will take up 3 or 4 inches of water in a few hours. We may therefore reckon that sugar requires on an average, (in addition to what it gets from the rains) 50 cubic yards per acre for 300 days; or 15,000 cubic yards in all. The value of the crop in highly cultivated rich land, may be taken at Rs. 120 (£12) an acre, and the cost of cultivation (including land tax) at Rs. 70 (£7); leaving Rs. 50 (£5) as the value of the water, or 1 Rupee (2*s.*) per 300 cubic yards. In the delta of the Godavery, water for this purpose used to be raised from the river or from wells, at a cost of about 500 cubic yards per Rupee, or Rs. 30 (£3) per acre, leaving Rs. 20 (£2) as the profit; but the price at which water is now extensively purchased for irrigation, is of course an unanswerable proof that it is worth more than that. Millions of cubic yards of water are purchased annually in the Madras Presidency, at prices varying from 1,000 to 300 cubic yards per Rupee (2*s.*); (the cost of raising it from wells and rivers, exclusive of the interest of the cost of the well and apparatus;) which is the most clear and certain proof of the value of water.

It is not necessary here to attempt to estimate the value of water for innumerable other products, such as plantains, cocoanuts, betel, &c.; but I think we are quite safe in reckoning its value for irrigation even in ordinary seasons in the Madras Presidency generally, at 1 Rupee (2*s.*) per 500 cubic yards. Of the value of water stored up, in seasons when the local rains fail, who can form any judgment? If 1,000 cubic yards would secure the crop on an acre of cholum, thus providing 1,000 lbs. of food, more than sufficient to feed two individuals for 12 months, and in time of scarcity to preserve the lives of perhaps a dozen, till rain falls; then, every 100 cubic yards of water may be the means of saving the life of one person.

Thus in different ways we attain to a certainty, that water when applied to the land is worth (even in ordinary seasons,) at least 1 Rupee (2*s.*) per 500 cubic yards; and as every square mile of land in India, receives from the rains on an average, probably at least $\frac{3}{4}$ yard more water than is consumed in evaporation, the rains supply 2 million cubic yards to be stored for use: which at the above rate, (500 cubic yards for 1 Rupee) (2*s.*) would be worth Rs. 4,000 (£400) per annum.

It may be well to add some remarks on the present state of irrigation in the Madras Presidency, both in order to show what has already been done, and also in order to meet some of the principal objections continually urged against this fundamental means of improvement, though refuted a hundred times.

The extent of irrigated land in Madras, is given at $2\frac{1}{4}$ millions of acres, (exclusive of a considerable quantity of free and zemindary lands) which (including the two crop lands) may probably produce on an average 2,000 lbs. of rice per acre; and this, at the rate of $1\frac{1}{2}$ lb. per head per day, would supply food for about 8 millions of people, (rather more than a third of the population of the Presidency;)

the food for the remaining two-thirds, and all other agricultural produce, such as cotton, oil-seeds, gram, &c., being grown on *un*irrigated lands.

A considerable portion of the irrigated land, however, is dependent for water on tanks filled solely by the local rains; which being very uncertain, it follows that the supply of a proportion of the above quantity of food (for one-third of the population) is at all times precarious, and in bad seasons often lost. The rest of the irrigated land, amounting to perhaps one-half, is supplied either from large rivers or tanks, which never fail. Part also of the dry cultivation, (*un*irrigated land) is situated where the local rains have never been known to fail; but other parts again are liable to entire failures of the monsoon.

It will thus be seen how very far we yet are, from having such an extent of certain irrigation, as will secure a full supply of food for the whole population; which alone appears to me in itself an ample answer to those, who from a secret dislike of all improvement, are continually expressing their dread of extending irrigation.

A great portion of the present irrigation also requires to be ensured by the addition of two classes of works;

1st. Channels leading from large rivers, which rising in the western ghauts never fail, and have a continuous supply for some months.

2d. Very large tanks to be filled by the flood waters of the rivers and thus store up a supply of water for the summer rice, in those months when there would otherwise be an insufficient quantity.

Besides thus securing a never-failing supply of water to the land at present irrigated, we may by the employment of the same means on an extended scale, water almost any extent of new land. This has reference so far, to the prevention of actual famine by securing a supply of food to the whole population; but the next point is, by growing food from irrigated rather than dry land, to procure it at a less cost.

One of the most extraordinary ideas on the subject of irrigation is, that by means of it *too much food* will be grown; and thus entail many fancied evils. It seems strange that such ideas should be entertained; but so it is, and they are constantly being repeated and brought forward. I reply, that no body wants to carry irrigation to such an extent that more food shall be grown than can be consumed; nor indeed is that possible, for no one can imagine, that people will go on growing grain for which there are no purchasers: the moment men find there is no profit in growing grain, they will turn to something else. We may just as well be afraid, that the country will some day be ruined in consequence of too many ploughs being made. All we want to do is, first, to try and place the supply of food beyond the reach of the bad seasons to which the country is ordinarily liable; and secondly, to secure that food with as little labor as possible. Probably two-thirds of the food of the country is at present grown on dry land, which even in the most favorable seasons, requires in order to produce a certain quantity of food, three or four times as much labor, as irrigated land. Does it not seem wonderful then, that any one should imagine, that the country or the treasury will be impoverished, by enabling the people to grow food by a less expensive means, even when the produce is also less precarious. We need have no fear of extending irrigation too far, not only while two-thirds of the people are fed by grain grown on dry lands, but also, so long as one single acre of land remains unirrigated.

It may seem absurd to occupy time in repeating such arguments; but it is too certain that even intelligent men are often carried away by these fancies, for want of opportunities of enquiring into the subject.

Another form in which the objections to irrigation are put

is, "What is the use of growing more food than can be con-"sumed on the spot, unless there be communications to pro-"vide for its being taken to other markets."* First it may be remarked, that the very persons who object to extended irrigation when that is proposed, most readily find a reason for objecting to extension of communications when that is proposed; and secondly, the substitution of irrigated for dry cultivation has, nothing whatever to do with communications. The two things are perfectly distinct, so that the argument for extended irrigation, is equally applicable to a country *without* communications, as to one *with* them.

Let us suppose ten men wrecked on an island, and that at first nine of them are constantly employed in procuring food for the whole number; but that after many discussions, one succeeds in persuading them, that it would be best to employ their spare tenth day in cutting a channel which would enable them to grow food with one half of the labour they did before; so that from this time forward, instead of living in the most comfortless way, with a bare subsistence, they have five men available to build houses, and do all sorts of things conducive to health and comfort. It will surely be admitted by all, that this is quite independent of communications either in their own island, or with other lands; and we may surely suppose, that our islanders are not so senseless as to go on employing nine of their party in growing food, after discovering a way of growing enough to feed the whole number, by the labour of only five. Having accomplished this, they will surely next lay the foundation of many kinds of improvement; setting apart a time for study &c. &c. and employing some of their party in making internal communications, or building a boat to trade with other islands and so on. If by communications with another island,

* Even Mr. Chapman does not hesitate to say that it is perfectly useless extending irrigation unless communications were made at the same time.

they can obtain some article more easily than in their own, it will of course be a further advantage; but this is entirely distinct from *raising food in the easiest manner.*

Again it is said, that food if plentiful, is cheaper, and low prices endanger the Revenue; but this is as much as to say, that a district containing a million of people out of whom 800,000 are employed in growing food for the whole on dry land, will be better able to pay certain Revenues, than if only 400,000 could grow the same quantity on irrigated land. How should it be possible, that compelling the people to grow food in a more laborious manner, should make them better able to pay the Revenue?

The only way in which men can arrive at such untenable conclusions, seems to be this.

When food is scarce it is dear.

When food is dear the cultivator can easily pay his tax.

Therefore when food is scarce, the Revenue is easily paid.

Who cannot see where the fallacy lies in this case? The man who has *grain to sell* is of course the better for high prices; but high prices exist only because there are *few* who have grain to sell, and consequently high prices imply an impoverished state of the community *upon the whole,* and less ability to pay the Revenue. Who cannot see that the same reasoning which tends to prove that irrigation should be restricted, equally tends to show that there should be no irrigation at all; and much more than this, that all ploughs even, should be destroyed? Irrigation is nothing but a means of growing food cheaper, that is, with less labour; and ploughs, and bullocks are exactly similar. If it be to our advantage to grow grain with a greater amount of labour, by adhering to dry cultivation, it must be still more advantageous to prohibit ploughs, and when they are gone, to prevent the people from using hoes or even pointed sticks to turn up the soil: for these inferior means of facilitating labour, are exactly the same in principle as the Ganges Canals. What an astonishing proof of the wide difference still existing between the ideas of old Indians and of real Englishmen, that it should be necessary to say, much more to put on paper such things as these!

Then again it is said, that grain has at times fallen so low in price, as to be almost unsaleable. In reply, we may observe in the first place, that if a country be so well supplied, that in no year however bad, will the food be greatly deficient, there must certainly be some years when it will be superabundant, and prices will consequently fall even disproportionately low; especially among a people who having no capital, cannot afford to keep some of their grain for another year. But which of the two is best? to have occasional temporary inconvenience from low prices, or to have real impoverishment and misery from deficiency of grain, even though the few who have grain for sale, may get high prices? And as to supposing that people will continue to grow more food than they can consume or sell, one would imagine it impossible that such a fancy could be entertained. The correct mode of reasoning appears to be this:

Food is grown with less labour on irrigated, than on dry land.

The less labour is required for growing food, the more remains for all the comforts and conveniences of life.

Therefore the whole food of the community should be grown on irrigated, rather than on dry land.

There is such strange confusion of ideas on this subject, apparent in innumerable books and papers, that it seems very necessary to make one more attempt to place the matter in a clear light. The question of facilitating the growth of food by irrigation, is perfectly distinct from that of communications, though it is true at the same time, that the full benefits of irrigation connot be realised without communications; whereas, if there be cheap transit, the people of a tract of country possessing peculiar water advantages, will not only grow their own food on irrigated land, but will also grow food for other parts of the country less advantageously circumstanced in this respect; and thus, each district will grow chiefly food, cotton, or other articles for which their climate and soil are best adapted, according to what they can sell with most profit, and without reference to what can be consumed on the spot. It is self-evident that if a revenue be received in bullion, and a part of it is constantly being sent away while the district produces none, the people must have the means of sending something it does produce, to bring back the balance of the bullion; but what can this have to do with the question, whether the inhabitants shall grow food on irrigated or on dry land? or how can it help to keep up the supply of bullion, to have the people growing their food with a greater expenditure of labour, rather than with less? On the contrary, the growth of food on irrigated land, does directly facilitate the recovery of the exported bullion; because less time and labour being employed in growing food for consumption on the spot, the people have more time to spare, for the growth or manufacture of articles to be sold to those who have superfluous bullion, and can also afford to sell at a lower price.

There are moreover, two plain and visible refutations of all that has been said and written, against the extension of irrigation in the Madras Presidency.

1st. That the only district that has invariably prospered, and increased in wealth and revenue, (Tanjore) is the only one that has been anything like fully irrigated.

2nd. That there is at this time a dreadful scarcity of food, extending almost throughout the Presidency; which would not have been the case to the smallest extent, if the country had been properly irrigated.

There is little doubt that in this one year (in spite of high prices) there will be lost in Revenue and property, a sum sufficient to have secured the country for ever from serious deficiency of food, if expended on works of irrigation ; or sufficient to have supplied the country with a magnificent system of cheap communications. It is estimated that in one district alone, there will be a loss of *Revenue* of 7 lacks, (£70,000) implying a loss of *property* of at least 20 lacks (£200,000) ; and yet, when it is proposed to spend 2 or 3 lacks a year (£20,000 or 30,000) in such a district on Public Works, the proposition is considered utterly visionary, on account of expense. In fact the loss of 100 lacks (one million sterling) to the Government and people, in Revenue and property, has hitherto been considered of far less moment, than the direct outlay by Government, of 5 lacks (£50,000).

In reference to the importance of this subject, as measured by the amount of Revenue dependent upon the present irrigated lands, I must first remark, that there is no means of correctly ascertaining that amount ; because the Revenue actually received (of which alone we have returns) is, in consequence of the irrigation works being so much out of repair, very much less than would otherwise be derived from the land. The portion at present irrigated (about $2\frac{1}{4}$ million acres) pays a Revenue of 130 lacks, (£1,300,000) even with the present very defective means of irrigation ; whilst the unirrigated land (80 millions of acres cultivated and waste) pays in all only 230 lacks (£2,300,000) ; so that the irrigated land, though comprising only about $\frac{1}{40}$ of the whole area of the country, yet pays rather more than a third of the whole land Revenue ; and if the existing irrigation works were only put in proper repair, the irrigated land would undoubtedly yield an additional Revenue, equal probably to half that at present derived from unirrigated land.

How remarkable it is then, that works, upon which so much of the Revenue and yet more of the welfare of the people depend, should have been thought so utterly unworthy of attention, that 30 years ago only 4 Officers (not one fiftieth of the number really required for superintendence,) were nominated to take charge both of these works and the communications of the country; and although the department has been constantly increasing since then, there are not even now one-fifth of the number of superintendents really required. It is evident indeed that there is still no right apprehension of the matter, from the fact, that though the increase of the Corps of Engineers has been urged by every body concerned for more than 20 years past, a Despatch has lately been received from the Court of Directors on the subject, speaking it is true of some future augmentation, but still avoiding the actual question of immediate increase to the establishment; and thus after all the agitation of this subject, we are only just where we were 20 years ago in this respect. We do not want Despatches saying that the Corps *shall be* augmented, these we have had I believe before; but what is really wanted, is either an actual and immediate increase by 3 Battalions at least, to be filled up as fast as Officers can be obtained, or some equally efficient provision for the supply of European Superintendents for Public Works. The question is not, "Has the increase of Engineers been talked of, written about, or promised?" India will never be a bit the better for this system; it has been tried for 30 years in this Presidency, and has totally failed. The question is; "Has the number actually been increased?" In this as in many other cases nothing can be more true than the saying, "where there is a will there is a way." There are now about 30 Military Engineers in this Presidency; and besides the Railway Engineers, there are upwards of 30 Officers (not trained Engineers) employed on Public Works, but still not one-fourth of the number required to put the country in a decent state within a long series of years. Why not permanently withdraw some Officers from these Regiments, for employment of this nature? There ought to be at least a million sterling spent annually on Public Works in this Presidency, and we should require about 300 Engineers, besides subordinate Europeans, properly to superintend such an outlay. Supposing that only 1 lack (£10,000) a year ought to have been allowed for Public Works in each district ever since we obtained possession of it, we are now at least half a million sterling in arrears for each district, or 10 millions for the whole Presidency.

What we now have to do, is,

1st. To *secure* an ample supply of food by means of thorough irrigation.

2nd. By the same means, to provide for that food being grown with a moderate expenditure of labour.

At present about three out of four of the population are employed in raising food, or are dying for want of it, according to whether the season is good or bad; but before we can do much to improve the state of the country, we must so arrange, that 1 out of 4 will be sufficient to provide food for the whole without danger of famine, excepting under such circumstances as cannot be foreseen. This must be the foundation of everything, because people must eat; *and so long as nearly the whole population are employed in providing food, there can be no room for any great improvement in the circumstances of the people.*

3rd. We have to provide by communications, ports, &c., for the transport of things, which can be bought cheaper or sold dearer at a distance, than at hand.

In order to ensure a constant and abundant supply of food from irrigated land, for the population of the whole of India, we must have 200,000 millions of cubic yards of water stored up, for distribution as required over the land; for which purpose, a capital of about 100 millions sterling would be required. This however is only sufficient to ensure the necessary quantity of *food* for the present population ; besides which, we must of course provide food to meet the wants of the rapidly increasing population, as well as water for the irrigation of sugar, indigo, and other kinds of produce, which would involve a further outlay of suppose 50 millions sterling. Further, we have to construct at least 100,000 miles of low speed communications, which if costing on an average only Rs 10,000 (£1,000) a mile, would amount to 100 millions sterling for the whole; and then there are the ports as yet untouched; so that in order to develop the resources of the country, we should have no difficulty in spending to advantage 300 millions sterling, even without reckoning a system of high speed Railways which we must add when we have first provided for our *necessities,* by ensuring *cheap* food and *cheap* transit.

When speaking of the *whole food* of the country being grown by means of irrigation, we must not be understood to mean, that this food should consist entirely of rice ; for irrigation may be used for all other kinds of grains, as advantageously as for rice. It is worthy of remark, that though under the present system, in the Madras Presidency, many things besides rice are grown on land artificially irrigated by the people themselves, rice *only* is grown on lands irrigated by means of water supplied by Government; for this most remarkable reason, that no opening is given for the growth of other things, in consequence of the high tax on irrigated land. Whilst dry land is assessed at 1 Rupee (2*s.*) per acre, *irrigated* land pays Rs. 10 or 20 (£1 to £2), so that the cultivator has no option but to grow the crop which will make the best use of the greatest quantity of water, and yield the greatest amount of produce on *a certain space.* The question with him therefore is not, "how can a certain quantity of water" (for the provision of which capital has been required) "be employed to the best advantage?" that is, whether by applying it in large quantities to a small extent of land as for rice, or in less quantities to a greater extent as for other articles of produce? He pays so much per *acre*, and not so much per cubic yard of water; so the great question with him is of course, how to get the greatest quantity of produce out of a small extent of land. For all we know, the same quantity of water might be ten times as profitably employed on 10 acres of indigo, cholum, or oil-seeds, &c., as on 1 acre of rice. This has been a very great mistake, and ought at once to be remedied. In most parts of the country there is plenty of land waiting to be cultivated, which Government can supply to the cultivator without outlay; but all the water Government has to dispose of, has cost money. The *water* therefore should be sold, and little more than a nominal rent charged on the land, which indeed when the water applied to it is paid for, might be entirely free; and the cultivators would then of course apply the water in the way most profitable to themselves, and consequently to the community. It is more than probable that this system would add a vast amount to the prosperity of the community; by turning to account a vast extent of land at present lying waste, and enabling the people to apply the water to any crop, and in any way they may find most profitable. Indigo for instance, though requiring little water, is at present a very precarious crop, and might probably be made prodigiously more profitable, if the cultivator had in hand only a comparatively small supply of water to provide against an interval in the rains. Each acre would require for one good watering, say about 400 cubic yards, which would cost the Government only about 3 P. ($\frac{3}{8}$*d.*); and if charged at ten times that rate, it would still only cost the cultivator 2½ Annas (3¾*d.*) per acre, whilst it might make the difference of securing a crop worth Rs. 5 or 10 (10*s.* or £1) which would otherwise be entirely lost, or might least at increase the value of a crop by Rs. 2 or 3 (4 or 6*s.*).

A little experience of this kind, would no doubt lead to much better arrangements about the distribution of water than we have at present; but at any rate it is not to be imagined, that we are to continue the *slovenly, wasteful* system hitherto pursued.

It must be borne in mind further, that the benefit of irrigation is not merely in moistening the spot of ground to which water is led; this is only a part of the subject, for water not only assists the growth of a plant as far as moisture is concerned, but further actually conveys to it a large portion of the nourishment it requires, even when the water flows off nearly clear from a tank in which it has deposited most of the matter brought down from the uplands in a state of suspension, and retains only what is chemically combined with it; and this is proved by the fact that in general such irrigated lands are not manured. But in the case of land irrigated from river channels, the benefits derived are of course much greater; for as the water reaches it without having been stationary at all, a large quantity of the richest manure is carried in a state of nearly mechanical mixture with the water, and deposited on the land; and the consequent saving of expense in cultivation is enormous. Lands in Tanjore have thus borne two white grain crops annually for centuries, without any other manure. Supposing that 1 million cubic yards of water per hour are distributed by means of the Godavery works, then, probably 1,000 tons of solid manure are every hour deposited on the land, without the cost of either carriage or of spreading; and we leave the farmer to calculate the value of this. Now the Godavery actually conveys to the sea about 150 million cubic yards of water per hour, in a high fresh, containing probably 150,000 tons of manure; and if we value it at only one-tenth of that of Guano, we find that manure to the value of £150,000 per hour, or 3½ million sterling per day, is constantly being carried into the sea. Land is even *made* by this process ; that is, worthless land thus irrigated from rivers, is in a few years converted permanently into land of the highest fertility.

Again, every square mile of irrigation is a benefit to the whole neighbourhood, both by moderating the temperature, and causing dew ; and thus also every mile of canal, independent of the irrigation from it and the transit by it, is a public benefit as contributing to the means of supplying water and forage for cattle. In most parts of India, during the dry season, the cattle have to go several miles for water ; and this at the time too, when they can scarcely find any thing in the shape of herbage to eat.

I may here also speak of the use of water in cotton cultivation ; Colonel Grant, Major Lawford and others have testified to the excellent effect of irrigation upon this crop, and there can of course be no question, but that the cotton is constantly comparatively deficient in produce, for want of water at some period of its growth. I have shown that the cost of fully supplying the Godavery Delta with water, providing for one or even two crops of rice and reserving a considerable quantity of water for the rest of the year, will be annually only about 3 Annas (4½*d.*) per acre ; supplying about 8,000 cubic yards. One watering of an acre when the land is very dry, may be taken to require 250 cubic yards (2 inches depth of water), so that to provide one watering for a crop of cotton would cost about $\frac{1}{30}$ part of (4½*d.*) somewhere about ⅐*d.* ; and if this increased the crop to the extent of one-tenth, making an addition of suppose 10 lbs. of cotton (worth on the spot 1*s.* 3*d.*) then the benefit derived, would be worth 115 times the cost of the water. I need not here go into further detail about this ; but if the papers of the American cotton planters employed in India be examined, it will be seen how strongly they insist upon the deterioration in the quality of cotton, as well as deficiency in quantity, caused by drought.

Navigation.

We may next estimate the value of water for navigation. There are three ways in which water may be so used,

1st. In keeping the rivers navigable.

2nd. In supplying canals which are kept on a dead level, so that the only consumption of water is in evaporation, and lockage.

3rd. For flowing canals.

As the use of water for the artificial supply of rivers for navigation, is not in practice in England or America, and has never (so far as I know) been even suggested in Engineering works in those countries, until of late by Mr. Ellet, in his admirable papers on the navigation of the Mississipi; it will be necessary to go as fully into it here, as our present data will allow. I should mention, that I remember many years ago hearing, that in Russia some rivers are made navigable upon this principle, though only in an imperfect manner. Water stored in lakes or reservoirs, is discharged at certain fixed intervals into the streams, so as to give a flush for a few days, which is taken advantage of by the boats which have previously been collecting in the line of navigation; and this is precisely the plan I would propose, excepting that the supply should be made constant. That this plan should never have been adopted in England, is perhaps owing partly to the considerable fall per mile which the rivers there generally have, and also to the value of land and consequent expense of reservoirs; but is more probably owing to the idea never having occurred to Engineers there. Mr. Ellet seems to have been the first to suggest the plan in America, and whether it has yet been acted upon I do not know; but his report is one of the ablest papers ever written by an Engineer, and will one day assuredly be duly appreciated. In a lake country like Wales and others, there are peculiar facilities for such an undertaking; because, by closing the mouths of the lakes, large bodies of water may be retained at a comparatively small cost; and in this way, it was suggested by an Indian Engineer some years ago, to improve the Severn navigation. In Van Dieman's Land the experiment was tried many years ago, by placing a slight dam at the mouth of one of the innumerable lakes there, so as to secure during the summer a better supply of water for the mills situated on the river that flows from the lake. A very complete work of this sort was also executed in that Island (at the suggestion of an Indian Engineer) at the head of another river; a large lagoon situated high up in the hills, being dammed up by a high and strong earthen bund, furnished with a sluice, so as to form a tank, and secure a very considerable body of water. In that part of the Island the fall of rain is extraordinarily small, and the river issuing from this lagoon was always dry for five months in the year, and sometimes had scarcely any water in it, even in the winter; but since the year 1839, (when the bund was built) till it was last heard of, in 1848, the river had never been without a large stream in it, and in one year when there was an almost total failure of rain, the supply of water from the tank was sufficient to keep up the stream through a whole winter and following summer, with scarcely any other accession of water.

This mode of improving the navigation of Indian rivers, has been singularly lost sight of; and what makes it still more remarkable, is, that the abstraction of water from navigated rivers for purposes of irrigation, to the endangering of the navigation, has to a certain extent roused attention to the subject; so much so, that a few years ago an experiment was made in the Jumna, to try what effect the abstraction of the water had upon that river. By merely closing the canals that lead from it, for four days in the dry season, the water in the river was raised 1¼ feet, and would probably have risen more, had the canals been kept closed for a longer time; since it appears from the diagrams given in the report published, that the river continued to rise up to the last moment before it began to fall again, in consequence of the canals being re-opened. Had the canals been kept closed sufficiently long, the river would have remained stationary for a time, when at its highest. The quantity turned into it, was about $\frac{1}{2}$ a million cubic yards per hour, showing that 12 millions of cubic yards a day or 360 millions a month, would in the low state of the river have afforded an additional depth of $1\frac{1}{2}$ feet; and supposing the river to have had 2 feet depth in its previous state, this additional depth would make the difference between a stream scarcely navigable, and one quite available even for steamers. This is a highly important experiment, as giving the positive effect of a known quantity of water in an ordinary Indian river of a certain size; but it is unfortunate that no observations were made as to the effect of this addition, in the Ganges below the confluence of the Jumna. No doubt however the effect would not have been less than $\frac{3}{4}$ of a foot on the depth of the main river; for although the lower Ganges is much wider, its fall per mile is less than that of the Jumna. The report of this experiment is published in the papers of the Agra Presidency; but one reason probably, why even this did not awaken attention to this most important subject, is, that public attention in England has of late years been wholly absorbed by railroads as means of communication, and the impression upon people's minds generally, and even upon those of many Engineers, has been that we have done for ever with internal water communication, and that railroads have entirely taken their place. This idea is however, entirely without foundation; for railroads probably never can supply the place of water communication, because as far as yet appears, the cost of working them will far exceed that of navigable rivers or canals. Railways cannot contend with canals in cheapness, even where they have the immense advantage over them of steam power; and steam canals, such as are now in use in Canada and the United States, are worked so cheaply as to leave scarcely any possibility of railroads ever competing with them in this respect; which is the main point as regards the great mass of traffic everywhere.

It is from a misapprehension on this point, I conclude, that even when the subject was so nearly brought forward, in consequence of the canals in the N. W. being led off from navigated rivers, it still escaped thorough investigation; although a few minutes' calculation would have shown, that the subject was well worthy of the closest scrutiny. The Ganges is the grand artery of Bengal and the N. W. Provinces, and upon cheap transit by means of it, hangs the whole present state of things there. Not a tenth part of the goods carried down it, could bear the cost of 500 miles of land carriage, nor even the doubling of the present cost 4 P. (½*d.*) per ton per mile; so that without this cheap line, *the trade of Calcutta and the Revenue of Bengal and the North West, would fall to a small fraction of what they now are.*

We will now proceed to form an estimate of the value of water for the navigation of rivers, from such data as we have; beginning with the Jumna, as we have already an approach to an experiment, in the effect of a certain quantity of water on it. It is stated in the railway pamphlets, that the traffic above Allahabad is 1 million tons a year; and if we take this as equally divided between the Jumna and the Ganges, or 500,000 tons to each, and reckon the present cost of transit at 4 P. (½*d.*) per ton per mile, and the mean distance of transit, at 300 miles, it will be found, that a sum of 30 lacks (£300,000) is annually paid for transit on the Jumna. But additional water thrown into the Jumna also raises the Ganges, and the cost of traffic on that river below the confluence, (calculating about 2,000,000 tons for 550 miles at 4 P. (½*d.*) per ton per mile,) amounts to about 230 lacks (2¼ million sterling). If this traffic were equally distributed over the whole 1,200 miles of navigation from Delhi to Calcutta, it would give 1¼ million of tons carried the whole distance at a cost of Rs. 18,000 (£1,800) per mile ; and if we suppose half of this to be carried during the six driest months, when the river is injuriously low, we have 600,000 tons, carried the whole distance at a rate of Rs. 12,500 (£1,250) per mile ; or on the whole length of navigation, a total of 1½ million sterling, affected by the state of the river. Any increase or diminution of depth, which affected the cost of transit to the extent of 1 P. (⅛*d.*) per ton per mile, (one-fourth of the present rate,) would therefore increase or diminish the sum expended on transit, to the extent of nearly £400,000, or 40 lacks a year. So important is this magnificent line of navigation ; but this difference of rate of transit would in reality produce a much greater effect than shown by this sum of money, in so far as it would materially increase or diminish the amount of traffic. Many kinds of goods which would be worth moving, if carried at 4 P. (½*d.*) per ton, or Rs. 20 (£2) for the whole average distance of 950 miles, would not bear a charge of 5 P. (⅝*d.*) a mile or Rs. 25 (£2-10*s.*) for the whole distance ; and on the other hand, many things that are not worth a transit cost of Rs. 20 (£2) a ton, would afford a merchant an ample profit, if carried at Rs. 15 (£1-10*s.*). So immense is the effect of the cost of transit indeed, that a difference of 1 Rupee (2*s.*) a ton, on a distance of 1,000 miles, would often be sufficient to turn the scale, and render an article saleable at a distant market, or otherwise.

The question then remains, What increase of depth of water, is sufficient to effect a diminution of one-fourth, or 1 P. (⅛*d.*) per ton, in the present cost of transit? Supposing the Jumna to be on the average of the six dry months, 2½ feet deep at the shallows, and that the above quantity of water (12 millions of cubic yards a day, or 360 millions a month) raised the river 1 foot on an average of the same time, (thus providing a depth of 3½ feet) this may fairly be supposed to allow of the boats carrying double what they would, when drawing only 2½ feet; and a double load on the same boat, would of course nearly, if not quite, halve the cost per ton of working it, for besides the additional load, there would be the advantage of much less delay and risk from running aground. In the Ganges, the difference of depth would be less, perhaps on an average about ½ foot; but we shall be within the mark, if we calculate that this addition of water would reduce the cost of transit by one-fourth, making a difference of 1 P. (⅛*d.*) per ton per mile, and producing a total saving of 40 lacks (£400,000) a year, besides all the profit in the new traffic created by the reduction of rates. The quantity of water required (as above) to produce this effect, is 12 millions of cubic yards per day for 180 days, or in all 2,160 millions of cubic yards; and this divided between 40 lacks (£400,000) gives 540 cubic yards per Rupee (2*s.*). But this is certainly a very low estimate; and in the case of the Ganges and its feeders, we may therefore confidently reckon water worth 1 Rupee (2*s.*) per 500 cubic yards.

Let us now take another river. The Godavery is at present not navigated at all by boats, owing mainly to the uncontrolled powers of the petty Zemindars on its banks throughout the Hyderabad Country, who assume the right of demanding dues on every thing that passes;* and the vexations thus endured by the owners of timber and bamboos rafted down the river, are quite enough to prevent any traffic by boats. It has however at a previous period been navigated for six months in the year, viz. from the middle of June to December; and

* In the late voyage of a Cargo Boat, eight or ten of these Zemindars demanded tolls, one of them to the amount of 30 per cent. on the value of the Cargo, and this is not at all the limit; they take upon themselves the authority to demand as much more as they please.

probably during this time there is never less than 3 feet at the shallows, as far as Wooni on the Wurdah, 400 miles from the sea. In December there is an average flow of about 600,000 cubic yards per hour; and when the river is at the lowest about 100,000. To keep up a depth of 3 feet throughout the dry season, would probably require an average addition of 400,000 cubic yards per hour; or for the six months 1,800 millions. Our data at present are far from sufficient to enable us to calculate with certainty, but we shall probably be quite safe in allowing that 3,000 millions, would give at least 700,000 cubic yards per hour, throughout the year.

The traffic from the upper part of the basin of the Godavery towards Bombay and the Ganges, appears from the statements given by the Railway Engineers, to be at least 100,000 tons a year, of goods merely seeking the cheapest access to a port; and which would consequently be all carried by the Godavery, if the navigation were open. In such a case as this however, it is evident, that the present amount of traffic cannot in the remotest degree indicate the amount of traffic there would be by the river, if easily navigated. At present, goods are either carried from the upper part of the Godavery basin to Bombay, over 300 miles of land, at 3 Annas (4½*d.*) per ton per mile, equal to Rs. 56 (£5-12*s.*) per ton for the whole distance; or else conveyed 400 miles by land to the Ganges, at about Rs. 70 (£7) per ton *for the whole distance*, and thence by the latter river 600 miles to Calcutta at 4 P. (½*d.*) per ton per mile, or Rs. 12 (£1-4*s.*) per ton for the voyage; making a total from Berar to Calcutta, of about Rs. 80 (£8) a ton. On the Godavery, if that navigation were put in order, the cost would be only about 2 P. (¼*d.*) per ton per mile, or a total charge of nearly Rs. 5 (10*s.*) per ton, for carriage from Berar to the Port of Coringa. And if to this we add an average of 30 miles of land carriage (which would take in a great range of country) it would add only Rs. 5¼ (10*s.* 6*d.*) per ton; so that the total charge would be not more than Rs. 10¼ (£1-0-6*d.*) per ton, about *one-seventh* of the present average cost of carriage to Bombay or Calcutta. If the river were opened, no doubt the land communications leading to it would soon be improved, and the total cost reduced much below this; but I take the cost by land as at present. Now if instead of a traffic of 100,000 tons, we suppose 500,000 tons to be conveyed at this reduced rate of one-seventh of the present cost of transit, then, calculating the saving at only Rs. 50 (£5) a ton, there would be a total of saving, 250 lacks (2½ millions sterling) a year; which divided by 450 miles of navigation, would be Rs. 55,000 (£5,500) per mile; and supposing that half of this traffic were carried during the six months of the year when the river is now navigable, it would still leave half that sum or Rs. 27,500 (£2,750) a mile per annum, as the direct saving effected by throwing water into the river. Besides this, a great portion of the other half also should be credited to the improvement, because the keeping the river navigable throughout the year, would be the principal thing to lead to its navigation generally; and we may therefore safely allow Rs. 35,000 (£3,500) per mile as the value of the water; or 140 lacks (nearly 1½ millions sterling) a year, for the whole distance of 400 miles.

If we require (as above calculated) 3,000 millions of cubic yards of water thus to improve the navigation of the Godavery, this, divided among the 140 lacks (1½ millions sterling) saved, gives 200 cubic yards per Rupee (2*s.*) against 500 cubic yards per Rupee (2*s.*) calculated as the value of additional water in the Ganges; which is not out of proportion, because the whole traffic of the Godavery basin being at present carried by land, the saving by water-carriage is of course much greater, even on a smaller amount of traffic.

We may next try to calculate the value of water used for navigation, in an ordinary canal. We have some data for the cost of a canal, in the case of the Ganges project, where 850 miles of canal varying from 60 to 10 yards wide, and from 10 to 6 feet deep, is expected to cost 160 lacks (£1,600,000) or about Rs. 20,000 (£2,000) a mile. This canal has very few locks; but it has some very heavy works near its head. From this, as well as from general experience in Hydraulic works, I think we may safely allow, that a vast extent of complete steam canals 25 yards broad and 3 deep, with locks, to admit screw steamers of 300 tons, might be executed in India at Rs. 15,000 (£1,500) a mile. There are of course tracts of country where they would cost much more than this; but we need only at present occupy ourselves with those where such works could be executed, without excessive expense. We may take for example the line connecting the two coasts of the Peninsula, from Negapatam in Tanjore, to Ponany on the West Coast, a distance of 350 miles, one of the most important lines that could be found.

1st. As passing through a vast population, having near its line, towns of 20,000, 30,000, 60,000, 100,000 (Trichinopoly) and perhaps 40,000 (Coimbatore) inhabitants; so that within 50 miles on either side, there are probably 4 millions of inhabitants.

2nd. As connecting two coasts, each of which are closed to trade for about three months of the year; but at different seasons, so that by means of very cheap water transit between the two, the produce of one coast could be shipped at the opposite coast, at that season when the one is open to trade and the other closed. On this line there is not a single serious Engineering obstacle; there is an ascent of about 900 feet to the water shed, which would require, on each side about 90 locks, or nearly one in two miles; but near the water shed, they might be placed by two or three together. They would cost about Rs. 10,000 (£1,000) for every 10 foot of lift, or about Rs. 5,000 (£500) a mile. The excavation, &c., on this easy line, could be done at a cost of Rs. 10,000 (£1,000) a mile; making in all Rs. 15,000 (£1,500) a mile for the whole length of canal. If the locks were 150 feet long by 15 broad, the water consumed by them, allowing a traffic of 300,000 tons (1,500 boats of 200 tons each,) at 1,000 cubic yards per lock-full, would be $1\frac{1}{2}$ million cubic yards; or 4,000 cubic yards per mile of canal. And the consumption of water by evaporation, allowing a breadth of 25 yards, at 2 yards per annum, or an average of $\frac{1}{5}$ inch a day throughout the year, would be $25 \times 1{,}800 \times 2 = 90{,}000$ cubic yards per mile, or including leakage, say 100,000 cubic yards per mile. The loss by leakage would however be very small; for in the Peninsula if good slopes are allowed, tanks and channels become soon puddled by the sediment from the water. If the traffic were 300,000 tons a year, (which it would certainly be on this line, including the immense passenger traffic there would be,) then, taking the present cost of carriage at $2\frac{1}{2}$ Annas ($3\frac{3}{4}d.$) per ton per mile, and the charge on the canal at 1 P. ($\frac{1}{8}d.$), the saving in transit by the canal would be Rs. 46,000 (£4,600) a year, for a consumption of 100,000 cubic yards of water, or 2 cubic yards per Rupee (2*s.*). But in this case there would be required for the canal, a capital of 1 Rupee (2*s.*) for every 5 cubic yards of water; in addition to the cost of storing it.

Though these calculations are far from showing accurately the value of water for different purposes, yet they undoubtedly give it sufficiently near for our present purpose, viz. to show that its *value* is extraordinarily high as compared with its *cost*; which last we now proceed to estimate.

There are two methods of obtaining a command of water for irrigation, &c.; 1st, by diverting it from rivers, by means of weirs, and channels; 2nd, by damming up small streams with earthern bunds, and thus forming tanks, in which it is stored up during the local rains.

Godavery Irrigation.

We have a good instance of the first mode, in the Godavery works. Up to the present time about 18 lacks (£180,000) have been spent on these works, (besides annual repairs,) and probably 7 lacks (£70,000) more, in all 25 lacks (£250,000) will complete the whole undertaking, including the making all but the very small channels navigable; so that there will be about 1,200,000 acres irrigated and drained, and almost 1,000 miles of good navigation. The total cost of the water so distributed, may be thus estimated.

4 per cent. on 25 lacks (£250,000). .	Rs. 1,00,000	(£10,000)
Repairs and management	„ 1,20,000	(£12,000)
Total annual expense. .	Rs. 2,20,000	(£22,000)

The total quantity of water distributed for this sum, will be as below.

1,200,000 cubic yards per hour for 5 months.	4,300	millions of cubic yards.
400,000 cubic yards per hour for 7 months. . . . . =	2,100	„ „ „ „
Total per annum.	6,400	millions of cubic yards.

This divided between the above Rs. 2,20,000 (£22,000) gives 30,000 cubic yards per Rupee (2*s.*). But this includes the cost of both irrigation and navigation; and if the benefit of the latter be only one-fourth of that of the former, it will leave the *cost* of the water for irrigation at about 1 Rupee (2*s.*) per 40,000 cubic yards, against from 300 to 1,000 cubic yards per Rupee (2*s.*) for its *value*.

We may observe that there cannot be much room for error in this calculation; because the works are now so far advanced as to enable us to form a very fair judgment of their total cost.

Who can be surprised at Hydraulic works being profitable both to Government and the people, when we find that the *cost* of the water is only $\frac{1}{50}$ part of its *value!* It must be remembered that this water is applied to the richest alluvial land, and that in the freshes it comes down loaded with such a rich sediment, as perfectly to renovate the land annually. In Tanjore the land has borne either one or two crops of rice annually, for centuries, without any manure; although a great part of the soil is of very inferior quality.

The Godavery is it must be allowed, a case of river irrigation on a very large scale, and gives perhaps the lowest rate at which water could be obtained for irrigation in this way. The works are however heavy; the weir having a clear water way over it of $2\frac{1}{4}$ miles broad, besides six large sets of sluices, 3 locks, wingwalls, &c., in a river with a bed of loose sand, and 29 feet deep in the freshes. The three main channels will together have a breadth of about 130 yards at their heads, and there will probably be 1,500 miles of channel, 5,000 irrigating sluices, and 50 locks, besides small weirs, aqueducts, tunnels, bridges, groynes, &c., to restrain the river.

Tanks.

The cost of obtaining water by the second means, viz., by constructing tanks to collect it during the local rains, may be shown thus.

It is evident that if the fall of the country be only 8 feet a mile, which is much above the average fall in India, a bund ten yards high would retain water, of a breadth at the surface of nearly 4 miles or 7,000 yards; and as its mean depth would be half of that at the bund, the quantity of water stored per running yard of bund, would be $\frac{7,000 \times 10}{2} = 35,000$ cubic yards. This is the simplest form of the question. In practice, sites for tanks would always be chosen where the form of the ground assisted the operation; that is, where a natural rise or a hill, would form part of the bund ; and allowing that with such assistance, the capacity of the tank in comparison of the length of the bund would be doubled, (which is probable) this would give 70,000 cubic yards for every lineal yard of bund. To retain water ten yards deep, would require a bund about 13 yards high, 5 yards broad at the top, and 60 at bottom, containing about 400 cubic yards of earth for every running yard, which in the Peninsula would cost about 1 Anna (1½*d.*) per cubic yard, or Rs. 25 (£2-10*s.*) per lineal yard of bund. This must be lined with loose stone at a cost of about Rs. 5 (10*s.*) for 10 cubic yards (at ½ Rupee (1*s.*) per cubic yard) which added to the above Rs. 25, makes up Rs. 30 (£3) per yard lineal of bund. To this must be added something for a waste weir and sluices ; suppose Rs. 10 (£1) makes a total of Rs. 40.

The annual cost would then be, as below,

	Rs.	A.	£	*s.*	*d.*
4 per cent. on Rs. 40 (£4)....	1	10	(0	3	3)
Repairs, &c. at 2 per cent....	0	13	(0	1	7½)
Annual cost per yard of bund..	2	7	(0	4	10½)

or about Rs. 2½ for 70,000 cubic yards of water; equivalent to 28,000 cubic yards per Rupee (2*s.*).

If the whole of the water is to be used for one crop of rice, or in a time little longer than the rains last, we may safely add to its contents 50 per cent. for the water that will be added after it is first filled, to replace the water drawn from it for irrigation. This will therefore make the cost Rupee 1 (2*s.*) for 42,000 cubic yards.

But if, as in the case of large tanks from which irrigation is carried on all the year, an allowance is to be made for evaporation, we may reckon that the gain by refilling during the monsoon, about balances the quantity withdrawn.

Every square mile of country gives as above shown 2 millions of cubic yards of water; and consequently for a tank containing 100 millions, (the capacity of the Veranum tank in South Arcot,) the drainage of 50 square miles or an area of 7 miles square, would be required.

Ganges Irrigation.

Let us next see what the cost of water is in the N. W. Provinces.

According to Captain Baird Smith's estimate, the cost of water for irrigation there, is as follows.

The Ganges canal is estimated to cost 160 lacks (£1,600,000) and to supply 900,000 cubic yards of water an hour, or 8,000 millions per annum, which would show an expenditure of capital of 1 Rupee (2*s.*) for 500 cubic yards per acre; and if we allow 4½ lacks (£45,000) a year for current expenses (7*d.* per acre) the actual cost of water at the present rate of interest will be as follows:

4 per cent. on 160 lacks (£1,600,000)	Rs. 6,40,000	(£ 64,000)
Annual expenses................	„ 4,50,000	(£ 45,000)
Total Rs..	10,90,000	(£109,000)

which divided among 8,000 million cubic yards, gives 7,300 cubic yards for each Rupee (2*s.*).

The cost of the Western Jumna canals has been (as appears from the same authority) 12 lacks (£120,000) for a supply of 300,000 cubic yards per hour; and the current expenses are Rs. 90,000 (£9,000) per annum; showing the cost of water to be as below.

4 per cent. on 12 lacks (£120,000)..	Rs. 48,000	(£ 4,800)
Annual expenses..................	„ 90,000	(£ 9,000)
Total Rs..	138,000	(£13,800)

which, divided between 2,500 million cubic yards, gives 18,000 cubic yards per Rupee (2*s.*)

The cost in the N. W. is therefore from 7,300, to 18,000 cubic yards per Rupee (2*s.*) against about 27,000 cubic yards per Rupee in Rajahmundry. The cause of this excess of cost in the N. W. is partly from the difference in the nature of the works necessary there to lead the water to the surface of the land; and partly from the works being executed upon a more expensive plan.

Of the cost of water in the N. W. if obtained by means of large tanks, we have no account, as such works have not yet been executed by our Government; and I have no calculation of the cost and capacity of the small tanks constructed in that part of the country in former years. I think however that in a country with so moderate a fall as that part has, water could be stored in tanks much more cheaply than it could be drawn from the river; but this would involve the great disadvantage, that the tanks would not suffice to prevent a famine, unless a supply was always left in them sufficient for the second year, in case of a failure of the local rains, and for this purpose it would be necessary to make them of a capacity to contain about three times the quantity required to irrigate the lands dependent on them for one year, so as to provide for two years consumption, as well as for the great evaporation there would be in a year of drought. If however these tanks could be made to retain water, at a cost of 22,000 cubic yards per Rupee (*2s.*) they would still be as cheap as the Ganges canal irrigation works; and would have the immense advantage over the latter, of leaving the river navigation entirely uninjured (except in the case of a drought); which is the most important part of the whole question.

Ganges Navigation.

When we take into consideration the river navigation in calculating the cost of water in the N. W. it entirely alters the case. In the above calculation of 7,300 cubic yards per Rupee (*2s.*), we suppose that the water while in the river is of no value; but in estimating the value of water for navigation in the Ganges, we find, as above shown, that it is probably worth not less than 1 Rupee (2*s*.) per 500 cubic yards. But indeed, the real value of the water for this purpose cannot be correctly calculated. It is not merely that the diminution of water in the river, would add a million sterling to the cost of transit of the present traffic; but that such an increase of cost would destroy a very large proportion of the trade. If the present traffic is on an average 1½ millions of tons, and the average value of the goods is Rs. 100 (£10) a ton, the total value is 15 millions sterling. An increase of one-fourth in the cost of transit, say from Rs. 20 to 25 (from £2 to £2-10*s*.) might very possibly take off the profit of one-half the goods, or reduce the traffic by one-half; say to the amount of 7½ millions sterling. It seems highly probable that the profit on one-half of the goods does not exceed Rs. 5 (10*s*.) a ton.

When therefore we add to the cost of leading the water from the river, its value for navigation, it seems almost certain, that its abstraction from the river, is, excepting in case of famine, the gain of a loss unless the canal were continued to Calcutta; but this point must be further considered hereafter.

Captain Smith further supplies the following data for estimating the *value* of the water in the N. W.

He reckons the increase of produce due to irrigation at 640lbs., or 10⅔ bushels per acre for one crop; making, at the rate of ¾ Rupee (1*s*.-6*d*.) per bushel, Rs. 8 (16*s*.) in all; and allowing a similar increase for the other crop, we have a total of Rs. 16 (£1-12*s*.) per acre per annum; and as the consumption of water is ⅔ cubic yards per hour, or 6,000 cubic yards per annum, the value of water would be 1 Rupee (2*s*.) for 400 cubic yards, supposing that the irrigated cultivation entails no more expense than that of land not irrigated. No data are supplied on this point; but even if we allow for the expenses of cultivation so large an addition as Rs. 6 (12*s*.) per acre, it would still give the value of water at 600 cubic yards per Rupee (2*s*.). There is however a difficulty here, for the

Government water rent is only 1 Rupee (2*s.*) per acre, and if we reckon that there is a clear annual profit to the cultivator of Rs. 10 (£1) per acre, the Government charge seems to be disproportionately small; and irrigated land having so great an advantage over unirrigated land, it would appear as if there could be no competition between the two.

Upon these data however, we have 600 cubic yards per Rupee (2*s.*) as the value of water for irrigation in the N. W. Provinces, against 500 cubic yards per Rupee (2*s.*) in Madras.

Ganges Canal Navigation.

We have now to reckon the additional value given to the same water, by its being used for navigation in the canal. If, as originally planned, the canal be continued to Allahabad, there will be 450 miles of navigation in one line. The present traffic by the river is estimated at 1 million tons, and the cost is about 4 P. ($\frac{1}{2}$*d.*) per ton per mile; which makes the total expenditure in transit on this line, amount to 90 lacks (£900,000). I have no doubt that in the canal, with towing paths and a current in the direction of the main trade, and an ample depth of water so that large vessels could be used, the cost of transit would not be more than $\frac{1}{2}$ P. ($\frac{1}{16}$*d.*) per ton per mile. On the Mississipi, where money is only one-tenth of the value it is in the N. W., the charge is sometimes 1 P. ($\frac{1}{8}$*d.*) a ton. The cost on the Rajahmundry canals is 1 P. or 1$\frac{1}{4}$ P. ($\frac{1}{8}$*d.* or $\frac{1}{6}$*d.*) though they are far from being in complete order; and this is for very short trips, so that for trips of 200 or 300 miles, the cost would probably not exceed $\frac{1}{2}$ P. ($\frac{1}{16}$*d.*) per ton. The saving therefore by using the canal instead of the river, would probably be 3$\frac{1}{2}$ P. ($\frac{1}{2}$*d.*) nearly per ton per mile, or nearly 80 lacks (£800,000) a year on the whole present traffic; and this divided among 8,000 million cubic yards, gives 1,000 cubic yards per Rupee (2*s.*) for the value of water for navigation, in addition to that for irrigation.

But even this does not give its full value, for if the cost of transit were reduced to one-eighth of what it is at present, a very large increase would take place in the traffic. If the canal were continued to Calcutta, the increase would be immense; but even if only to Allahabad, the augmentation will still be very great, and we may safely allow as profit on this new traffic, about half the sum saved in transit on the old traffic, or 40 lacks (£400,000) which, with the above saving of 80 lacks in transit, would make a total saving of 120 lacks ($1\frac{1}{5}$ million sterling) as the return for 5,000 million cubic yards of water; giving 660 cubic yards per Rupee (*2s.*).

It must be observed however, that this calculation supposes no increase of cost of transit to take place in the lower Ganges, from the abstraction of water; or, that some means are found to compensate for it, for it is evident, that as so large a portion of the upper Ganges traffic, either goes to or comes from Calcutta, whatever increases the cost of transit in the lower Ganges, will check the traffic in the canal above Allahabad.

There can be no question but that if the canal were continued to Calcutta, making the average cost of transit for 1,000 miles $\frac{1}{2}$ P. ($\frac{1}{16}$*d.*) per ton per mile, or Rs. $2\frac{1}{2}$ (*5s.*) per ton for the whole distance, several millions of tons a year would be added to the traffic, and the trade of the Port of Calcutta would be increased manifold. No system of railroads could possibly produce such effects, because they could probably never be worked at less than four times the cost of a canal.

If we now add together the value of water in the Ganges canal for irrigation, viz. 1 Rupee (*2s.*) per 600 cubic yards, and the value of the same for navigation, viz. 1 Rupee (*2s.*) per 660 cubic yards, we find the total value to be 1 Rupee (*2s.*) for 315 cubic yards. And this shows the great economy of making irrigating canals navigable in this country; in this case it just doubles the profit upon the expenditure.

Perhaps, wherever a fresh water canal is made for navigation, it would be advisable to use it for irrigation also: and in the same way there can be no question but that where a canal is made for irrigation primarily, it should further be made navigable.

Rajahmundry Navigation.

If we add to the value of water for irrigation in Rajahmundry (as calculated above), its value for navigation (in the same manner as I have estimated it for the Ganges canal) the calculated results of that undertaking will be greatly increased. First, there will be at least 1,000 miles of navigation connected with the annicut. We have no sure grounds for estimating the traffic at present over the whole; but on some of the principal channels, it is about 4,000 tons a month, or 50,000 tons a year.* As yet however no part of the district has been put fully in order, and not half of it has received water; so that the traffic is a mere trifle of what it will be, if the Delta continues to prosper. Probably the main channels will before long have a traffic of 500 tons a day, or 150,000 tons a year, and the average traffic of the whole may be half that quantity, that is 75,000 tons a year, making a total of 75 million tons conveyed one mile, which if carried by land at 2 Annas (*3d.*) per ton, would cost about 94 lacks (£940,000) a mile, but when carried by the channels will not cost, at the utmost, more than 1 P. ($\frac{1}{8}$*d.*) per ton, or in all 4 lacks (£40,000) a mile; thus producing an annual saving of 90 lacks (£900,000) per mile on the whole traffic: which, divided between 6,000 million cubic yards, gives 700 cubic yards per Rupee (*2s.*). It is evident that this way of calculating the gain by navigation, must give it far too low; but it is in fact impossible to calculate the real extent of the advantage obtained, by enabling the people to grow and sell things, which but for cheap transit would be unprofitable. Taking the mean

* On one channel the last monthly return shows 1,100 boats, properly 10,000 tons, or at the rate of 120,000 tons a year; perhaps already 10 times what the traffic was 3 or 4 years ago.

distance from the point of production in the Delta, to the Port or place of consumption within the district, or to the boundary, if exported by land, at 50 miles, the saving by water transit, would be about Rs. 6 (12*s.*) per ton. So that by means of canals, a vast trade might be carried on in articles which, for want of means of cheap transport would be quite valueless unless consumed on the spot. We shall therefore be far within the mark in allowing an additional value of 1 Rupee (2*s.*) per 700 cubic yards, as given to the water by the use of it for navigation; making its total value about 1 Rupee (2*s.*) per 300 cubic yards. I have here supposed that the traffic on the channels, increases from 150 tons a day (its present average) to 500 tons; which is surely not too much, if we take the following circumstances into consideration.

1st. That the supply of boats is at present so totally inadequate that the charge for freight is about 5 P. ($\frac{5}{8}$*d.*) while the cost of working them is only about $1\frac{1}{4}$ P. ($\frac{1}{6}$*d.*).

2nd. That not a fourth part of the land is yet watered.

3rd. That most of the channels in use, have only been opened a few months.

4th. That only very little European capital and influence, have yet been brought to bear on the province.

5th. That the Delta is not yet one-third filled with population.

A curious confirmation of the above estimated value of water for irrigation, is found in the case of a poor man who had a small garden, which he cultivated and watered himself. His time was equally divided between the two, and he earned 2 Annas (3*d.*) a day by the produce. He raised the water 16 feet, and used 70 cubic yards in two days; and his gain being 2 Annas (3*d.*) a day, this makes the value of the water to him, 560 cubic yards per Rupee (2*s.*). Now if instead of raising this water himself at the cost of a day's labour, he had obtained it from the Government, who by providing it on a large scale could sell it at 30,000 cubic yards per Rupee (2*s.*), he might have had the 70 cubic yards for $\frac{1}{400}$ Rupee or $\frac{1}{2}$ P. ($\frac{1}{10}$*d.*); that is, for $\frac{1}{50}$ part of the sum he received from it as profit.

Cost and value of Water.

We thus find, that when provided on a large scale, water can be obtained in India for $\frac{1}{50}$ part of what it is worth; that Government do actually obtain it at about 30,000 cubic yards per Rupee (2*s.*); and that when applied to the land and to navigation, it is worth at least 1 Rupee (2*s.*) per 500 cubic yards.

Is it then surprising, that the new works of irrigation executed in Madras within the last 13 years, should yield on an average 70 per cent. to Government in direct Revenue; besides the amount of indirect Revenue, arising from the increase of duties on articles which the improved condition of the people enables them to consume? Or is it surprising that in Tanjore, 1½ millions sterling have been added to the saleable value of the land, since the construction of the Colleroon weirs? Those works were executed in 1836, and up to the present time there has been expended on them and on various other improvements in the Delta of Tanjore, perhaps 10 lacks (£100,000) (besides the outlay for necessary repairs); and the Revenue has increased from 42 to 52 lacks (from £420,000 to £520,000). The increase of value of land has been, so far as I have been able to ascertain, from about Rs. 20 (£2) an acre, to Rs. 40 or 45 (£4 to 4-10*s.*), making a difference on 700,000 acres, of at least 1½ millions sterling; and I think this is below the actual present price. The result of this expenditure of 10 lacks or (£100,000) may therefore be thus calculated:

Capital represented by an annual interest of £100,000 at 4 per cent.......	2½ millions sterling.
Increased value of property..........	1½ „ „
Total. .	4 millions sterling.

And the increase of value given to the land, is yielding from 5 to 6 per cent. Thus, this outlay of £100,000 has produced the interest of upwards of 4 millions sterling; or, the *value* of the water is more than forty times its *cost*. After many examinations of the case, I feel confident that this is a true calculation, and no exaggeration; and it remarkably agrees with the former calculations of the cost and value of water taken from other data.

Now if a community can purchase water at a certain price, and sell it again in the shape of rice, sugar, indigo, tobacco, pulse, cotton, &c., in unlimited quantities for fifty times as much, one would suppose that the question of how to make both ends meet was settled. And such is undoubtedly the actual state of things in India. The prices of all exportable articles, whether rice or cotton for instance, are equally made up of the cost of food and clothing. And if water be applied to diminish labour in raising articles of food, the portion of the population thereby set free, will of course employ themselves in raising whatever their country is best suited to produce for foreign countries; and any amount of cotton and other things can be sold to Europe, China, &c.

Port Phillip has been loaded with wealth, by discovering a thing which can be obtained at one-fourth of its value, while India continues poor, with a thing which can be obtained at one-fiftieth of its value.* What is the difference between the two countries that produces such a strange anomaly? The sole reason is, that the P. Phillippians make use of their treasure, which the Indians, or rather their European rulers, do not. A man in P. Phillip who could earn previously £40 a year on an average, went to the diggings and obtained in one year about £140 worth of gold. As soon as this was known, more than half the population were

* It has been estimated that every man employed at the diggings, obtains on an average 50 oz. of gold, worth £140 a year.

employed in digging gold, and last year they obtained about 14 millions sterling. In India, supposing that at this moment 25 lacks (£250,000) a year are being spent on new Hydraulic works, we may calculate that about 60,000 people are so employed; or not more than $\frac{1}{2500}$ part of the population, and not a thousandth part of the proportion employed in P. Phillip, in securing the treasures there discovered.

Nothing therefore can be more evident, than that it is not the having a treasure in the country that makes it rich, but the taking advantage of it. It was not the gold under ground that made P. Phillip rich, since the people were none the better for it for many years; but rather the digging it up, and giving it in exchange for consumable things, &c. In the same way India will continue poor, even if water were ten times its present value, so long as it is not made use of, but still allowed to flow into the sea by millions of tons per second. The water that flows off in this way by the Godavery, is sometimes as much as 4,000 million cubic yards per day, worth 80 lacks (£800,000), or three times the whole Revenue of Rajahmundry for a year; but till it is made use of, the country continues just the same as if it had no such treasure.

How strange it seems, that whilst the dullest labourer can perfectly understand the value of gold, the wisest statesman cannot perceive the value of that which is exchangeable for gold; so that though £100 worth of gold in the form of water can be obtained in India at a cost of only £2-10*s*., no Indian statesman has yet been found wise enough to set a thousandth part of the population at work to obtain it; whereas in P. Phillip, when it was discovered that £100 of gold could be obtained for £25 worth of labour, more than half the population were immediately employed in digging it up. Whenever this subject is started, the defence is, "but see what we are now doing; look at the "Ganges canal and the Godavery and Kistnah works." Suppose the P. Phillippians had continued as poor as they were, and upon somebody taunting them with neglecting their great treasure, they were to say in defence ; " what shameful " misrepresentations ! out of our 60,000 people, we have got " 12 people digging at Bullarat, and 12 at Mount Alexan- " der ;" what should we think of their sense and activity ? And yet, 24 diggers bear the same proportion to the population of Port Phillip, as the 60,000 employed in Hydraulic works, bear to the whole population of India.

Upon what imaginable principle is it then, that only certain parts of 3 or 4 districts out of 100, are to be thus improved ? The objection of want of money, has been shown over and over again to be without a vestige of foundation. Did the P. Phillippians wait till they were rich, before they went to the diggings ? How many of those who traversed the country to reach the spots where this treasure was known to be, had any surplus cash ? They went there because they were poor, not because they were rich. And the case is exactly the same in India. How much surplus Revenue has it taken to furnish Rajahmundry with Hydraulic works ? While 20 lacks (£200,000) have been spent, 30 lacks (£300,000) have already been obtained in return. The same with Tanjore and to a still greater extent, for with an outlay of only Rs. 40,000 (£4,000) a year, a permanent increase of Revenue of 2 lacks (£20,000) a year was obtained ; so that in ten years, 4 lacks (£40,000) had been paid, whilst 20 lacks (£200,000) had been received. How astonishing it is then, that in the face of these notorious facts, this plea of *want of money* should be continually advanced, just as if nobody knew of them. Suppose the Marquis of Tweeddale, instead of having the Godavery works commenced some years since, had urged the Court to wait till the district yielded a surplus Revenue out of which they could be carried on, can there be a doubt that the district would have remained in its poverty for ever ? And on the other hand, how much better and more just would it have been to execute the new works by borrowed capital, rather than to levy all this additional Revenue at once. This money if left in the hands of the people, would have been laid out so as to yield 50 or 100 per cent., while only 4 per cent. would have been paid for the loan.

There is only one district in the whole Indian Empire (Tanjore) that has never for more than 50 years past, caused the Government an anxious thought about finance; that has from the first up to the present time, been a source of real satisfaction in this respect; about which no body has ever had to say "how shall we make both ends meet?" and that has even provided in its increase of Revenue, ten or twenty times its share of the war expenses of India. And this is the only district where money has throughout been spent in increasing the supply of water. Has this district in any one single year been a drain on the treasury? Has any one yet been heard to say, "these are certainly grand and profitable "works, but how can we find money for them? no doubt at "some future time they will pay well, but in the meantime "what possible contrivance can we discover to enable us to "provide the money?" Nothing of this sort has ever been thought of. The district itself has throughout provided the money for every thing from year to year, and an enormous surplus besides. And yet the moment it is proposed to do the same thing in the next district, it is said, "these ruinous "wars keep us so poor that we cannot afford it; and not "only that, we cannot even afford to have the old works kept "in repair." For there is not a district in the Madras Presidency except Tanjore, in which the old works are generally in good repair.*

* Just as in Rajahmundry, so in Tanjore, if it had been said, "we will wait till we have a surplus Revenue before we commence upon improvement," the district would have been without surplus Revenue to this day; and if money had been borrowed at once, to give the district a really complete system of works, it would have been ten times as rich as it now is.

It is not the ruinous wars then that have kept us poor, but the most unaccountable neglect; a neglect the more extraordinary, because it is not endured for a moment in other things. Let any man propose to provide money for wars, by leaving buildings to go to ruin, and he would be thought mad; and yet this is only what is systematically done, with works upon which the food of the people and the Revenue depend.

India is like the field after an Indian battle; there is but one cry, "*water, water.*" All that is wanted is water; and this want supplied, every thing else will almost follow of course. Water for irrigation, and water for transit, will provide for every thing else. Water is the universal solvent, and can solve that which has puzzled all the Indian wise men, from Lord Cornwallis down to the present time, viz., the Revenue Settlement question. *It has solved* that question in Tanjore, the only district where it has been tried. When a man has to pay only Rs. 6 (12*s.*) a year for an acre of land saleable at Rs. 45 (£4-10*s.*), the question is substantially solved. There may of course be a thousand questions of secondary importance about that, as about every thing else; but the essential difficulty is gone. The real difficulty all along has been this, how to get Rs. 6 (12*s.*) of Revenue out of land on which the total profit was only Rs. 5 (10*s.*), and nothing but water could solve this; and it will assuredly do the same in every district of India where it is applied, by the simple process of making the profit on the land Rs. 10 or 15 (£1 or 1-10*s.*) per acre.

The total amount of treasure in the country, in the shape of water, may be thus calculated. If we allow on an average 2 feet of rain to run off the face of the country annually, then, after allowing for evaporation, there will still be 2 millions of cubic yards available per square mile; besides what falls on ground under cultivation, of which of course the profit is not lost. Thus the water that flows off every square mile, is worth (at the rate of 500 cubic yards per Rupee,

2s.,) Rs. 4,000 (£400) a year. The present population of India averages about 100 per square mile; but if the whole of the water that falls were made use of, no doubt the country would bear at least 400 to the square mile. The water then turned to account would be worth Rs. 10 (£1) a head per annum, and as there would be in all India 600 millions of people, the total value of the water would be 60,000 lacks a year, or 600 millions sterling.

Again, allowing that 7,500 cubic yards per acre would be sufficient for a rice crop, and 2,500 for what are called dry crops, (as above calculated) and that one-fourth of the country is cultivated with rice and three-fourths with other crops, it would take on an average 4,000 cubic yards per acre; which would allow of 500 acres being cultivated in every square mile, which is no doubt the proportion of the whole country that is fit for culture.

With the present population, one-fourth of the whole of this water might be turned to account, and by that means a clear additional income of 150 millions sterling, six times the whole present Revenue would be obtained. Hence we see how utterly insignificant, as compared with its income, would be the cost of governing the country, provided only the same were done here that has been done in P. Phillip; that is, if the treasure we possess were made use of.*

Can any body assign any reason why the same that has taken place in Tanjore, should not take place in every district, if the same means were used? That district is yet by no means improved to the fullest extent, and yet the po-

* Let us take a specific example of the effects of attention to Public Works, compared with those of economizing in expenditure. On roads near Madras, more than Rs. 30,000 (£3,000) a mile are paid for transit. A canal would cost, suppose even Rs. 20,000 (£2,000) a mile, or Rs. 800 (£80) a year for interest, and the same transit by it would cost Rs. 1,000 (£100) a mile, or, there would be a saving of Rs. 29,000 (£2,900) a mile. If only half of this were charged as tolls, every two miles would provide the salary of a Collector or three Revenue subordinates; so that 40 miles so improved, would provide for double the number of European Revenue men throughout the districts of the Madras Presidency.

pulation has doubled within perhaps 25 years, and is now about 500 per square mile. Were water thus made use of generally throughout the country, the population would certainly increase as fast every where ; the state of the people there has greatly improved in respect of their physical circumstances, and this also would be universal.

We may next examine more particularly into the state of the question, as respects the use of water for navigation. This involves the great question of the comparative value and importance of internal navigation, and land communications ; especially with reference to India. Not a single paper has yet been written about canals and railways in India, that does not show a fundamental misapprehension of this subject. Universally, railways are spoken of as substitutes for canals; though nothing can be more false than this idea. Canals as at present worked, even where steam is not used, are the cheapest of all communications : but railways afford the highest speed. There is not the slightest probability of railways ever beating canals in cheapness, nor of canals beating railways in speed. This at once reduces the question between the two works to this ; which in any particular circumstance is most required, speed or cheapness? or in other words, which is the most serious loss, that of time, or that of money in increased cost of transit? Or again, is the time saved by a railway purchased at more than its real value, considering the extra cost of transit? A very simple calculation will show that this may be the case. Suppose goods carried by a railway 1,000 miles in three days, at 14 miles an hour ; or the same distance by a steam canal in fourteen days, at 3 miles an hour night and day so that the loss of time by the latter is eleven days. Now if these goods are of the value of £3 a ton, grain for instance, the loss in interest at 8 per cent. for eleven days, is 15 P. (2*d.*) equal to $\frac{1}{70}$ P. ($\frac{1}{560}$*d.*) per ton per mile; and if the railway be worked at 4 P. ($\frac{1}{2}$*d.*) and the canal at 1 P. ($\frac{1}{8}$*d.*), it is clear that an addition of 3 P. ($\frac{3}{8}$*d.*) is paid for a benefit of the value of $\frac{1}{70}$ P. ($\frac{1}{500}$*d.*); or, we pay for our whistle 200 times what it is worth. This is quite sufficient to show that railways are not *substitutes* for canals; and that to talk of these latter, as the substitution of a second-rate for a first-rate means of commercial intercourse, as is so universally done, is a complete mistake. It is exactly as if we should insist that no more carts should be built, because carriages had been invented.

Thus the question is an open one still, "Under such and such circumstances, what kind of communication is most suitable?"

Before going further however, it will greatly help us in investigating this most important point, if we consider the more obvious oversights clearly observable, in the mode in which this subject has hitherto been treated.

First, all our ideas on the question, are based upon the two kinds of work as seen in existence in England, and thus, we compare canals constructed at a cost of £10,000 a mile, before steam and the value of time were discovered, with railways costing £45,000 a mile, and arranged to be worked by steam and to economize time to the utmost. But how does this settle the question between two systems of communication, in both of which the power of steam would of course be adopted?

In England moreover, the only canals at present in existence, are winding ones fitted with confined locks, which take a long time to fill and empty, are often closed for weeks by frost, and always worked at 2 or 3 miles an hour by horse power. And yet with all these enormous disadvantages, are railways in England a substitute for the canals? Not at all. All the great lines of canal are in full operation to this day, and are I believe without exception, yielding much larger profits on their cost than any railways. What is the actual amount of traffic on most of the English canals, I have not the means of ascertaining; but on the Manchester and Liverpool canals it is 2 millions of tons a year, and on the Grand Junction canal 1,100,000 tons; and when we see by Lardner's Treatise, that the goods traffic on the railways varies from 68 to 631 tons a day, it is quite certain that the great bulk of goods must be still carried by the canals. And when it is considered, that railways although having the prodigious advantage of steam power in their favour, yet carry so small a proportion of the traffic, nothing can be more evident, than that railways cannot be *substitutes* for canals.

If we want fully to compare railways and canals, we should consider how the case would stand even in England, if a new canal perfectly suited to the use of steam powers were now cut. I will not take the cost at £45,000 a mile, like the great railways, (or 4½ times the actual cost of a canal); but at £20,000 or £30,000 a mile, the canal with few windings, and with capacious locks capable of being filled and emptied in a few seconds, and of being navigated by screw steamers of 300 tons or of 300 H. P. for passengers: and we should then see a real comparison between these two classes of communication in England. It seems almost certain, that a railway on the same line as such a canal, would not obtain employment enough to pay one-tenth of the interest of its cost; because passengers could be conveyed by the canal at 15 or 20 miles an hour, and the great mass would be conveyed with a speed of 10 or 12 miles an hour at so very low a cost, as to leave probably only the very highest class of passengers for the railway; whilst goods would be carried at such a speed as would best suit each kind.

Thus in comparing canals and railways, we take our ideas only from the state of things in England, where there is steam power on one side, and animal power on the other, besides many other disadvantages in the canals, such as frost, a very winding course, locks very slowly filled, &c.; which are by no means a necessary part of a system of inland navigation, and would not be met with here.

2nd. We have lost sight of the effect of long distances upon transit. In England (according to Dr. Lardner) goods in general are carried on an average by railway a distance of not more than 22½ miles and there of course, cheapness forms a far less important item than in a country where goods are carried from 100 to 1,000 miles; but even there, cheapness is so far important, that as we have already seen, the great mass of goods is carried by the cheapest means of communication although at a low speed. In America and India however, all other points are comparatively insignificant as compared with cheapness. In England, a thing worth £40 a ton, is carried the average distance of 22½ miles at the rate of 2*d.* per ton per mile, whereby only 3*s.* 9*d.* or less than ½ per cent. is added to its value; and if conveyed at 1*d.* a mile, the addition would be only £1 in £400. But if in India an article worth £10, (a high value for the common articles of traffic here) be carried 500 miles at 2*d.* per mile, more than £4 or 40 per cent., is at once added to its cost; and if carried 1,000 miles £8 or 80 per cent. Even if it could be carried at 1*d.* a mile, there would still be an addition of from £2 to £4, or from 20 or 40 per cent. to the first cost; and as a difference of ¼ per cent. often makes a great difference in the demand for an article, the reduction of even one-tenth part of the above 20 or 40 per cent., may easily make the difference of a vast demand for an article, or none at all. And hence we see, that although this question were finally settled in England, that would by no means close it as regards India, even if there were only this one point of difference.

3rd. The question has never been discussed in England, whether railways or canals should be constructed there, as the main means of communication. The question there was, *whether railways should be added to other existing means of communication;* and therefore the two cases are totally different. The country was already provided with a complete system of *cheap* communications, and the only question was, whether it could afford to *add* to them, a system of costly high speed communications. England could much better do without its railways, than without its canals; *for if the canals were destroyed, the railways could not in their present state, carry on the amount of traffic which is indispensable.* If the high speed trains were continued, then, in order to accommodate the mass of traffic now carried by canals, additional lines of rails must be laid down, at a far greater outlay both in capital and current expenses, than the previous cost of construction.

Hence again, even though it were clearly proved that people were right in adding railways to canals in England, this does not decide the question, whether in a country without either roads or canals, we should first construct railways.

4th. The large amount of traffic to be provided for in India, has been totally lost sight of. The busiest railway in England only carries 630 tons a day; the ten principal ones on an average only 288 tons, and the average of the whole is probably not as much as 200 tons a day. How then can this settle the question for a traffic of 7,000 tons a day, (like that on the line from Calcutta to the interior,) which will undoubtedly increase to 20,000 tons, when the country is improved as it now soon will be. We might as well say that because my Lord and his Lady find a carriage sufficient to carry their own persons, therefore all the farmers on the estate, ought to carry their hundreds of tons of goods in a gentleman's carriage, instead of in waggons. It by no means follows, that because railways answer for such comparatively insignificant traffic as that conveyed by them in England, that means of communication would therefore be sufficient or suitable for the enormous traffic of India, even in its present paralyzed state. But it does *not* answer even in England; for while 180,000 tons are carried between Manchester and Liverpool by the railway, 2 millions of tons are carried by the canal on the same line. It is quite clear, that if a double railway had to convey 100 trains a day of 100 tons each, they must at least all go at one speed, and I suppose it would be found absolutely necessary, in order to allow of the necessary repairs being made, to have a third way; so that if fast trains were also to be used, the railway must have five pairs of rails, which in England would cost on an average £100,000 per mile. But if we only consider what would be the effects of occasional accidents on a line worked by 100 trains, it appears more probable, that a railway with even five pairs of rails could not any thing like perform the work of a line of traffic of 10,000 tons a day, besides quick passenger transit.

The question therefore still remains open, " What kind of " communication is best, for a country with such an enor- " mous traffic as we have to expect and provide for in In- " dia?"

5th. In England, the time occupied in constructing, was a comparatively unimportant consideration. Up to this time perhaps 7,000 miles, including a great length of secondary lines, have been constructed; and in the meanwhile the country had the use of a complete system of common turnpike roads and canals, (about 100,000 miles of the former and 5,000 miles of the latter, I believe) besides sea and river communication within 50 or 60 miles of every point in the country. But in India, we want at least 20,000 miles of main and 100,000 of secondary lines, or 15 times the length required in England; and have in the meantime, no cheap and moderately expeditious means of transit, excepting one single internal line (that of the Ganges), and the Coast line of the Peninsula.

The question of the *quickest mode of opening out communications,* is therefore a vital one to India.

It is not like the railway question in England, which was merely the introduction of a great improvement, when the main interests of traffic were already substantially provided for. Rapidity in the execution of a system of communications is here the great fundamental point of the whole question; 20 years were occupied in laying down the principal railways in England; but as India cannot afford to be 300 years in providing herself with the corresponding 120,000 miles of communication she requires, India *must* find some more expeditious way of proceeding.

6th. England had no internal facilities of any importance for forming internal water communications; having only a few short lines of improvable rivers. India on the other hand has a vast extent of rivers capable of being made perfectly available for steam navigation throughout the year, at a cost not exceeding $\frac{1}{50}$ of what railways will cost; and consequently capable of being brought into use, in at most $\frac{1}{10}$ part of the time that it would take to execute the same extent of railway. Thus we have on several lines, the choice between opening in one year 300 miles at a cost of Rs. 1,000 (£100) per mile, by improving a river; and constructing a railway in 20 years, at suppose Rs. 50,000 (£5,000) a mile. The *most* important lines can all be opened at once by the former trifling expenditure of time and money. What madness then to throw away our immense natural advantages, merely because another country was compelled for want of such advantages, to incur enormous loss of time and money!

7th. The false impressions respecting canals as compared with railways, have arisen in part at least, from what upon a little further enquiry, proves to be one of the strongest things in their favour; namely, the alarm or actual loss of canal proprietors in consequence of the competition of the railways. What placed them in this predicament, was the enormous profits on the canals, some of which I believe yielded 20 per cent. or more upon their original cost, and in consequence their saleable value rose to 4 or 5 times that cost. Thus the modern shareholders paid perhaps £1,000 for a share which originally cost £200, and it was necessary, in order for them to get 4 per cent. for their capital, that the canal should yield 20 per cent. upon its cost. Of course a concern in such a predicament, was in danger from any new competing work ; and a new canal would have ruined the shareholders as effectually as a railway. When the profits on a work are great, the market value of shares corresponds, and if a work which cost £10,000 a mile, has to provide interest for £50,000, it must needs contend at a tremendous disadvantage with a new work which has only to provide a profit on its actual cost. The abstraction of a small proportion of the traffic may easily reduce the profit to the present shareholders below that of the national interest of money ; or, they may be deprived of half their income, while still the great mass of the traffic is conveyed by the canal, and the profits of the work are, say 10 per cent. on its actual cost. The mere fact therefore of a new work injuring the property in the other, or even ruining the owners, proves nothing as to the superiority of one to the other. A steam canal worked at 20 miles an hour at ¼*d.* a head per mile for passengers, and at ¼*d.* a ton for goods, would effectually ruin any railway in England that it competed with.

8th. The settlement of the question between railways and water communications in England, would not tend to decide anything here, for another century at least ; on account of the difference in the nature of the surface of the country. Wherever the variations of level are great, the advantage is proportionably in favour of the construction of railways as compared with canals. But there can be no comparison between the surface of the country in England, and that in India ; the amount of work required on a given length of communication in India, being probably not one-tenth of what it is in England, taking the main portion of India. Hence on many lines, a canal may be almost as straight as a railway ; and the labour of constructing a steam canal altogether, would not be more than that of preparing a line for rails. On many lines therefore, a steam canal could be made for a tenth of what a railway would cost.

It must be observed that all these remarks refer to *high speed* railways, such as are now talked of for India, and are under construction.

9th. In England the comparative cost of earth, masonry, &c., as well as iron and machinery, is so totally different from the same in India, that a conclusion reached by means of data obtained in the former country, cannot be trusted to for India. Supposing rails to cost in England £6 per ton, and earth 1*s*. per cubic yard, whilst in India the latter costs 1*d*. and the former £8, it is very evident that although in England the cost of a canal may be one-fourth of that of a railroad, in India it may cost only one-tenth ; even, without making any allowance for the difference in the surface of the country.

We may thus sum up the points which have hitherto been lost sight of or misapprehended, with reference to the use of water communications in India.

1st. Effects of the application of steam.

2nd. Extent of country for which means of transit must be provided.

3rd. Railways not as the only communications, but as an *addition* to a system of cheap water transit.

4th. Amount of traffic to be carried.

5th. Importance of time occupied in constructing a system of communications.

6th. Facilities for internal navigation in India.

7th. Original cost of canals in England as compared with present value.

8th. Comparative nature of the surface of the country in India and England.

9th. Comparative cost of iron, &c., and of labour, in India and England respectively.

We thus find, that the state of things in England affords no data for the decision of the question respecting the comparative advantages of land or water communications in India, at least in regard to most of its fundamental points; and consequently, if we trust to our preconceived notions in this case, we shall most assuredly draw wrong conclusions. In the first place, there are no steam water communications of any consequence in England. There are such however, both natural and artificial, in America; 160 miles for instance on the Hudson, from Albany to New York, and Mr. Mackay informs us* that on this line, a barrel of flour is conveyed for 2*d.* including landing charges, &c.; which is equivalent to $\frac{1}{7}$*d.*, a little more than 1 P. per ton per mile. And if this can be done in America with the low value of money there, it could certainly be done in India for $\frac{1}{4}$ P. or $\frac{1}{32}$*d.* per ton per mile. Now compare this with the proposed railway rates in India, varying from 1*d.* (8 P.) to 2$\frac{3}{4}$*d.* (2 As. nearly) per ton per mile, and the great difference will at once be made clear. As regards speed, the Hudson line is regularly worked at 18 and 20 miles an hour, with steamers drawing 4 feet; and there is no doubt that this speed will go on increasing. Thus we have an actual case of inland steam navigation, with a very small depth of water, a speed of 18 or 20 miles an hour, and a charge for goods corresponding with $\frac{1}{4}$ P. ($\frac{1}{32}$*d.*) per ton per mile in India. The common charge too for first class passengers is $\frac{1}{2}$ Dollar, or 1 Rupee per head per mile, equal to 1$\frac{1}{4}$ P. ($\frac{1}{8}$*d.*) in India. Can any man be found to deny, that such a communication would be immeasureably more valuable for India, than one on which the very few first class passengers could travel at 40 miles an hour, but on which the great mass of travellers and the whole amount of goods, must pay ten or twenty times as much as need be charged on a navigation line?

Again, Mr. Ellet states, that goods are sometimes carried

* Vide Mackay's "*Western World.*"

on the Mississipi at 1 P. ($\frac{1}{8}d.$) per ton per mile; and although he does not state the general rate, it would doubtless not be much more than that.

Of artificial steam navigations, we have that of the St. Lawrence and its canals. On this line, (according to Mr. Mackay,) the charge is $2s.$ $4d.$ for a barrel of flour of 200lbs. carried 650 miles, which gives 4 P. ($\frac{1}{2}d.$) per ton per mile (including canal dues); and he also states that after some further improvements, this charge will be reduced to about $2\frac{1}{2}$ P. ($\frac{1}{3}d.$) per ton. This traffic is carried on by 300 ton screw steamers at an average rate of $6\frac{1}{2}$ miles an hour, night and day, including stoppages. The above charge corresponds with about $\frac{1}{2}$ P. in India, or even less, allowing for the difference in the value of money; and at a speed of 3 miles an hour, the cost would not be half that.

Thus we have undeniable proofs, upon the unexceptionable authority of Mr. Mackay, of the value of inland steam navigation, both with respect to the grand fundamental desideratum in transit, *cheapness*, and also with respect to speed. But even were it otherwise as regards speed, it is most certain that in the present state of India, no speed in the world could make amends for the cost of transit of goods, being increased eight or ten-fold.

We have next from the same authority, some account of the navigation by the Erie canal, from lake Erie to Albany on the Hudson (365 miles) worked by horses. This canal was first cut in 1822 at a cost of about 7 million dollars (150 lacks or $1\frac{1}{2}$ million sterling); and in 1840, (ten years after the value of railways was clearly seen,) its enlargement was commenced and carried out at a further cost of 24 million dollars, so that its total cost has been 31 million dollars (700 lacks or 7 millions sterling) on the whole; or about Rs. 180,000 (£18,000) a mile. Lardner in his account makes the cost Rs. 137,000 (£13,700) a mile, and the average cost of railways in the States, is given by the same authority at Rs.

81,000 (£8,100) a mile; so that even after the effects of railways were fully known, and several thousand miles had been constructed in the States, it was not thought a mistake to enlarge a canal, by spending on it three times its original cost, making a total per mile of more than 1½ times the cost of railway; and that too, in a country where *frost stops water communication for five months in every year.*

In a chapter entirely devoted to the subject of the transit between the upper valley of the Mississipi and the Atlantic, in which Mr. Mackay describes the struggle between the States and Canada to secure its passing through each of those countries, *railways are never once mentioned;* a highly significant fact in connection with this investigation. The fact is, that railways do not in the slightest degree affect the question. Their usual charge for goods is 1½*d.* (1 Anna) per ton, and even though they have the immense advantage of being open all the year round, while canals (in America) are only open for seven months, the whole question still turns upon the comparative advantages of the two lines of *navigation;* and Mr. Mackay shows, that Canada having steam power, the other has no chance with it. Dr. Lardner states that it was in contemplation when he wrote, again to enlarge this canal, in order to allow of the use of steamers on it, so that it will probably eventually cost much more than treble the railroads in America; and this after the fullest experience of the two kinds of communication. This leaves no room whatever for doubt, that it is a complete mistake to look upon a canal as universally and simply a second rate means of communication, which ought never to be substituted for a first-rate one, like a railway. Here is an actual case, where there cannot be the smallest question of the superiority over a railway, of a steam canal, or even one worked by horses, and where the railway is constructed, not as a substitute, but as an addition; and *that* no doubt chiefly on account of the canal having been hitherto worked at only 3 miles an hour by horses, and being entirely stopped for 5 months in the year. The cost of transit on the Erie canal line is stated to be (including tolls) $\frac{9}{10}$*d.* (7 P.) per ton per mile; which, (considering the difference in the value of money) corresponds with about $\frac{1}{5}$*d.* (1$\frac{1}{2}$ P.) in India; but as interest on so large a sum as Rs. 137,000 (£13,700) a mile, is provided out of this, at 5$\frac{1}{2}$ per cent., and by a traffic confined to 7 months in the year, the actual cost of draft can be only a small part of the whole charge.

In speaking of the railways in the States, Dr. Lardner says, "*But little merchandize is transported by them, the* "*cost of transit by them being greater than goods in general* "*are capable of paying.*" And in his tables he shows, that the average distance that goods are carried by rail, is 38 miles; clearly proving, that the great mass of the distant traffic is scarcely touched by railways, although they exist on many lines where there is no water communication. The real fact is, *where goods cannot be carried by water, they are not carried at all except for very short distances.* Let this be well considered in investigating the subject of communications for India. Dr. Lardner gives the average charge for goods in America, at 1$\frac{3}{4}$*d.* per ton, corresponding with about $\frac{3}{8}$*d.* (3 P.) per ton in India; and *this cost is sufficient to prevent distant traffic.* Dr. Lardner says also, in regard to the Hudson navigation carried on in steamers drawing at most only 4$\frac{1}{2}$ feet, "when the splendour and magnitude of "the accommodation is considered, the cheapness of the "table, &c., it will be admitted that no similar example of "cheap locomotion can be found in any part of the world. "Passengers may there be transported in a floating palace, "surrounded with all the conveniences and luxuries of the "most splendid hotel, at the rate of 20 miles an hour, at "$\frac{1}{6}$*d.* per head per mile; corresponding with about $\frac{1}{6}$ P. in India. Now if there were a line of steam canals in India, suited to steamers drawing 4$\frac{1}{2}$ feet, worked at 20 miles an hour for passengers at a charge of $\frac{1}{6}$ P. ($\frac{1}{48}d.$) per head, and conveying goods at $\frac{1}{5}$ P. ($\frac{1}{40}d.$) per ton per mile, how much traffic would be left for a railway on the same line?

The following tables extracted from the Report of the Select Committee of the House of Commons on railways and canals, will show how far the railways are, even in England, *substitutes* for canals.

Statement of the traffic by water between Manchester and Liverpool, from the year 1839 to 1852 inclusive; and by Railway from the year 1838 to 1848 inclusive.

Year.	Gross Total by the Bridge water Canal, and by the Mersey and Irwell navigation.	By Railway.
1839	318,894	—
1840	338,300	164,625
1841	323,860	
1842	327,819	Average.
1843	413,005	
1844	429,742	190,914
1845	464,710	200,239
1846	498,028	217,416
1847	413,781	191,144
1848	429,937	181,968
1849	478,644	
1850	413,583	
1851	349,718	
1852	318,904	

Statement of the Gross traffic on the navigation of the Bridgewater Trustees, inclusive of the Staffordshire trade.

Year.	Total.
1839	1,174,214 Tons.
1840	1,228,234 "
1841	1,169,522 "
1842	1,161,250 "
1843	1,272,567 "
1844	1,537,547 "
1845	1,750,939 "
1846	1,823,811 "
1847	1,744,179 "
1848	1,608,223 "
1849	1,939,935 "
1850	1,910,247 "
1851	1,900,926 "
1852	1,980,266 "

Here we see that after several years competition, notwithstanding the enormous power of the Railway Companies from the immense capital under the management of a single body, notwithstanding the prodigious advantage possessed by railways over canals in being originally constructed for *steam power* instead of for *animal power* only, notwithstanding the very low rate of speed on the canals, their being annually closed by frost for several months, and their being divided under so many different Companies, and finally, notwithstanding that some of the railways have been allowed to get possession of certain canals, forming links of an extended chain of communication—yet, by far the greater mass of the traffic is still carried on by the canals. The Manchester and Liverpool canals carry 2 million tons a year or more than 6,000 tons a day, and the Grand Junction canal carries 1,110,000 tons a year or 3,600 tons a day; whilst according to Dr. Lardner, the most crowded railway in England does not carry 700 tons a day. If this be the case in a country where the distances are very small, so that the cost of transit is a small item, and where the value of goods is great; what must be the case in India, where distances are ten times as great, and where the goods are perhaps only one-tenth the value of those in England?

We may further judge of what inland steam navigation may be, from the statement of the expenses, &c., of the Austrian Lloyd's Company's Mediterranean fleet for 1852-3.

The expenses of their whole fleet of 58 vessels, for the year, while running 580,000 miles was as follows:

	Florins or Rupees.	Pounds Sterling.
Pay, victualling, fuel and expenses, &c.	2,100,000	(£210,000)
Administration..................	300,000	(30,000)
Depreciation of vessels............	70,000	(7,000)
Rs..	2,470,000	(£247,000)
Dividend at 8 per cent............	240,000	(24,000)
Rs..	2,700,000	(£270,000)

This divided over 580,000 miles, gives Rs. $4\frac{2}{3}$ (9*s.* 4*d.*) per mile per vessel, which, allowing 4 to 1 for the difference in the value of money in the Mediterranean and in India, is equivalent to Rs. $1\frac{1}{4}$ (2*s.* 6*d.*) per mile in the latter; including profit at 8 per cent.

The sum of Rs. 240,000 (£24,000) being interest at 8 per cent., implies a capital of 30 lacks, (£300,000) or about Rs. 50,000 (£5,000) for the cost of each vessel, which may therefore probably average 100 horse power and 300 tons.

The cost per horse power per mile will then be,

$\frac{4\frac{11}{16}}{100}$ Rupee = 9 P. ($1\frac{1}{8}$*d.*) equivalent to $2\frac{1}{4}$ P. ($3\frac{1}{4}$*d.*) in India.

And the cost per ton of vessel per mile is,

$\frac{4\frac{11}{16}}{300}$ Rupee = 3 P. ($\frac{3}{8}$*d.*) equivalent to $\frac{3}{4}$ P. ($\frac{1}{11}$*d.*) in India.

And this being the actual expense of working ocean steamers, which allowing for the difference of vessel and engines, the difference in the wear and tear, and other contingent expenses, must certainly be double that of working vessels of the same size and speed on inland waters; we may arrive at the conclusion, that such vessels could be worked inland, at the rate of 10 or 12 land miles per hour, at 10 As. (1*s.* 3*d.*) per mile.

This will give a very clear idea of the difference that water communication by steam power, would make in India; a vessel of 300 tons and 100 horse power going at the rate of 10 miles an hour, costing exactly the same as two palanquins or four bullock bandies. If there were such a communication from Madras through Tanjore and Trichinopoly, (to which there is not the least obstacle,) a gentleman and his wife might hire a whole steamer of 300 tons, and reach the foot of the Neilgherry Hills in 40 hours, for the same money that they now pay to go there by palanquin in 8 days. Or, if content with merely a cabin to themselves, supposing there were only 20 first class passengers who paid one-fourth of the total expenses, (the rest being paid by second class passengers and goods) they would have to pay only $1\frac{3}{5}$ P. ($\frac{1}{5}$*d.*) a mile each; or Rs. 6 (12*s.*) for both for the whole distance, instead of Rs. 250 (£25) as at present by palanquin.

And supposing the merchant who had to send 300 tons of goods to Madras, paid half the hire of the vessel, (the rest being paid by passengers,) the goods would be charged at the rate of only $\frac{1}{5}$ P. ($\frac{1}{40}$*d.*) per ton per mile, or 11 As. (1*s.* $4\frac{1}{2}$*d.*) per ton for the whole distance; making a total of only Rs. 200 (£20) for the whole 300 tons conveyed to Madras in 40 hours, instead of as at present, paying the hire of 600 bandies, at 1 Anna (1½*d.*) a mile each, total Rs. 15,000 (£1,500) to have it conveyed to the port in 30 days, with much risk; so that what is now an unprofitable venture to a merchant, would with the steam canal, give him a profit of £1,480 that being the amount saved on the carriage alone.

From such calculations as these, based on unimpeachable data, one cannot but see what India is losing for want of cheap water communications.

It is remarkable how the above calculation from ocean steamers on an extensive scale, agrees with the actual cost of working a 20 horse power steam tug on the Godavery, viz., 4 As. (6*d.*) per mile, or 3 P. (⅓*d.*) per horse power per mile; just the cost of the ocean steamers, after allowing for the difference in the value of money, viz. 4 to 1; the small vessels on inland waters thus costing the same per horse power as the large vessels at sea.

Such a steam canal could certainly be cut on the line above mentioned, viz., from Madras to the Western Coast through Coimbatore, at a cost of Rs. 15,000 (£1,500) per mile; making the most liberal estimate.

Now let us suppose instead, a high speed railway with double lines of rails, (which would be absolutely necessary to accommodate the traffic) costing Rs. 70,000 (£7,000) per mile; and allowing that it were worked at half the lowest rate estimated by the railway men, viz., 4 P. (½*d.*) per mile, or 20 times the cost of working the canal, can there be any doubt which should be selected? Ask the merchant which he would prefer, to go up to Coimbatore by canal in 20 hours travelling at the rate of 15 or 20 miles an hour, and send his goods back at 11 As. (1*s.* 4½*d.*) a ton, or to travel himself by the railroad in 10 hours, and then send his goods back at Rs. 50 (£5) a ton. And this too being only obtained by an outlay of 280 lacks (£2,800,000) for the railway, whilst 80 lacks (£800,000) would suffice for the canal.

We find therefore abundance of undeniable data, which leaves no possible room to question the suitableness of water communication to this, and indeed all other countries, or its immeasurable superiority to any other means; at least until a country can afford to *add* communications giving a still higher speed. Moreover, we are not yet at the limit of speed by water; it has already exceeded 20 miles an hour in 4½ feet water, and nothing is more certain than that it will go on increasing. The vessels on the Hudson for instance have attained a speed of 22 miles an hour, and would easily carry a second engine as large as the first, and then run at about 27 miles an hour. And from the lately published accounts of the screw, it appears almost certain, that the same power of engine, working screws instead of paddles, would give a much higher speed; probably at least 30 miles an hour, *or half as much again as the present average speed of the American railways.*

It must not be forgotten, that now after 20 years' experience it is fully ascertained that as a *speculation* the high speed railways have totally failed, even in England. It has been stated by one of the best informed Engineers in England, that the real profits on all the railways do not average more than 1½ per cent. I do not at all mean to give it as my opinion that the system of high speed railways has on the whole been a loss to the country; I believe that in a country in the present state of England, speed up to perhaps 20 miles an hour, is worth almost any money; but it is quite certain now, that the cost of the very high speeds of English railways has hitherto been quite under-estimated.

Let us again suppose the river navigation here, to be improved to the utmost, so as to make all rivers with a fall of 2 or 3 feet a mile and under, as complete lines of navigation as possible. I have before reckoned that a stream of 1 million cubic yards an hour, would secure a depth of 3 or 4 feet every where in the Godavery, and that tanks containing

3,000 millions of cubic yards would be ample for this purpose, and would cost about 15 lacks (£150,000). If treble this quantity were stored, so as to give a depth of full 6 feet in the river, and if the bed were perfectly cleared of rocks, so as to allow of the freest passage for steamers, then vessels of any power might be used, and I have little doubt that if the rivers are kept at this regulated depth, excepting during the freshes, they could be worked by night as well as by day; and if very high speeds were required, a mean current of suppose 2 miles an hour, would be no obstacle to such vessels as would be worked. A vessel with a speed of 20 miles an hour for instance, would go up at the rate of 18, and come down at 22 miles an hour. Now the cost of storing 9,000 millions of cubic yards of water, might be 45 lacks (£450,000); and allowing 5 lacks (£50,000) to be spent on the bed of the river, &c., we should have ½ million sterling as the cost of at least 700 miles of inland river navigation,* besides making the branch rivers available for small vessels to a much higher point; which would be an outlay at the rate of only Rs. 7,000 (£700) per mile, against Rs. 15,000 (£1,500) per mile for a steam canal, or Rs. 70,000 (£7,000) for a railway. And it would have this vast advantage, that in the very first year, the river would be available throughout; and each year the whole navigation would be improved to the full extent of the amount expended. This is precisely what India wants, viz., to have whole lines of transit at once improved to a certain extent. If a high speed railway were laid on this line, it would be many years before the cotton country would be really accessible, and in the meantime, at least ten times the whole cost of the work would be lost for want of means of transit; whereas, 5 lacks (£50,000) laid out on the river, would in the first year provide a thoroughly good and exceedingly cheap communication from the heart of Berar to the Coast, while the same sum laid out

* Including the branch rivers.

on even a single line of high speed railway, would provide for only perhaps 30 miles out of the 400 required: and if only 100,000 tons were carried per annum, there would be a loss of 50 lacks (½ million sterling) for every year that the opening of the communication was delayed.

This shows the real state of the case as regards the Bombay railway, and the Godavery navigation. To reach the centre of the cotton country will require about 400 miles of railway. What has already been done, has been at the rate of 10 miles a year, and Rs. 70,000 (£7,000) a mile; and continuing at the same rate, we should, if it were not for those plaguy ghauts, reach the Wurdah in 40 years, after spending about 280 lacks (£2,800,000) on the line; and allowing only a traffic of 100,000 tons a year for half the time, or 20 years, at Rs. 60 (£6) per ton, there would be an outlay of 1,300 lacks (£1,300,000) on transit alone. And the account would stand thus at the end of 40 years, even supposing the trade did not increase on the Godavery, and that goods were carried for nothing by the railroad.

RAILWAY.

400 miles at Rs. 70,000 (£7,000)..	280 lacks	(£ 2,800,000)
100,000 tons per annum for 20 years at Rs. 60 (£6) per ton........	1,200 ,,	(£12,000,000)
Total expenditure..	1,480 lacks	(£14,800,000)

GODAVERY.

Improving river so as to give a constant depth of 6 feet.......	50 lacks	(£ 500,000)
100,000 tons for 40 years at Rs. 3 per ton.....................	120 ,,	(£1,200,000)
Total expenditure..	170 lacks	(£1,700,000)

But the railways expect to be able to carry goods at 1¾ As. (2½*d.*) per ton, which for 400 miles would be Rs. 40 (£4) per ton, or ⅔ of what it now is; in which case 800 lacks

(£8,000,000) more must be placed against the railway, making the expenditure on that line 2,300 lacks (23 millions sterling), against 170 lacks ($1\frac{3}{4}$ millions sterling) by the river; or 13 times as much as the latter. Even allowing the railway to be worked for nothing, there would still be a difference of 1,300 lacks (13 millions sterling) in favour of the river.

And this too supposes that the river traffic would *not* increase, whereas if carried at Rs. 5 (10*s.*) per ton, it would probably before ten years were over, increase to 500,000 tons a year; and were the river improved to the extent above proposed, the rate of transit would not exceed Rs. 3 (6*s.*) per ton.

Even if we suppose the ghauts to cause no delay in the railway, and that it be henceforward carried on at three times the rate hitherto, that is, at a cost of about 20 lacks (£200,000) a year, (a large extent of operation for India, corresponding with £1,200,000 in England,) still, it will take no less than 13 years to reach the centre of the cotton country. And if we allow that the railway is worked at $\frac{1}{5}$ of the sum at present calculated by the railway men, or 4 P. ($\frac{1}{2}$*d.*) per ton per mile, equal to Rs. 8 (16*s.*) for the whole distance, whilst the Godavery is worked at from Rs. 5 (10*s.*) gradually diminishing as it is improved to 1 Rupee (2*s.*), or at an average on the whole of Rs. 3 (6*s.*) per ton per mile, then, the account for the 13 years, would stand thus:

RAILWAY.

400 miles at Rs. 70,000 (£7,000)....	280 lacks	(£2,800,000)
100,000 tons a year for $6\frac{1}{2}$ years carried by common road at Rs. 60 (£6) per ton........................	390 ,,	(£3,900,000)
100,000 tons a year for $6\frac{1}{2}$ years carried by railway at Rs. 8 (16*s.*) per ton...	52 ,,	(£ 520,000)
Total expenditure..	722 lacks	(£7,220,000)

GODAVERY.

Improving river..................	50 lacks	(£ 500,000)
100,000 tons a year for 13 years carried by river at Rs. 3 (6*s.*) per ton..	39 „	(£ 390,000)
Total expenditure..	89 lacks	(£ 890,000)
Saving by Godavery..	633 lacks	(£6,330,000)

But besides this, the traffic on the Godavery may be reckoned to increase by that time to 500,000 tons a year; while that on the railroad, being carried at eight times the cost, would certainly not have increased in proportion beyond 200,000 tons. So that after losing at least 630 lacks, (6¼ millions sterling) we should be left in the one case with a traffic of 200,000 tons, carried to the coast at Rs. 8 (16*s.*) per ton, and in the other with a traffic of 500,000 tons carried at 1 Rupee (2*s.*) per ton; the extreme rate of transit by railway being perhaps 40 miles an hour, against 20 by the river. I think this may fairly be considered paying too dearly, for an additional speed of 20 miles an hour for the very small proportion of passengers to whom this would be an object worth mentioning; and I suspect that even those who advocate a high speed, would when it came to the point, rather go at 20 miles an hour, than pay the difference of cost for speed.

This also entirely leaves out of view the extremely important point, that by the Godavery, Berar can be supplied with food from Rajahmundry at one-fourth of the present cost; an advantage on the side of the river line, which it would not be easy to over-estimate. This would give a further stimulus to the cotton cultivation, almost equal to that caused by the cheap transit; and thus, at the end of 5 years, when the railway would not yet have reached up half way to Berar (even allowing it to proceed three times as fast as hitherto), the Godavery would have been a line of immense traffic for 4 years, every one of which would much more than pay for the whole cost of making it a 6 feet navigation.

One would suppose that nothing could be more obvious, than that a country lying just half way between two coasts, with on the one side, a river already navigable for 6 or 8 months in the year, (a longer line than the Erie canal, upon which the Americans have spent 7 millions sterling, or Rs. 180,000 (£18,000) a mile) and on the other a line of ghauts 3,000 feet high which render a railway a very difficult undertaking, should first be connected with the port to which the river flows, by making that navigation available, rather than with the other coast by means of an expensive railway. But men can only hold one idea at a time; and if their minds are already occupied with that of a railway, it is impossible to force in that of a navigation too.

If we could only have a ship-load of East India Directors, Manchester Merchants, Indian Reformers, and others interested in this matter, landed at Bombay, carried 20 miles by the railway, and then on horses and in palanquins 300 miles to the Wurdah (a journey of from 10 to 20 days) at an expense of Rs. 100 (£10) each; and on arriving there placed in a steamer and floated down to Coringa in 30 or 40 hours for 1 Rupee (2*s.*) each, then they would probably return to England, with a more correct notion of the real state of the case; particularly as on the way up, they would have met with thousands of worn-out bullocks and drivers, carrying cotton at the rate of 10 miles a day and a cost of Rs. 60 (£6) per ton, whilst in the boats in which they descended the river, there would probably be 100 tons of cotton on freight at Rs. 5 (10*s.*) a ton. Reaching the end of the railway after a journey of 20 miles, when it had already been 2 years in progress, and then seeing the frowning ghauts immediately before them, would also be a highly instructive circumstance, that would tend greatly to clear their sight;

and there would also be plenty of time for true impressions to be received, while on their long weary journey of 10 or 20 days to the Wurdah, through a country without roads, and across rivers without bridges. What a lively idea they would have of the advantage of inland steam navigation, long before they reached the Wurdah; and with what entire satisfaction would they resign themselves to the sofas in the steamer, and consider themselves as good as at their journey's end.

I should mention that the river runs through, or near forest country all the way, so that firewood could be obtained every where at the bank of the river, at $\frac{1}{2}$ Rupee (1*s.*) per ton, (equivalent to about Rs. $1\frac{1}{4}$ (2*s.* 6*d.*) for coal) or less; so that a 100 horse power steamer would cost about 3 As. ($4\frac{1}{2}$*d.*) for fuel per mile going up stream, and she would never have to carry a large quantity. Coal also has been found at two spots, and it is supposed to exist at a third, which the Natives have hitherto contrived to conceal from Europeans.

Besides the effects on navigation and irrigation, already mentioned as resulting from thus storing water in tanks, other points will be gained. First, 3,000 million cubic yards retained in the tanks, would lower the water of the Godavery in the Delta during floods, 1 foot for 500 hours or 21 days; and as the floods never continue at their highest more than 8 or 10 days, these tanks would probably keep the river a foot lower than otherwise on such occasions, which would greatly diminish the danger to the embankments, and the extent of mischief in case of breaches. A further value would be given to the water, by its use for water power in the Delta; after entering the minor irrigating channels, it will fall 33 feet to tide water, and allowing $\frac{1}{3}$ of this on an average as available for power, 1,200,000 cubic yards per hour will provide 7,000 horse power for the whole 24 hours, throughout the year, reckoning by the standard of 33,000 lbs.

through 1 foot for a horse power. But as good steam engines now usually *exert* a force of 60,000 lbs. for every nominal horse power, the above quantity of water and extent of fall will give only 4,000 horse power, assuming as the standard of measurement, the present usual nominal horse power of steam engines.

This amount of power being available for the whole 24 hours, would be equal to the daily work of 42,000 pairs of bullocks, allowing their effective work to be 16,000 lbs. per minute, and time of labour 8 hours per day; and the value of this, at 5 As. (7½*d.*) a day per pair of bullocks, would be Rs. 13,000 (£1,300) a day, or more than 40 lacks (£400,000) a year; besides rendering unnecessary the provision of a capital of 12 lacks (£120,000) for the purchase of bullocks.

If the comparison be made with steam power, we shall find that it would cost about 20 lacks (£200,000) to establish engines of the united powers of 4,000 horses; they must be worked night and day, and the cost of working them in that locality would be about 8 lacks (£80,000) a year, allowing wood fuel in the Delta at 1 Rupee (2*s.*) a ton, and including wear and tear, interest, &c. Thus, the cost of steam power, calculating upon large engines, would not exceed one-fifth of the cost of bullock labour. This is the value of the water power throughout the year; but only a third of it will be the effect of the 3,000 millions of cubic yards supposed to be stored in tanks for the purpose of improving the navigation, and therefore only the sum of 2½ lacks (£25,000) a year, should be credited on this account.

But it is evident that here also, the money difference is far from correctly measuring the value of this water power, inasmuch as it would be much more convenient than steam, both by rendering unnecessary the erection of steam engines at a cost of 20 lacks (£200,000), and also by the great superiority of water over steam power, in its certainty, manageableness, and safety.

The water stored in tanks, would thus be of value in four different ways.

1st. In lowering the river in floods, and thereby diminishing the risk to the crops and other property in the district; which however cannot be measured in money.

2nd. In improving navigation, which has been calculated at 1 Rupee (2*s.*) per 200 cubic yards, or 150 lacks (£1,500,000) for 3,000 millions of cubic yards.

3rd. For irrigation during the dry months, which, calculated (as above) at 1 Rupee (2*s.*) per 300 cubic yards, gives a total of 100 lacks (1 million sterling) for the 3,000 millions of cubic yards.

4th. For water power in the Delta, calculated (as above) at 2½ lacks (£25,000) a year, when compared with steam power.

Thus, we have more than 250 lacks (2½ millions sterling) as the total annual *value* of 3,000 millions of cubic yards of water when fully employed; while the *cost* of storing that quantity (at 28,000 cubic yards per Rupee, (2*s.*) would be only Rs. 110,000 (£11,000) a year, or a little more than 1 lack (£10,000).

Now let us stop a moment to consider, what we may, I think it will be allowed, fairly expect to be the effect in the basin of the Godavery, of thus turning to account this invaluable treasure, water.

We have at present a vast extent of country on the Upper Godavery, (about 120,000 square miles) occupied by perhaps 100 inhabitants to the square mile, who are almost entirely cut off from the products of the coast and from foreign trade, by a cost of transit of Rs. 50 or 60 (£5 or £6) a ton. They can grow most beautiful cotton cheaper than any country in the world, and have thus in their possession one of the very first desiderata of the wealthiest country in the world, England; but of this they at present sell only about 20,000 tons (worth 40 lacks, (£400,000) the produce of about 700 square miles, or $\frac{1}{170}$ part of the area of the basin; while England is ready to buy of them at least 250,000 tons, besides which, China could take an unknown quantity at such a price as they could afford to sell it for.

The people of this tract at present pay for rice about Rs. 120 (£12) a ton, while with cheap transit they could get it from the irrigated Delta for Rs. 30 (£3), and they also pay Rs. 100 (£10) a ton for salt, which they could get by the river, for Rs. 35 (£3-10*s.*) Again, they can grow wheat at Rs. 20 (£2) a ton, which if conveyed to the coast by the river, would be there made into flour by the water power, and would then be worth about Rs. 80 (£8) a ton; whilst the cost of transit and grinding, and loss in weight, would not exceed Rs. 15 (£1-10*s.*) a ton.

In the Delta of the Godavery there are about 600,000 people occupying an area of 3,000 square miles of the richest land, perfectly capable of bearing 2 millions of people. Before the new Hydraulic works were commenced, their foreign trade amounted to only 3 or 4 lacks, (£30,000 or £40,000) per annum; there were scarcely any European inhabitants, and to pay a revenue of 19 lacks (£190,000) a year, there was an annual drain of specie from the district, that is to say, the revenue was actually paid in part out of capital. There were no internal communications whatever, excepting a very irregular one by the river, which was almost impracticable during high freshes and in the dry season; and which of course from its distance, was of no use at all to by far the greater part of the Delta.

There is an excellent port at Coringa: but owing to there being only 9 feet of water over the bar of the river, it can scarcely be made any use of for repairs; and thus, the district is almost entirely shut out from European enterprize and capital.

Now let the following sums be expended upon water works, viz.:

Storing 3,000 million cubic yards of water, improvements in the bed in the river, &c.	20	lacks	(£200,000)
Hydraulic Works in the Delta	25	"	(£250,000)
Deepening bars, &c.	5	"	(£ 50,000)
Total..	50	lacks	(£500,000)

or ½ million sterling.

The following may then be the changes that will take place.

A trade in cotton, of at least 150,000 tons a year, will rapidly spring up, bringing in an income of 300 lacks (3 millions sterling) to the upper Godavery districts. An equal quantity of rice will probably be imported, causing a saving to the people nearly 150 lacks (1½ million sterling) a year; and even the present population would consume about 100,000 tons of salt, in which there would be a saving of 65 lacks (£650,000) a year. They would also sell perhaps 100,000 tons of wheat; producing an income of 20 lacks (£200,000), even at the present rate. With this vast export and import trade of 4 millions sterling in value of goods, there would of course be an extensive settlement of European merchants throughout that fine country; which though excessively hot for three months in the year, has an exceedingly pleasant climate for the other nine. Thus the foundations would be laid, for bringing European influence to bear fully upon the Native population; and an immense demand for every kind of English manufactures, would inevitably spring up, for as soon as the people become sellers they must needs become buyers also. Would not this connection with Europeans, lead through God's providence, to the improvement of the people in every respect?

Again, were the people in the Delta provided with an unlimited supply of water for irrigation, and with 1,000 miles of water-communication within the Delta, having thus the means of growing sugar, rice, chillies, &c., at prices which must give them the command of almost all markets, with an immense demand from the upper parts of the basin, for all their peculiar products, salt, &c., with a safe port affording advantages for repairs of shipping beyond almost any port in the world, on account of the cheapness of labour, &c.; a people so situated must necessarily soon become a wealthy community, and increase so as fully to occupy the whole Delta. A vast mercantile city with a trade of 2 or 3 millions sterling would be formed on the Bay of Coringa; extensive establishments for building and repairing ships, would folow, and numerous sugar manufactories, and water power mills for grinding and various purposes, would also be erected.

Have we not fair ground for believing that all this prodigious change would take place, solely by turning to account 3,000 million cubic yards of water (less than a single day's discharge of the river) that now flows uselessly into the sea?

I may also mention two facts, bearing upon the case. One is, that within a few months of the time that the water was turned into one of the Talooks of the Delta where sugar was an article of produce, the cultivation was increased *four-fold*, though only a small extent of canal was cut. The other is a statement of the requirements in the way of transit, of one of the sugar works in the Delta, which while manufacturing 2,000 tons of sugar per year, requires to convey the following quantity of goods annually.

		Tons.
3,000 tons of jaggery,	35 miles ..	105,000 for 1 mile.
2,000 " " sugar,	" " ..	70,000 " " "
10,000 " " firewood,	" " ..	350,000 " " "
	Total....	525,000 for 1 mile.

This is now all carried by water; but to convey it by land (when the country is dry enough for it to be moved at all) would cost 2 As. (3*d.*) a mile more by land, than by water;

or, Rs. 66,000 (£6,600) for the whole distance: equivalent to a charge of £3 a ton on the sugar, and sufficient to make the difference of the works being highly profitable, or to cause a total loss of the capital sunk.

If this fact be not sufficient of itself to prove what India loses from want of cheap transit, what could prove it? These works are not situated 500 or 1,000 miles in the interior, but in one of the coast districts, and only 35 miles from the port, and yet the want of water carriage would alone be sufficient to turn the scale, whether capital invested in this way would bring in a large profit, or whether the whole would be lost. This difference in the cost of carriage would be 13 per cent. upon a capital of £50,000, which may have been the sum invested. And of course this sum of money saved, does not fully measure the value of the water carriage which is always available because before, when the Delta was under cultivation, and flooded in all directions by the monsoon, goods could not be carried at all by land, on account of there being no practicable road. In a neighbouring district there are works capable of making 10,000 tons of sugar a year, situated about 40 miles from the coast, and some of the jaggery is carried thither from a very great distance; water carriage for those works would probably make a difference of more than £10,000 a year. Even if that district were fully provided with railways, there would still be a loss to the owners of these works of more than £3,000 a year, as compared with water carriage, even supposing the railways worked at the lowest rates proposed by their advocates, viz. 8 P. (1*d.*) per ton.

I may here also call attention to the small importance of cheap water power for manufactures, &c., as compared with the application of the same water to cheapening transit, and produce. The same quantity of water which by the above calculations would be the means of saving 250 lacks (2½ millions sterling) a year, when applied to navigation and irrigation, would only save 8 lacks (£80,000) a year, by substituting water power for steam, to the extent of 4,000 horse power for the whole 24 hours ; or 40 lacks (£400,000) if substituted for the same amount of bullock power. At these rates, the Godavery navigation would be equal in value, to 76,000 steam horse power working the whole 24 hours. And the use of 9,000 million cubic yards in the Delta for irrigation, would (at the rate of 300 cubic yards per Rupee, (2*s.*) be equal in value to 150,000 steam horse power. We give this calculation in order to show the immense comparative importance of cheap transit and produce to a country, above steam power for manufacturing, &c. ; even if it could be had for nothing.

It would seem almost impossible for any person to examine the circumstances of this basin of the Godavery, without being convinced, that no known mine in the world could compare with the value of this water-mine. We may safely reckon that 50 lacks (½ million sterling) spent on it, will within a few years produce property to the value of 250 lacks (2½ millions sterling) a year, the interest of 60 millions sterling, or 120 times the amount expended; while the gold mines of Port Phillip only produce four times the amount expended in working them; and this too without the tremendous evils connected with gold digging.

In this enquiry I have not touched upon the subject of iron and coal. We know that iron ore of the first quality, and in the utmost abundance is found in the line of the Wine Gunga, and that it is now worked to a great extent by the Natives in their miserably defective way. We know that coal exists in three localities, though we have no satisfactory evidence as to its quality or accessibility in those sites; and last year a largo mass of very good coal was brought down to Rajahmundry, but, we have not been able to ascertain where it was found. We know however that coal in abundance is found at no great distance from the site of the iron ore, that is, near the Nerbudda: a quantity of this was quarried by Captain Fenwick, and conveyed to Bombay, and there I am informed pronounced to be of very good quality, and all particulars respecting it are no doubt to be found recorded at Bombay.

We have thus every reason to believe, that in addition to all the other sources of wealth in the basin of the Godavery, it will become the seat of an immense coal and iron manufacture one of the grand desiderata for India.

It may be here noticed, that when once a weir is constructed across any river, the whole upper part of the basin of that river becomes available for storing water; and an immense extent of country being open for the selection of sites for reservoirs to retain water for irrigation, it is no longer necessary to construct an irrigation tank on every spot where cultivation is to be carried on. Wherever a site can be found which will afford great capacity with a short bund, water may be stored, and allowed to flow down the natural water-courses and the river; to the weir, from which it will be led by channels to the cultivable land. Many of the large rivers of the Peninsula are so circumstanced; for instance the Tambrapoorney, the Vigay, the Cauvery with its branches, (the Ambravutty, the Noel, and the Bowany,) the Vellaur, the Cheyar, the Toombuddra, and the Godavery; and weirs are now building on the Kistnah and the Pennaur, and estimated for on the Pallaur. This opens an unbounded field for improvement; and were there but one-fifth part of the number of Engineers that are required in the Presidency, the country ought immediately to be examined with a view to such sites for tanks. In connection with this subject, and as a specimen of the difficulties that Engineers had to contend with in times past in trying to get the Government to take advantage of the magnificent capabilities of the country, it may be mentioned here, that at one time the construction of such tanks on the Neilgherries, where there are remarkably fine basins available, was pressed upon the authorities; and besides many almost equally ludicrous objections to the project, officially put forward, the question was triumphantly asked, "How could it be known where the water from such "tanks would flow to?" the objector being perfectly satisfied in his own mind, that it was beyond the capacity of man to ascertain whether a certain stream flowed towards the East or the West coast. Upon exactly such grounds as this, have innumerable plans for improving the country been rejected, by those who were fully satisfied that they were the ablest men of their day, and who looked down with extreme contempt on the poor creatures who put forward such senseless schemes as these. In this respect, almost the whole Peninsula is ready for the construction of magnificent reservoirs on all its great rivers; the water of which would be at once applied to the land, by means of the rivers and channels already existing in the plain country, which channels are at present but imperfectly supplied with water even during the rainy season, and are either very partially or not at all supplied, during the dry season.

As another example, a sketch may here be given of what may yet be done by means of water, even for the best irrigated district in India, *Tanjore;* already so often referred to. This district contains 7 or 8 thousand acres of irrigated land which are pretty well supplied with water for six months in the year, though not without occasional deficiencies; but for three or four months scarcely any water flows through it.

Some use is made of the Cauvery and Coleroon and their branches in this Delta, for navigation; but this is precarious even during the rainy season, and quite stopped during the dry months. At least 1 million cubic yards of water per hour, could be profitably employed in this district for six months of the year, in addition to its present supply; besides a considerable quantity in reserve, to supply occasional deficiencies during the rains.

Thus, 5,000 millions of cubic yards of water, could with immense advantage be stored up, even for this already highly irrigated district; and this would not only allow of the cultivation of sugar to any extent, (which is at present almost impracticable from the supply of water not continuing long enough for a 10 or 11 months crop,) and thus give the district its grand desideratum, a new article of foreign commerce, but would also furnish several lines of river navigation running through the very heart of the district, to the coast. The rivers within the limits of the district, have a fall diminishing from 3 feet to 1 foot per mile, and though not affording any thing like such a navigation as would be obtained by means of a steam canal, would still at once be the means of effectually relieving the district from its present intolerable burthen of land transit, 2½ As. (3¾*d.*) per ton. As a specimen of what this burthen is, on one item of trade which exists notwithstanding such a hinderance, we may mention that about 60,000 tons of rice annually exported to Ceylon are carried on an average 30 miles, at a cost of nearly 3 lacks (£30,000) a year; whereas five-sixths of this might certainly be saved, if the rivers were made permanently navigable.

Now a stream of 1 million cubic yards an hour, would not only be the means of rendering navigable the branches of the river within the Delta, but would also enable the navigation to be extended inland to near Bowany in Coimbatore, about 180 miles from the sea, from which point it is now navigated at intervals during the freshes by means of basket boats; and thus, with the new stream within the Delta, at least 500 miles of river navigation would be provided through one of the most densely populated tracts in the world. A line of canal (about 50 miles in length) has already been formed, running in the direction of Madras from the heart of the district, and connected with the Cauvery; and the extension of this along the coast for 20 miles, has now been ordered.

About 100 miles of exceedingly easy country along the line of backwaters to Madras, would connect all this system of river navigation with Madras, and thus unite the place of greatest consumption in this Presidency, with the richest producing tract.

To store 5,000 millions of cubic yards for this purpose, would cost about 30 lacks (£300,000); and perhaps 1 lack (£10,000) more, might be spent with advantage in trifling improvements in the rivers. It would not of course be advisable to go to great expense in improving the rivers for navigation, because it would be better ultimately to make regular canals; but in providing this water for the improvement of irrigation, the great object of relieving the country from the main part of the burthen of cost of transit, would be attained. Though I have stated the cost of the whole supply of 5,000 million cubic yards of water at 31 lacks (£310,000), yet it must be remembered, that a very small part of this, about 3 lacks (£30,000), would suffice to keep the rivers steadily supplied to a good depth during the present cultivating season, or for about 7 months of the year; thus securing the present crops from drought, and keeping the navigation constantly open for that period at least. So that about 3 lacks (£30,000) spent on the remaining line of the coast canal to Madras, and 5 lacks (£50,000) on an increased supply of water, would, even if nothing further were done, make an immense difference to this important district in money receipts; and the effect of a rapid steam communication with the city of Madras, would be matter of far greater importance.

This then is a sketch of what is still wanted in the way of water improvements, even in the only district in India at all tolerably supplied with that fundamental necessary.

An outlay of only 5 lacks (£50,000) would give, besides this vast addition of water for irrigation, 300 miles of inland navigation for 7 months of the year; while New York has been content to pay 31 millions of dollars, (700 lacks or 7 millions sterling) for 365 miles of canal, open during only the same period of the year. And if only 50,000 tons a year were carried over the 300 miles, it would be a saving to this part of the country, of 35 lacks (£350,000) a year, as compared with land carriage; and the additional water for irrigation, (1,000 million cubic yards) would be worth 10 or 15 lacks (£100,000 or £150,000) a year.

Salt Water.

While writing about water in India, however, it ought not to be forgotten that fresh water is not her only treasure; the salt water is also of incalculable value.

Salt has been hitherto obtained at a very low cost, viz., about Rs. 2 (4*s.*) a ton, by the native method, without the least hint from Europeans; but this native mode of manufacturing is open to the same objections as their other operations, viz., that of carrying it on upon too confined a scale, and without capital. They think it impossible to manufacture salt excepting in the very lowest lands, on account of the expense of conveying and raising the sea water; and they consequently incur many far greater expenses, especially in respect to the liability to have the whole harvest destroyed by floods.

The following calculations will show in what enormous quantities salt may be manufactured, of the purest quality and at the most trifling cost. Sea water contains 3 per cent. of salt; or a cubic yard weighing 1,700 lbs., yields 50 lbs.; and fully saturated brine contains 30 per cent., or 500 lbs. per cubic yard. A square mile of plain is equal to three million square yards, and consequently a square mile of area one yard deep, will yield nearly 70,000 tons of salt; or we may allow 60,000. The evaporation in the Carnatic during the months of March, April, and May, is nearly half an inch a day on an average; and probably in extensive and very shallow reservoirs, it would be quite as much as that, so that we may safely reckon a yard of depth to be evaporated in less than three months. If therefore a convenient plain 1 mile square, and from 5 to 10 feet above the sea, were chosen and enclosed by a bank a 1 or 2 feet high, and if adjoining to that, a second area of about one-tenth the extent or 550 yards square were enclosed, the sea water might be raised to the first plain in such quantities as to keep it always near the point of saturation, and it might as fast as it reached that point, flow off into the smaller area, where it would be allowed to evaporate entirely; so that when the amount of evaporation amounted to one yard in depth, there would be 500 lbs. of salt on every square yard of ground.

Care should be taken to obtain the water in the first instance as clear as possible; and while standing in the first reservoir it would deposit every remaining particle of *Silt*, and flow off into the smaller one in a state of great purity.

The total quantity of water that must be raised in order to give this quantity of 60,000 tons of salt, would be 3 millions of cubic yards, or 5,000 million of pounds; and as a one horse power engine will raise at least 3 million pounds 1 foot high per hour, it would only require one horse power for 1,700 hours or 140 days, to raise the whole quantity 1 foot, or for 700 days to raise it 5 feet; or 8 horse power to do the same work in three months. The cost of working an 8 horse engine in such situations, would be about Rs. 400 (£40) a month; allowing 20 per cent. for interest and wear and tear, and charging the year's interest, to the three months. This gives Rs. 1,200 (£120) for the cost of raising to the height of 5 feet, water sufficient to yield 60,000 tons of salt, or on an average 50 tons for 1 Rupee (*2s.*) or 4 P. ($\frac{1}{2}$*d.*) per ton. And if bullock power be used, we may take it at 800 cubic yards raised 5 feet for 1 Rupee (*2s.*) or Rs. 4,000 (£400) for 60,000 tons of salt; equal to about 1 Anna (1½*d.*) per ton, which shows that the cost of raising the water, is an insignificant item.

Again, to lead the water to a convenient place would be but a trifling expense. To cut a channel 1 yard wide at the bottom and 2 yards deep, would cost about Rs. 300 (£30) a mile, so that even if it had to be cut several miles and were only used for one year, the cost would still only amount to 1 or 2 P. (⅛*d.* or ¼*d.*) per ton, on a manufacture of the extent of 60,000 tons. The expenses of collecting also, from a surface of something more than ¼ mile square, would be equally trifling.

If the site chosen for the manufacture were a few feet above the level of tide water, it would not be liable to be submerged, and the only evil arising from untimely rains would be, that the reservoirs would receive 2 or 3 inches of water, which would take a few days to evaporate. There are vast plains suitable for such works along the coast. In Tanjore especially, near Point Calymere, there is a plain containing perhaps 50 square miles, in which salt could be manufactured on a magnificent scale, and probably at 3 or 4 As. (4½ or 6*d.*) per ton. That tract has also the advantage of water from the Bay of Tondi, where from its sheltered position, it is as clear as crystal; and the coast there is also peculiarly favorable for shipping the salt, as there is smooth water and consequently no surf. The coast canal, when completed, will materially facilitate the manufacture, because almost any point on the whole extent of coast may be taken, wherever the circumstances are most favorable, and whence the salt can be conveyed to any other point, at the rate of about 1 Rupee (2*s.*) per ton, for a distance of 400 miles. The idea of Cheshire competing with India for this trade is most absurd, unless some advantage, direct or indirect, be granted to the former.

There is only one important caution to be given on this subject, and that is, that fresh water must never be used.

The salt manufacturers recently reported to the Collector of Masulipatam, that they had commenced their operations as usual, that the evaporation had proceeded just as in former years, but that not a particle of salt was produced; and on careful investigation it was found, that the creeks from which the salt manufacturers had been in the habit of obtaining their supplies of water, were in that year all filled with fresh water from the channels leading from the Annicut in the Godavery, which was the only way in which this phenomenon could be accounted for.

This part of the paper may well be closed with a few lines on the water works in Rajpootana, as described in Colonel Dixon's work on Marwar. These consist chiefly of tanks, and though on a very small scale and constructed in a very expensive manner, have yet produced such magnificent results not only in rescuing the population from all the horrors of a state of disorganization, poverty and liability to famine, but even in direct and immediate returns in money to the State, that they furnish another clear and undeniable proof of the value of water. These tanks were chiefly formed by very massive walls of rubble in mortar; generally backed by earthen embankments. The largest of those in Marwarree, is stated to cover a third of a square mile, and to be about 8 yards deep at the lowest point of the bed. The capacity is not given, but the mean depth would probably be thus above 2½ yards, and the contents 2½ millions of cubic yards. The total area of all the tanks constructed in Marwarree, is given at 15 square miles, and taking the mean depth of the whole at 2 yards, the total quantity of water stored in them would be 90 millions of cubic yards, and the cost being stated at £24,000, would give 375 cubic yards per Rupee (2*s.*) of capital; or, taking interest at 4 per cent., the cost of water would be 9,400 cubic yards per Rupee (2*s.*), which, allowing for the very small scale, and the very expensive mode of construction, agrees well enough with the cost of water as already calculated in other parts of India.

The results of this expenditure, also fully support all that is said of the value of water in India, as deduced from results in the Peninsula and in the N. W. The income to Government in Revenue had in 1847, reached £11,000 a year, or 47 per cent.; and taking the tax at one-third the produce as stated, this would imply a further profit to the people of 94 per cent., making the total returns on the capital amount to 141 per cent. There can be no doubt also that with more experience in such works, the same quantity of water might have been stored at one-half or perhaps one-third of the actual cost; in which case the returns would have been 300 or 400 per cent., even with tanks on so very small a scale as these, the largest of which appears not to have been the twentieth part of the size of many of the old tanks in the Peninsula.

Again, in the adjoining district of Ajmere, 112 tanks, covering an area of 20 square miles, and containing perhaps 120 millions of cubic yards of water, cost £38,000 and yielded an additional Revenue of £10,000 in the fourth year from the commencement; showing the cost of the water to be thus about 8,000 cubic yards per Rupee (2*s.*), allowing 4 per cent. for interest of capital, and the returns in Revenue to Government being about 26 per cent., or probably 100 per cent. in all, as Capt. Smith estimates the benefit to the people, at nearly three times the amount of increase of Revenue to Government.*

* The scope and success of Colonel Dixon's measures, have been sufficiently indicated in the preceding pages. Though much was done by his predecessor for the civilization of the Mairs, yet undoubtedly all this was most precarious, and their subsistence and employment were dependent upon most uncertain seasons; and the development of a great system of irrigation works, (by which the falling rain is economized to the utmost and distributed in time and place of need, instead of sweeping down the valleys and passing away in a useless torrent) has been the means of giving permanence and advancement to the people.

It is of the utmost importance to observe, that these, as well as other isolated improvements by means of water, have been made solely in consequence of the earnest applications of the local officers, or the subordinate Boards; and this is the evident reason why there has been no general system of irrigation improvements, carried on throughout the whole of India. Not only have these works not been suggested or ordered by the authorities at home, in the first instance; but even these wonderful results from every isolated case of improvement, have been totally insufficient to awaken the authorities to a sense of the importance of the subject.

Who would not suppose that such cases as these, of Marwarree and Ajmere, would at least lead to the question being asked, "May not these magnificent results, calculated "to benefit the people so immeasurably, and at once to re-"leave us from our intolerable load of anxiety about the "finances, be obtained by like means throughout India?" What has as yet been done in this way, has always been done at the personal risk of the individual, who has had no better knowledge of his own interests, than to insist upon this extravagant expenditure; and no one has yet been found bold enough to propose, that in addition to a Board of Revenue, (Collectors,) a Military Board, and a Judicial Board, there should be a Board of Irrigation and Navigation to facilitate the provision of the Revenue collected, and by which themselves and all the rest were to be paid. And yet until the matter is seen so far in its true light, as to lead to the appointment of such a Board, India will never flourish.

By these works the country has been fortified against the miseries of famine; tracts of wild jungle have been converted into fertile fields, dotted with villages and alive with rural industry; population and revenue have more than doubled; families which for generations had abandoned their native hills, have returned to seek their traditional landmarks; the inducement to constant migration and unsettled habits done away, and a taste acquired for the sweets of profitable toil. The wild unmastered Caterans of 1820 are thus found to have become in 1843, a thrifty, thriving, peaceful, and industrious peasantry, an example to their neighbours whose terror they once were.—*Captain B. Smith, p.* 425.

Sketch of water transit system for India.

It may be well here to say something specific about a system of water transit for India, though the data for such a project are at present very insufficient.

It would not suit this paper, to go systematically into the principles on which lines of communications should be selected, but we may just refer to the one fundamental principle which must ever be kept in view; viz., that each river basin will in general be the natural field of a system of communications complete in itself; the basis of the system being a main line leading generally along the line of the river, from near its source to the port at its mouth: because the densest part of the population is generally along that line, and there being great interchange of commodities produced in coast districts or imported from foreign countries, and those produced in the higher lands and either consumed by inhabitants near the coast, or exported. In providing communications for a vast extent of country like India, which is as yet entirely without them, we have the immeasurable advantage of a clear field on which we may bring to bear the great principles of science, with less interruption than in countries of smaller extent, where the natural course of things has already been interfered with by partial and isolated works, forming no necessary part of a well digested system.

A map of India, coloured according to the river basins, and marked by contour lines, is one of the first things to be provided before planning communications generally for this country; for with this before us, we shall always be reminded when we are inclined to work against nature.

We may point out with respect to the main features in the present case:

1st. That the river Ganges, with its branches the Gogra, Jumna, Chumbul, &c., the Burmpootra and other rivers in

Bengal and the North-west, as also the Mahanuddy, the Godavery with its branches, the Wurda, Weingunga, Indrawuttee, &c., the Kistnah (with its branches, the Beema, &c., from near the western ghauts as low down as Kurnool) and the Cauvery, have all such moderate falls (from ½ to 2 feet per mile) that they are already navigable for a part of the year, and could be made navigable throughout the whole year, at a comparatively moderate expense. To these perhaps may be added the Taptee and Nerbudda ; but of these the falls are greater, and they would therefore require a greater expenditure. At any rate however, at least 5,000 and perhaps 6,000 or 7,000 miles of navigation could thus be obtained ; and at the same cost as 100 or 200 miles of high speed railway. The Kistnah below Kurnool has a greater fall, and might require considerable works ; or else we might substitute a canal or low speed railway for 140 miles.

2nd. That there is a vast extent of country in India so favorable to the construction of such works, that many thousand miles of first class steam canals, might be constructed at the rate of Rs. 6,000 (£600) a mile, and under.

3rd. That Rs. 15,000 (£1,500) a mile for canals, would be sufficient to provide for their being carried almost entirely throughout the populous parts of the country.

4th. That the various systems of navigation in the basins of the different rivers, where the water sheds are too high to allow of the construction of canals without excessive expense, might be connected with each other by means of low speed railways ; so as to provide for very cheap conveyance of goods from every part of India to the other. Thus, goods might be conveyed by one kind of navigation from Cape Comorin to Nagpore, and then by a cheap railway across the basin of the Nerbudda to meet the system of navigation of Central India, the North-west and Punjaub ; so that by means of two continuous lines of water communication, 1,400 and 800 miles long respectively, connected by 300 miles of railway, goods could be cheaply conveyed for a distance of 2,500 miles; and allowing $\frac{1}{3}$ P. ($\frac{1}{18}$*d.*) per ton per mile for the water transit, and 2 P. ($\frac{1}{4}$*d.*) for the land transit, the cost would be only Rs. 9 (18*s.*) per ton for the whole distance; not more than equal to the present cost of conveying a ton of goods 50 miles, in most parts of the country.

It must be particularly pointed out however, that the connection of the different systems of navigation with each other, is a matter of comparatively very small importance; the transfer of goods from one river basin to another being an insignificant matter, compared with the collection of the produce of each basin and its conveyance to the coast, and the carriage of produce from the coast and its distribution through the basin. Thus, the communication across the water sheds, will always have a very small traffic compared with that on the communications leading from the upper parts of basins to the coast; and this brings us to another point, which seems to have been wonderfully misapprehended in the great question of communication. We hear continually of a railway from Bombay to Calcutta, or Agra, or Madras, though in point of fact, the connection of these places with each other, are matters of so small importance, that it ought not at present to be thought of. How many tons of goods, and even how many passengers would pass from one of those places to the other, as compared with the number passing from the interior of the country to each Presidency? I think we are safe in saying, not 1 ton of goods to a 100, and not 1 passenger to 50? No doubt one thing that has led very much to this misapprehension, is the political and military point of view in which this as well as all other Indian questions, have hitherto been viewed: and it is certainly a matter of importance that we should have the means of moving troops rapidly from one part of India to another, but still there are other considerations of moment.

1st. This even is chiefly a question of economy; that is, the object in view is to economize, by rendering a smaller force sufficient for defence, and if while making a certain line of railway to save a lack of Rupees a year in expenditure on soldiers, we are neglecting another line, by means of which we could obtain an increase of income of ten lacks by extended sale of produce, this is of course false economy. It is just the old mistake which has pervaded our whole Indian system, of thinking a hundred times as much about 1 lack (£10,000) of expenditure, as of 100 lacks (£1,000,000) of income; for the idea always seems to have been, that if we can only retard the money in oozing out, it will come in of itself without our help.

2nd. Even as respects military purposes, the transfer of troops from one capital to another, is comparatively of little importance; the point to be kept continually in view while we have an unimproved country of 1¼ million of square miles before us, is not, "Is such a work wanted? won't it be very beneficial? or will it pay?" but rather, "Is it the most important work we can have for our time and money?" Nor is the question "Will it diminish our yearly expenses?" but rather, "Will it either diminish our expenses, or increase our income, *more than any thing else?*" This is the first question with beggars such as we are; and when we have taken off the rough edge of our difficulties, by seizing every opening for obtaining great returns at a small cost, (with which a totally unimproved country must necessarily abound) then we may take in hand secondary projects.

North and South lines in the Peninsula, and lines about the water sheds in the interior will generally be quite out of the question at present, at least for railways; but it must not be forgotten that what may be very bad policy in a line of railway, may still be good for a canal for two reasons.

First, because of the difference in the cost of construction and of working; for goods may be carried 100 or 200 miles round by water, without much disadvantage, because the cost of transit is extremely small, whereas on a railway it will be a much more serious item. It is not at all likely that any very large quantity of goods would bear transferring from one Coast of the Peninsula to the other by railway, but this is quite supposable by canal.

The second reason is the great value of water, for irrigation and other purposes. A canal 25 yards broad and 3 deep, will, with a fall of 1 inch a mile, have a current of 1,200 yards an hour, and convey 90,000 cubic yards per hour: sufficient for 30,000 to 90,000 acres of rice; and in a great proportion of cases it will be most profitable to use the water for both navigation and irrigation, as is now done in the Godavery and Kistnah works. In planning communications for India, it must never be forgotten, that *every puddle is a valuable thing in a tropical climate in the dry season,* and thus every mile of canal throughout the country is entirely independent of the advantages of navigation, an incalculable blessing. It is true that this is one of the things, that a man who has never been out of England cannot fully realize; but if every man who takes a part in Indian affairs, were only to take a few walks in the middle of the day, with a land wind blowing, and the thermometer at 110°, he would have a very strong impression of the advantages of canals and tanks. Unfortunately however, even some Englishmen who have passed 20 or 30 years in India, have never taken this sort of practical lesson in Hydraulics; whilst the Natives who have, wonder that their rulers show so little interest about Hydraulic works, and even leave so many of the old ones in ruins.

As regards railways, even supposing 1,000 miles to be laid, it should not be in one continuous line the centre part of which would certainly have very little traffic, but should rather be laid in short lines of 100 or 200 miles, leading direct from ports to the interior, or from the interior to a canal. Thus, in the projected railway from Madras to the Western Coast near Cochin, the centre 200 miles running nearly N. and S. and along the trade shed of the country, will not have a twentieth part of the traffic on it, that it would have if laid on some line or lines leading from the coast into the interior. Even if the Government care nothing about these points, what will the shareholders say, to the returns on their whole capital being reduced in consequence of these barren portions of the line, to a quarter of what they might otherwise be? Our first object is then, to select those lines on which there is or would be the greatest traffic, rather than to aim at long lines, a great part of which would be comparatively unimportant; and to that end, let every line be brought distinctly to this test, viz., the probable amount of traffic on it. There can be no use in connecting two great places, if comparatively few goods or persons pass from one to the other. The main question is, *not* whether a certain line would be useful? but whether it be in proportion to its cost the *most* useful one we could undertake?

It is also to be observed, that the natural lines are often not the shortest; there are certain natural obstacles which cannot be altogether got rid of, though means may be found greatly to diminish the expense of passing through or over them; and though the force of gravity cannot be removed, the inconveniences caused by it may no doubt be greatly mitigated.

With so vast an extent of country under one paramount authority, and with the experience we now have from different countries, in irrigation, river and canal navigation, railways of different classes, and in harbour works, we ought to be able to plan such a system of communications and other works for India, as has never yet been seen in the world; and thus certainly make a near approach to that grand desideratum, *the annihilation of cost of transit.* If canals be used for irrigation as well as navigation, there can be no doubt that they will abundantly pay the interest of the money expended on their construction and repairs ; thus leaving as the cost of transit on them, only the bare expense of draft. By actual calculation from the data we have, it appears that on canals 6 feet deep and provided with locks 150 feet by 15, and with the low cost of fuel generally throughout India ($\frac{1}{3}$ Rupee a ton of wood), the actual cost of transit on long lines worked by steam would be, if the vessels have constant employment, about $\frac{1}{4}$ P. per ton per mile, or 1 Rupee per 800 miles, including interest on boats and engines at 10 per cent., wear and tear, &c. It appears from calculation, that the rate which will give a minimum cost of freight with steam power, in vessels of the size for the above locks, is about 5 miles an hour through still-water, and that a rate of 6 miles an hour would add very little to the cost ; so that allowing for delays at locks, the most economical speed for goods, where the trade is extensive, would be upwards of 100 miles a day (the canals being worked by night as well as day); and there is only a very small proportion of goods for which it would be worth while to pay a higher rate for conveyance 500 miles in one day, than the same distance in five days. This is partly proved by canals in England, which on the principal lines carry as much as $\frac{2}{10}$ of the goods, notwithstanding the higher speed of railways ; and although, owing to the canals and locks not having been made for steam power, the rate of transit is only about 2 miles an hour.

As some however may still object to the use of steam canals, on the ground that it has been tried in England and has not succeeded, it may be well to answer this objection here.

1st. Steam cannot be used on the old canals, for the simple reason that they were not made for it.

2nd. The Canada canals are navigated by 300 ton Steamers, at the rate of 6 or 7 miles an hour for goods.

3rd. The grand difficulty in England, viz., injury to the banks from the ripple, would be easily removed here; as it would not cost more than £200 a mile, to line them throughout with stone. And though canals not made for steam, cannot be worked by means of it, this is no reason why canals should not be made suitably for this power. The objection that locks cause so much detention, is equally untenable; it is true that locks made so as to take five minutes to fill and empty, do cause much detention; but there is no reason at all why a lock should not be filled in a few seconds, and the detention thus reduced to little more than the mere stopping and starting the boat. Where the traffic is very great, as it would be on some lines in India, separate locks should be made for the swift traffic, with all the necessary arrangements for a quick passage through them, without the smallest hinderance from the slow traffic. Such a canal would accommodate an almost unlimited extent of traffic, and if we reduce the cost of transit to ⅛ P. per ton per mile, we must be prepared for a traffic beyond any thing we have any idea of at present. It is in this respect especially that the necessity for canals will be seen. A traffic of 5 million tons a year, or 17,000 tons a day, on a canal fitted for boats of 170 tons, would only require a boat to pass the locks once in a quarter of an hour, and by the addition of a second lock, any amount of traffic might be provided for; and the repairs of the canal would not increase in proportion to the traffic. Now to accommodate such a traffic by railway, would require perhaps 5 lines of rails; but they would not indeed really be required, because railways never could be worked at so low a rate of toll, as to lead to so free a traffic. Some of the railways in England seem to have nearly reached the maximum of traffic (to judge from the accidents) though carrying only 200,000 tons a year; while some of the petty canals there, worked only by horses and furnished only with single locks, carry a million tons a year and upwards, and are probably capable of carrying much more. All plans for improved communications in India, that do not keep in view this main point, viz., the vast extent of traffic that will arise in consequence of the cost of transit being reduced as it ought to be, will be found equally inefficient; and there is not the slightest prospect of the high speed railways providing for any enormous traffic.

Erroneous ideas regarding Irrigation.

It seems of importance yet to speak on some further points connected with the use of water in India, and though it is of course impossible to meet beforehand all the erroneous ideas of persons quite unacquainted with the subject, which being the fruits of the imagination are innumerable, yet, amongst the many strange fancies prevalent in regard to irrigation, some of the most popular may be usefully remarked upon.

One is, that well irrigation should be encouraged; and even that the Government should dig wells for that purpose. It is however surely a sufficient answer on this point, to refer to the calculations given in the preceding pages, which show that the mere raising of filtered water from wells 12 to 15 feet, without including the expense incurred on account of the well, costs about 1 Rupee for 500 or 600 cubic yards; while water of much superior quality may be applied to the land by means of tanks and river channels, at a cost of 1 Rupee for from 20,000 to 40,000 cubic yards, or from $\frac{1}{40}$ to $\frac{1}{80}$ the cost of merely raising it from wells. Instead therefore of encouraging the people to construct private wells, at such an enormous waste of money, Government should do their utmost to render such waste impracticable, by providing water every where, and selling it at $\frac{1}{40}$ the cost, at which it can be obtained from wells.

Another fancy is, that tanks should be *cleared out*, that is that their beds should be excavated from time to time. Now it is evident, that for every cubic yard of earth thus excavated, one cubic yard of water per annum will be obtained; so that if 1*d*. per cubic yard be paid for excavation, and the interest of money be 4 per cent., we shall have to pay $\frac{1}{25}d$. per annum for every cubic yard of water, or 1 Rupee for 576 cubic yards; while it would cost only $\frac{1}{50}$ of that sum to obtain the same quantity of water by raising the old bund or making a new tank. "Then do you mean to say, that tanks are never to be *cleared out?*" Certainly not; that can never be done with advantage or economy, as it costs fifty times as much as the work is worth: but as tanks become filled up, their bunds must be raised, if they are to contain the same quantity of water. It seems not to be generally known, that excepting in tanks supplied by very small streams near their sources, the process of silting up is very slow; but be it slow or quick however, it should not be remedied by excavation, on account of the disproportionate cost.

Another of these apprehensions is, that it is a waste of money to expend it on magnificent works like those of the Godavery, and that money might be much more economically laid out, on a multitude of small works. On the contrary, however, it may be laid down as a general rule with respect to irrigation works, (as indeed with most things) that the larger the scale on which they are executed, the greater will be the proportional results. Further, a Delta offers peculiar facilities for irrigation, as it stands to reason that water can be distributed over a plain without undulations and with only a moderate slope in one direction of a foot a mile, far more cheaply than over a more uneven country; and no tract in India could probably be found, where water can be distributed at so small a cost, as in the Deltas of the Godavery and Kistnah, excepting indeed the Delta of the Ganges. Again, the Delta lands are generally the richest, and therefore will pay best for the supply of a given quantity of water; there is also the largest population in a given space, and consequently the water communications will provide for a greater traffic; and lastly, the larger the river the greater the extent of country it drains, and consequently the more certain is the supply of water.

Another popular idea is, that tanks are uncertain works for irrigation, and that river channels alone can be fully depended on. This is true in a certain sense; that is, small tanks filled by streams which only drain a small extent of country, are uncertain, and fail whenever there is a great failure of the local rains: and this is the case with $\frac{99}{100}$ of the old tanks of the country. But in the first place almost all these could be supplied at a moderate expense from the large rivers; and that this has not been done throughout the country, is one of the most grievous neglects of the British rule; and in the second place, not only ought all tanks to be supplied from large rivers, but the tanks ought to be almost universally of great capacity. The Natives from their peculiar circumstances, were generally compelled to make a multitude of these petty works; but this is no excuse for us, who have ample means and power to construct them on any scale. The sources of the great rivers of the Peninsula which never fail entirely, are all within the British dominions; and there need therefore be no want of water, as large tanks if connected with the great rivers, would always contain water all the year round. Many of the old tanks are noble works, both in respect of size and supply, some capable of containing 100 million cubic yards of water, and having very expensive channels led from the great rivers; but even they are not sufficient, and what we should now do is to construct tanks of far larger dimensions than any now existing; in the same way as we have formed systems of channel irrigation, on a scale far beyond the old Native works. The only novelty that I know of, to be introduced in the construction and use of these large tanks, is this: instead of irrigating lands immediately below their bunds (as is universally done in the old tanks) rather to discharge water into rivers when they are low, for the supply of any systems of channel irrigation connected with them. Every part of the country should be thus furnished with vast tanks, to be filled in the heavy bursts of the monsoon, and the water gradually discharged into the rivers according as they become too low; so as to keep up the supply of water for the irrigated land. Such tanks should contain from 1,000 to 5,000 million cubic yards; that is, tanks 50 yards deep and from 16 to 80 square miles in area, or from 2 miles broad by 8 long, to 5 miles broad by 16 long, would store water at a cost perhaps almost as low as that of the Delta irrigation, and would never fail. It is too late now, to use the old argument against these works, that no body ever heard of such things, after the execution of the Ganges canals 850 miles long, and the Godavery weir 2½ miles long. It is only proposed to do that with respect to tanks, which has already been done with respect to river channels; and with our Western knowledge and unbounded means, we should not think ourselves bound to *follow* the Natives, who had not a thousandth part of our advantages, and who, we may be quite sure from what they have done in times past, would not have followed such an example as we have set, if they had had our advantages. I doubt whether India has ever for a hundred years together, been destitute of men, who if only possessed of our science and resources, would have been ashamed to leave the country in the state in which we now see it.

Another idea is, that to supply navigable still-water canals with water all the year round, would be next to impossible; but this too is without the slightest foundation either of experience or calculation. The consumption of water in such a work would be from the following causes:

1st. Evaporation.
2d. Absorption.
3d. Lockage.

The evaporation in the Peninsula is about 2 yards a year, after deducting the fall of rain; that is, the difference between the fall of rain and the evaporation, is about 2 yards. A mile of canal 30 yards broad would therefore require 1,760 × 30 × 2 yards = 100,000 cubic yards per annum, which would require (at 1,000 cubic yards per Rupee (2*s.*) a capital of Rs. 100 (£10) a mile so that if the canal cost Rs. 10,000 (£1,000) a mile, the providing for the evaporation would cause an additional first outlay of one per cent., or, the annual cost of the water would be Rs. 4 (8*s.*) a mile (4 per cent. on Rs. 100 (£10) equivalent to a charge of $\frac{1}{10,000}d.$ per ton per mile, on a million tons per annum. This is one of the principal supposed obstacles to the construction of navigable canals in India.

We have abundance of experience on this point of absorption, from the innumerable tank bunds and channel banks now existing. The fact is, that if the slopes are sufficiently gentle for the silt to lodge, every Hydraulic work puddles itself immediately. I have seen a channel cut through the loosest sand, widened by cutting a trench by its side within a yard of the water's edge, and to the depth of 5 feet, without the least moisture being found in the excavation; so perfectly water-tight was the lining of silt that the channel had furnished itself with. The loss from this cause also would therefore be insignificant.

As regards Lockage. A lock 150 feet by 50, and with a fall of 3 yards, would require 2,500 cubic yards of water to pass a boat; and if the navigation were 100 miles in length in one slope (a very moderate supposition), it would require 25 cubic yards per boat per mile; as it is evident that a lockfull would be expended in the whole line. If the boats were of 200 tons, this would be $\frac{1}{8}$ cubic yard of water per ton per mile; which, supposing the water to cost (as elsewhere calculated) 20,000 cubic yards per Rupee (2*s.*), would be equivalent to a charge of $\frac{1}{160,000}$ Rupee or $\frac{1}{7,000}d.$ per ton of goods per mile. Or, the total quantity of water required for a million tons per annum would be 125,000 cubic yards for 100 miles, or 1,250 cubic yards per mile per annum; to store which would require a capital of Rs. $1\frac{1}{4}$ (2*s*.-6*d*.).

Such are the most serious obstacles that have yet been discovered to the establishment of permanent navigable canals in India. The total charge of transit on account of the cost of water might be (according to the above calculations,) $\frac{1}{3,000}d.$ per ton per mile, or 1 Rupee (2*s*.) for a ton carried 70,000 miles; so that if it were ten times as much as I have calculated, it would still be of no perceptible importance.

More of these fancied difficulties might be mentioned; but the explanations given above, will be sufficient to show those not conversant with the subject, that other difficulties which occur to them, may be capable of an equally complete and satisfactory solution.

Navigation and Irrigation Board.

Returning to the question of the necessity of appointing a Board of Irrigation and Navigation, we must observe that the plan now proposed, of placing an individual nominally at the head of the Department of Public Works, which in reality makes the Government Council itself the Board of works, will we fear aggravate all the former evils. Such questions *must* be *discussed*; they *must* be examined by both Engineers and Civilians, and consequently if there be only one individual at the head of the department, the Governor in Council will discuss them: and as the Council have fifty other things to do, every one of which they will think of more importance than tanks and canals, the latter will still be considered as mere bye-works, and the business will fall usually into the hands of a Secretary, who will not be the ostensible and responsible person. Of the absurdity of making the Council a Board of Works, and thus giving it duties to do which are quite foreign to it, we have a convincing proof in the case of the rejection of a proposed work, under the idea that a Lock would oblige all the boats to wait for the return of the tide, and would let all the water out of the canal when it was opened. Not being conversant in such matters, the Councillors did not know, that a Lock was a work to allow boats to pass, and keep the water in.

Nothing will do but a Board consisting of two or three persons besides an Engineer, *who shall have nothing else to attend to whatever*, but irrigation and communications; and this board should be charged with *all* works of this nature, and their whole thoughts, time and energies, should be concentrated upon this duty. Public Works never can be properly attended to till this is done, and it is impossible that the appointment of a single Engineer to such a charge should answer the purpose. Let the petty details connected with buildings, and especially all the minute pottering about Military buildings, be kept out of the hands of this Board, in order that they may be able to give all their time and energies to the fundamental and all-important general duties connected with Public Works throughout the country. But in order to prevent the confusion at present arising from there being in Madras no less than five different departments employed about these works, (besides the department of Military Buildings,) let them all be under the general control of this Board and subordinate to it; the executive and supervisory part however being confided to two distinct classes of officers, who have no part in the Board itself.

There are at present; 1st, The Board of Revenue, in charge of works of irrigation and part of the communications. 2nd, The Department of Roads; certain great trunk roads being nominally under a single Superintendent, but in reality immediately under the Governor in Council as a Board of Trunk Roads, with the Superintendent of Roads really an executive officer under them. 3rd, The Railway

Department, also under the Governor in Council, with an Officer as Consulting Engineer. 4th, The Electric Telegraph Department, on the same footing. 5th, The Paumbam Channel Works, under the Chief Engineer subordinate to the Governor in Council. The consequence of this confusion, is, that while one department is cutting a canal, and another a railway, a third is very busy making a grand road parallel with each. Fancy a private household in which the groom was entrusted with a small part of the cooking, the housemaid with another small portion, a third being entrusted to the butler, and the remainder left to the cook herself, excepting that which the master of the house in his wisdom kept in his own hands. Let any one imagine to themselves the utter confusion which would prevail in such an establishment, and they may then form an idea of the state of things in India, in connection with Public Works; where the Government is employed partly in trying to regulate a state of things essentially productive of nothing but disorder, and partly in doing itself some of the work belonging to the humblest subordinate executive officers.

The curse of the Indian system, is the continual effort on the part of the superior authorities to do every thing themselves, and to meddle with matters of detail for which they have neither time nor experience, and this is felt sufficiently even where a Board has charge of a Department. Not only is an individual not allowed to *do* any thing, but not even to *speak;* he is courteously told that his remarks are quite uncalled for, and if not then silenced, other more effectual means are taken to prevent his making known the results of his experience, local knowledge, &c.

Great objections have been made to Boards as being a machinery very slow in its operation; but matters *must* be discussed, and there need be no delay connected with a Board beyond what is really necessary from the nature of the subject under consideration, unless the Board be composed of inefficient men, or have executive duties in detail imposed on them, foreign to their proper functions. Undoubtedly a Board composed of ex-officio men, that is, of men having other duties to attend to, and who were not selected for the specific purpose on account of their qualifications, is an utter abomination. The Members of the Board we propose, should be *selected* for the peculiar duties of the Irrigation and Public Works department, and then if the arrangement does not work well the remedy is in the hands of Government, and is very simple; it is only to turn the members out, and put better men in their place. It is not to be supposed that a man is to be put into an office of such importance, and then to be considered immoveable. While he holds the office he should be treated as a gentleman, and a man of sense, honesty and capacity; but if he be found not to be so, then he should be at once replaced by one who is. The system of keeping a man through thick and thin in such a situation, and then gagging him and treating him at every step as a fool, and a man not fit to be trusted with 5 Rupees (10*s.*), will never do for a Board of Public Works, such as is now required in India. The Board must be left in a great measure to manage things their own way, a large portion of the outlay being left entirely at their own disposal, and Government only requiring constant reports of proceedings and results; every source of delay being avoided as far as possible, and especially that the greatest of all sources of delay, viz., superannuated members.

When we consider the magnitude of the field, and the trifling sum yet spent as compared with the outlay required, we are surely warranted in asserting, that Public Works have been almost entirely neglected throughout India. The work that ought to have been spread over the last hundred years, must therefore if we wish to redeem our character, be done in the next ten; and to accomplish this, will call for the utmost energies of men in full possession of all their faculties. Hitherto, the only mistake of any consequence that has not been guarded against, is that of *doing nothing*. The Board of Public Works ought to have written on the paper-stand in front of each Member and Secretary, in large letters, "Do IT, DO IT, DO IT." The motto hitherto has been, "*Do nothing, have nothing done, let no-" "body do any thing. Bear any loss, let the people die of" "famine, let hundreds of lacks be lost in Revenue, for want" "of water, or roads, rather than DO any thing.*" It is not the loss of money that we mind; that is nothing, we can afford to lose millions every year for want of Hydraulic works, and therefore to spend a few lacks of Rupees on such works would of course be nothing; but, nothing must be *done*. Before any thing is *done*, a matter must be brought before the Collector,* who has charge of the welfare and in a great measure the lives of a million of people, and of a Revenue of 30 or 40 lacks (£300,000 or £400,000) a year; but is still not permitted to spend £100 without superior sanction. He hands it on therefore, to the Board of Revenue: but they have no power to sanction an expenditure of £100. It then travels on from the Board of Revenue to

* This misnomer was pointed out more than thirty years ago, by Sir Thomas Munro. "He," said that great man, "who is called collector, exercises the whole of the internal administration of the province. His" "designation is an unfortunate one, and ought to be changed, as it leads" "to the belief that the collection of the revenue is his sole duty, and that" "he is a mere tax-gatherer; but the collection of the revenue is a very" "subordinate part of his duty; it extends to every branch of the finance," "and its influence is felt in the prosperity of the inhabitants. He watches" "the operation of the different existing taxes, points out such as are oppressive, that they may be lowered, or altogether abolished. In every" "country the amount and distribution of taxation are perhaps the most" "important concerns of public authority; there are no others on which," "as on them, the universal comfort and prosperity of the people depend." "In this country the management of taxation rests almost entirely with" "the collector; for he is the only channel through which the Government" "can obtain any tolerable correct information on the subject, and it is" "chiefly from his opinions that their own must be formed."

the Local Council; but the hands of that Council are tied if the project involves an expenditure beyond £1,000, so it must be passed on to the Supreme Council, who, dead to the wants and interests of those extensive kingdoms called "Minor Presidencies," are glad enough to avoid the inconveniences and responsibilites of expenditure, by referring the project to the Authorities at home: and on its arrival there, it has to undergo the ordeal of two more Boards, the consequence of which is, that nothing or next to nothing has been done, in comparison with what is needed.

Now it should be remembered, that even the youngest of the authorities mentioned above, have, owing to the effects of climate and advancing years, almost ceased to be men of action; and every step the matter is carried upwards, it gets more into the region of *counsel*, and more out of the reach of *action*, and has consequently less and less chance of being carried into execution. In the superior Boards and Councils, there is generally not a trace of that physical energy, which is essential to produce real healthy and vigorous action; and this habitual exclusion of men in the prime of life (we must except an occasional young Governor General), is undoubtedly one of the principal if not the principal defect of a system, which has led to the exhibition of the extraordinary phenomenon of the most inert, stationary, decrepid management of a country that was ever seen, by the most advanced and energetic race that has yet appeared in the world.

Who would not suppose, from the excessive precautions regarding expenditure mentioned above, that at least fifty districts had been ruined by works of irrigation and communication, and that now the only fear was, that anything further should be *done?* Who would believe that without half a dozen miles of real turnpike road, with communications generally in much the same state as in England two centuries ago, with periodical famines and a stagnant Revenue, the stereotyped answer to any one who urges on improvement is, "He is too much in a hurry," "He is too sanguine," "We must go on by degrees;" and this, too, in the face of the fact, that money laid out upon public works in India, has almost without exception, yielded money returns of 100, 200, 300 per cent., besides immeasurable other advantages to the community.

What should we think of the owner of a heavily mortgaged, but improveable estate in England, who, with means at his command of doubling his income, should be afraid of arriving at that result "too soon?" And yet the only difference between the private landlord in England and the public landlord in India, is, that whilst the one may have an interest in a single square mile, the interest of the other extends over a million of square miles. The more extensive the field is, surely the greater is the need for energy and enterprise. We have already all but lost one century, to the great damage of our finances, and the great injury of the people; and shall we now lose another century, by continuing to crawl, or shall we not rather make a strenuous effort to redeem the time we have lost, by working double tides, until we have fully developed the resources of our magnificent estate? The millions that we are about to spend upon a few costly and high speed railways, would suffice to accomplish that far more important object, to the great profit of the shareholders, of the people of India, and of the public treasury.

Precautions enough have assuredly hitherto been taken, against that dreaded thing, *action;* but no doubt such complication of means are necessary, so completely to keep down that innate energy of Englishmen which commonly breaks through all restraints; and it must be granted that no such success of this kind was ever achieved before. To keep down 5,000 or 6,000 Englishmen so effectually in the midst of such demands for exertion, and with the prospect of such results before them—a large proportion of them too, faithful and conscientious men who cannot bear to see the impoverished state of the people—this is no slight task, and to have succeeded in it, no doubt deserves the highest applause. The success has however not been so complete as could have been wished, after all. This irrepressible energy *has* oozed out here and there, and produced the few good results we have seen; and if I mistake not, these are sufficient too at length to rouse England to say; "This state of "things is at end. India shall no longer be kept in this "degraded state; effectual measures shall now be taken to "ensure to her a participation in those blessings which we "ourselves enjoy; and we will find men who will enter "heart and soul upon this great work."

APPENDIX.

*Conclusions.**

UPON the whole the main points connected with the question of communications for India, seem to be the following—

1st. That the great point of all to be kept in view, is, not to make the most perfect communication possible on some few hundred miles in the course of 20 or 30 years, leaving the remaining 100,000 miles untouched; but rather, to adopt a system of communications, by which the principal part of the cost of transit will be saved, to be executed throughout the whole country, in the shortest possible time.

2nd. That in order to accomplish this, we must for the present be content with less perfect communications than high speed railways; because it is impossible that the country can be covered with such, even on a few main lines only, within a hundred years.

3rd. That cheap railways and good common roads, will have the effect of greatly reducing the present cost of transit; the latter taking off about one-half, and the former probably much more; besides giving us a speed of 200 miles a day for first class travellers, and from 50 to 100 for goods.

4th. That a great extent of river navigation may be improved, and canals cut at a moderate expense, say from Rs. 1,000 (£100) to Rs. 3,000 (£300) a mile, so as to reduce the cost of transit on such lines, by nine-tenths.

* These Conclusions having appeared in the London Edition, are inserted almost verbatim in the Indian Edition, without having had the advantage of Colonel Cotton's revision, prior to embarkation for England.—*Note by the Publisher.*

5th. That the proposed rate of $2\frac{3}{4}d.$ or nearly 2 Annas per ton per mile for conveyance on the Bombay railroad, is really absurd; and that in order to give any thing like effectual relief to India, we must reduce the cost of transit to one-tenth of that sum, viz., 2 P. (about $\frac{1}{4}d.$) per ton which, (even without reckoning the difference in the value of money,) will correspond with about $1\frac{1}{4}d.$ per ton per mile in England; because an article must be carried at least five miles in India, for one mile that it is carried in England.

6th. That the rate of $2\frac{3}{4}d.$ per ton per mile, on a railroad that has cost Rs. 120,000 (£12,000) a mile, is actually three times the rate at which goods are now conveyed on the grand trunk road in Bengal; and half as much again as on the western road at Madras, which is still in quite an imperfect state.

7th. That in general throughout India, goods can be conveyed on good common roads, at an average of about 8 P. (1*d.*) per ton, exclusive of carriers' profit and interest, even as things are now managed; but that under European management they would be certainly carried for less.

8th. That with a traffic of 100,000 tons per annum on a common road costing Rs. 5,000 (£500) per mile, the interest at 10 per cent. would be 1 P. ($\frac{1}{8}d.$), repairs also 1 P., and allowing the same (1 P.) for carriers' profit, the total cost, including the above average of 8 P. (1*d.*) would be 11 P. or say $1\frac{1}{3}d.$; about half of what it is proposed to charge on the Bombay railroad.

9th. That on a cheap railroad worked by cattle, the cost of transit would certainly be less than a quarter of that on a common road; say about $\frac{1}{4}d.$ a ton including every thing.

10th. That on a steam canal, the cost of transit would not exceed $\frac{1}{2}$ P. ($\frac{1}{16}d.$) per ton, and the interest and repairs would not exceed $\frac{1}{2}$ P. more; or in all 1 P. ($\frac{1}{8}d.$) per ton per mile.

11th. That on an improved river with a constant depth of 3 feet, the cost of transit would not exceed 2 P. ($\frac{1}{4}$*d.*) per ton per mile, including every thing.

12th. That the average cost of transit in England may be taken at 1$\frac{1}{2}$*d.* per ton per mile; equivalent to 2 P. ($\frac{1}{4}$*d.*) in India, allowing for the difference in the value of money.

13th. That for every mile goods have to travel in England, they must be carried at least five miles in India.

14th. That the average value of goods carried in India, is much less than that of goods in England.

15th. Hence, that even if the cost of transit in India, were reduced to 2 P. ($\frac{1}{4}$*d.*) per ton per mile, it would still allowing for the difference in the value of money and in distance, be equivalent to five times the cost of transit in England; besides that cost being charged upon goods of inferior value, and therefore less able to bear it.

16th. That at present, the average cost of transit in India may be taken at 2$\frac{1}{2}$ Annas (3$\frac{3}{4}$*d.*) per ton per mile, which, allowing six-fold for difference in value of money, and five-fold for increased distance, is equivalent to 9*s.* 6*d.* a ton a mile in England, or 70 times what it is there: and that paid on less valuable goods.

17th. That a ton of cotton value £12 conveyed from Berar to Bombay, costs about £9 for transit, including interest, &c.; so that to convey it from the place of production to the place of shipment, adds 75 per cent. to its cost.

18th. That a ton of cloth, value suppose £40, conveyed from Manchester to Liverpool, costs only 5*s.* in conveyance from the place of production to that of shipment, equivalent to an ad valorem tax of only $\frac{5}{8}$ per cent. or not more than $\frac{1}{120}$ part of the tax paid by cotton in India; thus showing (as compared with 75 per cent.) the comparative state of transit in the two countries, taking into account increased cost per mile, increased time and risk, increased distance, and inferior value of goods.

19th. That there can be no sort of question, as to what is the main cause of the poverty and inertness of India, when we consider what would be the state of England, if the cost of transit there, were equivalent to an ad valorem duty on its goods 120 times greater than it now is.

20th. That in England, about 8 millions sterling, say $\frac{1}{7}$ of the whole amount of taxes, is paid for transit of goods, whilst in India probably not less than 15 millions sterling or about half of the amount of taxes, is paid for the same item.

21st. That allowing for the difference in the value of money, this sum (15 millions) is equivalent to 90 millions sterling in England; or eleven times the amount paid there for transit.

22d. That allowing the actual money cost of transit in India to be $3\frac{3}{4}$*d.* per ton per mile, or $2\frac{1}{2}$ times as much as in England, and the distances in India to be five times as great, $12\frac{1}{2}$ tons are carried in England at the same cost as 1 ton in India. And consequently that the 15 millions paid in India, indicates, for a population about six times as great, the transit of not more than one-fifth of the quantity of goods that the 8 millions paid in England gives; or, the proportion of goods moved in India, is, allowing for the difference of population, only $\frac{1}{30}$ of that moved in England. And undoubtedly, $\frac{29}{30}$ of the present traffic in England would be stopped, if attended with the same expense as in this country.

23d. That improved river navigation, canals, and cheap railways, could be formed to the extent of 20,000 miles, at an average cost of Rs. 3,500 (£350) a mile, or in all 7 millions sterling; which would provide for perhaps two-thirds of the present transit (the other third being conveyed by the feeders to the main lines,) and save $\frac{4}{5}$ of the present cost of transit, or 8 millions sterling per annum; but at these reduced rates, probably at least five times the quantity of goods now moved, would be carried.

24th. That a large proportion of this expenditure would be for iron, &c.; and as these canals and cheap railways might be begun at once in every district in India, they could be easily completed in five years.

25th. That 50,000 miles of cheap railway with temporary timber bridges at Rs. 3,000 (£300) a mile, could be made in the course of ten years at a cost of about 15 millions sterling; which would cause a saving of about 5 millions sterling in transit even on the present amount of traffic, and cause the traffic to increase perhaps four-fold, on all these lines.

26th. That if in this way, the grand point of the establishment of cheap transit throughout the country within a few years were secured, the present Railway Companies may if they please go on with their snail's-gallop of 20 miles a year, as that will do little harm; but if they are allowed to seal up any important lines of country to the present enormous rates of transit, or anything like it, they will do most serious mischief.

27th. That with respect to passenger traffic, the great mass must be carried at about 1 P. ($\frac{1}{8}d.$) a mile, or little will be gained.

28th. That if carried at this rate or less, the numbers will be immense. At present, over a vast extent of road there are from 1,000 to 3,000 travellers a day; and probably with an increased speed of from 20 to 100 miles a day, and a charge of only 1 P. ($\frac{1}{8}d.$) per mile, there would be a four-fold increase in the number.

39th. That the proportion of first class passengers, or those who can afford to pay much more for going at 700 miles a day than for going at 200, is utterly insignificant.

30th. That a speed of 200 miles a day for first class passengers and valuable goods, is abundantly sufficient for the present state of things in this country.

31st. That a very high speed is at present absolutely unattainable and in this respect the great railroads are a complete delusion; for in ten years, perhaps 500 miles at the utmost, may be opened, leaving the other 19,500 miles of main line, to be traversed at three miles an hour.

32d. That if we will be content with a moderate speed of 200 miles a day, we may have it all over India in 5 years; whereas, if we will not have this, we must for centuries to come go on at three miles an hour over the greater part of the country.

33d. That the present plan for opening India by high speed railroad, is like preparing a loaf by taking wheat grain by grain, and thus grinding, kneading, baking and eating it; so that with our food all the time before us, we are dying of famine. Thus, India will become more and more impoverished, while the railroads are constructing; and famine may even depopulate the country, before they are carried to any considerable extent.

34th. That the same money and time required to make one mile of high speed railway, will be sufficient to make 100 miles of good river navigation; 24 of first class steam canal, 12 of very good low speed railroad, 20 of an inferior kind of common road, and 40 of perfect common road with timber bridges, or 24 with masonry works.

35th. That we have to deal with a present direct burthen on the country in actual payments for transit, of probably at least 15 millions sterling a year, equal to three-fifths of the whole taxes; besides there being a loss of at least an equal amount, on goods not carried: in all 30 millions sterling, or much more than the whole revenue.

36th. That by a judicious expenditure on communications, such a portion of this may be saved, as will relieve the country to the extent of the whole of the present taxes; while its effects in stimulating traffic will be far greater than in the money saved.

37th. That the present railway between Bombay and Madras, if carried on at *both* ends at the rate of 10 miles a year, (as hitherto at the Bombay end,) will only be completed in 40 years, and will cost, for a single way, about 6 millions sterling, (Rs. 80,000 (£ 8,000) a mile for 300 miles); whilst in the meantime, there will have been spent on transit by the present tracks, about 16 millions sterling (Rs. 10,000 (£ 1,000) a year per mile, on 800 miles for half the time); sufficient to lay an excellent low speed railroad sixteen times over.

38th. That in a very rich country already provided with a complete system of *cheap transit, high speed of transit* is the grand object to be sought; but that in a very poor country, paralyzed by utter want of means of transit at a moderate cost, *speed in forming a general system of cheap transit,* is the grand desideratum to which every thing else should give way.

39th. That what is the best economy for a country like England, is ruinous to India in its present state; in the same way as a carriage and pair is the ruin of a young Apothecary with one patient a day, though it is a very economical expedient for a Physician with more patients than he can reach on foot.

40th. That a more effectual expedient could not have been fixed upon, to keep India in its present beggarly state, than to keep its rulers and all others interested in it amused with laying down annually 30 or 40 miles of fine railroads; while the whole country is starving for want of any thing in the shape of cheap communication of any kind.

41st. That one of the greatest evils India labours under, is the cumbrousness of its ruling apparatus; and to increase the difficulty, even railways are carried on under ten separate authorities.

1st. The Board of Controul,
2d. The Court of Directors,
3d. The General Government of India,
4th. The Local Government,
5th. The Shareholders,
6th. The Managing Committee at Home,

7th. The Consulting Engineer at Home,
8th. The Agent in India,
9th. The Government Inspecting Engineer,
10th. The Local Engineer.

And the progress hitherto, has been much what might be expected from such a complex system.

42d. That if we compare this, with the simple, effective plan followed in regard to the Electric Telegraph, the progress of which will no doubt correspond therewith—a single Officer, active in his movements as his own electric sparks, sent home to make all arrangements in direct communication with the Court—we can have no doubt as to which of the two plans is best suited to the circumstances of India, when demanding 100,000 miles, whether of communications or of Telegraph.

43d. That the interests of shareholders coincide with those of the country; as capital employed on cheap communications will return ten times that laid out on expensive ones. A lack of Rupees (£10,000) spent on a mile of high speed railway, would save Rs. 12,000 (£1,200) a year out of the Rs. 16,000 (£1,600) at present spent in the transit of 100,000 tons of goods: whereas, the same sum spent on 10 miles of cheap railway would save Rs. 100,000 (£10,000) a year; and if in both cases half the saving were taken by Government in tolls, the respective profits would still be 6, and 50 per cent.

44th. That the profits on money invested on common roads, would be as great as the above profit on cheap railways and much greater if invested in canals.

45th. That the field for employment of capital giving enormous returns, is unlimited in India; it is represented by 15 millions sterling clear saving that may be effected on the cost of the present transit; representing a capital of 150 millions at 10 per cent. The whole expenditure on railroads in England was about 200 millions sterling, yielding only 3 per cent. or 6 millions a year; and England has now before it a clear field for the employment of capital that will yield at least $2\frac{1}{2}$ times as much as the railway capital in England; and if content with only three or four times as much per cent. in profit as the English railways yield, the shareholders will still make India a present of many millions a year.

46th. That the present high-speed railways may demand 5,000 tons of rails a year, whilst the plan proposed of opening the country at once by means of cheap railways will take 50 or 100,000 tons a year; a quantity which must have a perceptible effect on the iron trade.

47th. That it is impossible to estimate the effects on England of throwing open all India by cheap transit, and relieving it from a burthen of 15 millions a year; thus making it at once a comparatively wealthy country, and universally a market for English manufactures.

48th. That all classes of people in Great Britain who care for the temporal and spiritual welfare of India, are interested in this undertaking. The East India Directors, the Abolitionists whose object is to take off the premium on slave labour by bringing in cheap Indian cotton, the Societies for spreading the Gospel through India, the Manchester, Sheffield, Birmingham, Yorkshire Manufacturers; is not almost every body in England in fact personally and deeply interested therein?

49th. That there is nothing to prevent this opening of the country being entered upon at once; the money, the materials, the country, the people, every thing is ready. The Court have but to issue the orders, and the communications may be commenced at one hundred points, and opened almost as soon as O'Shaughnessy can lay his Telegraph.

50th. That every thing depends upon our giving up this idol of *speed*. Besides some thousands of miles of good water communications, which can be had at a small outlay if speed is given up, cheap railways can be laid with steep gradients, sharp curves, light rails, a narrow guage, timber viaducts, &c., with little labour and at small cost; so that 3,000 or 4,000 miles can easily be completed in a year.

51st. That nobody is more interested in these cheap and rapidly laid railways, than the shareholders in the high speed railroad themselves; because by means of them, the great mass of the traffic may at once be brought upon such few miles of complete railroad as may be finished, instead of waiting for 40 or 50 years before one main line is completed. Wherever the high speed railway shareholders work therefore, they ought to begin by laying over the whole length of the line a cheap railway which would immediately give them enormous interest for their money.

52nd. That in respect of the main object in every country whether rich or poor, viz., *cheapness of transit*, nothing can compare with internal navigation; and that without this, a continental country must, owing to the great distances to be traversed in it, be almost entirely cut off from foreign commerce.

53rd. That even if there were railroads all over India, it would still be worth while, nay necessary, to open lines of navigation; because after all that can possibly be done with railroads, goods cannot be carried nearly so cheaply by rail, as by water.

54th. That generally the cost of transit by different communications in India may be thus estimated:

By the present unmade roads..........	3 As.	($4\frac{1}{2}$*d.*)
By perfect common roads..............	8 P.	(1*d.*)
By first class railroads (high speed)......	4 P.	($\frac{1}{2}$*d.*)
By cheap do. (low speed)......	2 P.	($\frac{1}{4}$*d.*)
By unimproved rivers................	4 P.	($\frac{1}{2}$*d.*)
By improved do.	2 P.	($\frac{1}{4}$*d.*)
By do. down stream............	1 P.	($\frac{1}{8}$*d.*)
By steam canals	$\frac{1}{2}$ P.	($\frac{1}{16}$*d.*)

55th. That the line of communication for goods between Europe and the upper valley of the Mississipi, depends entirely upon the inland water communications; whilst it is not in the least affected by the railway. The struggle is exclusively between the Erie and the St. Lawrence canals; and that too in a country *where canals are closed for* 5 *or* 6 *months in the year, by frost.*

56th. That Agra being only 500 feet above the sea, (1,200 miles up the river,) 40 annicuts (weirs) which might cost on an average 3 lacks (£30,000) in all 120 lacks (1⅕ millions sterling) would give, at the rate of Rs. 7,500 (£750) a mile, a perfect steam navigation with still water for 8 months in the year; much superior to the Mississipi, as being without its disadvantages.

57th. That in Berar, cotton is grown at 1¼*d.* a lb., while the people are fed on rice, which there costs four times the sum for which it could be brought from Rajahmundry by the Godavery; and it is the same with the salt they use.

58th. That in communications, we have this paradox, that a diminution of cost of transit however small, may produce an effect however great, in creating a demand. Upon a reduction of cost of transit by as little as Rs. 5 (10*s.*) a ton on 1,000 miles, may depend whether it is profitable or not to convey some great staple article of commerce to another mart. For instance, upon this may turn the sale and consequently the cultivation of an article of commerce to the amount of a million tons a year, thereby bringing in to a country an income of suppose 10 millions sterling a year.

59th. That in so cheap and populous a country as India, the whole foreign trade (to say nothing of that which is internal) hangs upon the *cost of internal transit.*

60th. That whatever is ultimately done, there is *at present* only one object to be kept in view, viz., *speed* in *making* communications, and that whatever is ultimately done, there is one thing that must *now* be rejected as destructive of all we aim at, viz., *great speed* in *working* the communications. If we give up this for the present, we can do any thing and throw open all India to every wholesome influence at once; but if we persist in aiming at this *first*, we can do nothing, however busy we may appear to be.